IMAGES
of America

ELSMERE AND ERLANGER

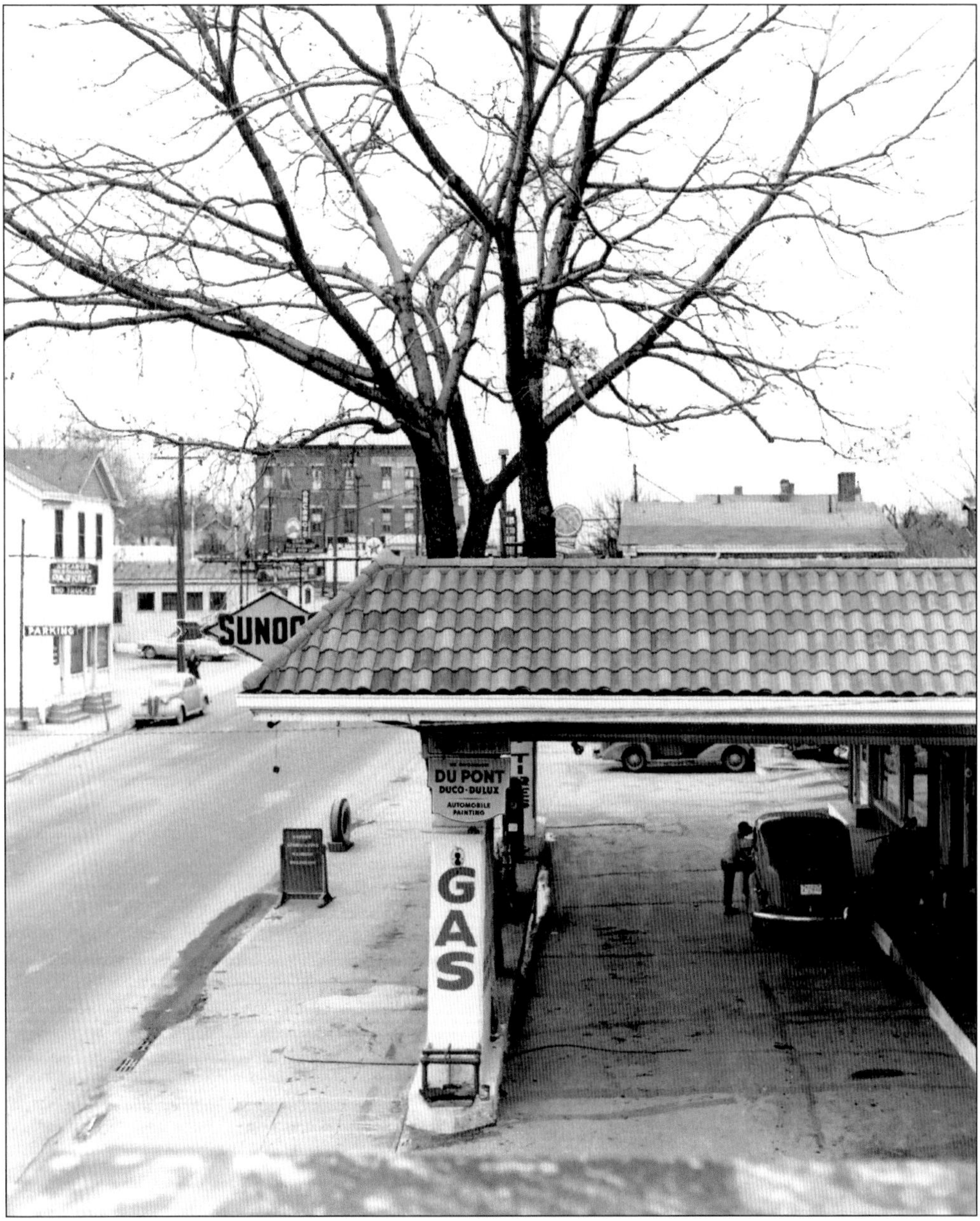

Historical Tree Dividing Cities. This elm tree stood for many years as the dividing spot between the cities of Elsmere and Erlanger. It was located on Dixie Highway. The Sunoco gas station owned by Joseph Michels in the 1950s was built in the 1900s by Bill Bentler. The gas station was built around the tree because they were not permitted to cut down the dividing tree.

On the Cover: The Erlanger Fairgrounds operated from about 1905 to about 1925. The Fair Association held fairs, horse races, and exhibitions. In 1925, the Erlanger Kennel Club brought dog racing to the fairgrounds. The courts ruled pari-mutuel betting to be illegal. The grounds were sold to the school board, and Lloyd High School was built on the grounds. (Courtesy of William Scheben.)

IMAGES
of America

ELSMERE AND ERLANGER

Elsmere and Erlanger Historical Societies

ARCADIA PUBLISHING

ISBN 978-0-7385-6663-4

Published by Arcadia Publishing
Charleston, South Carolina

Printed in the United States of America

Library of Congress Control Number: 2009932194

For all general information contact Arcadia Publishing at:
Telephone 843-853-2070
Fax 843-853-0044
E-mail sales@arcadiapublishing.com
For customer service and orders:
Toll-Free 1-888-313-2665

Visit us on the Internet at www.arcadiapublishing.com

The Erlanger and Elsmere Historical Societies would like to dedicate this book to our founding fathers who built their houses and captured the images of their lives on film for us. We hope that the youth of the community continue this work by preserving the present for our future generations.

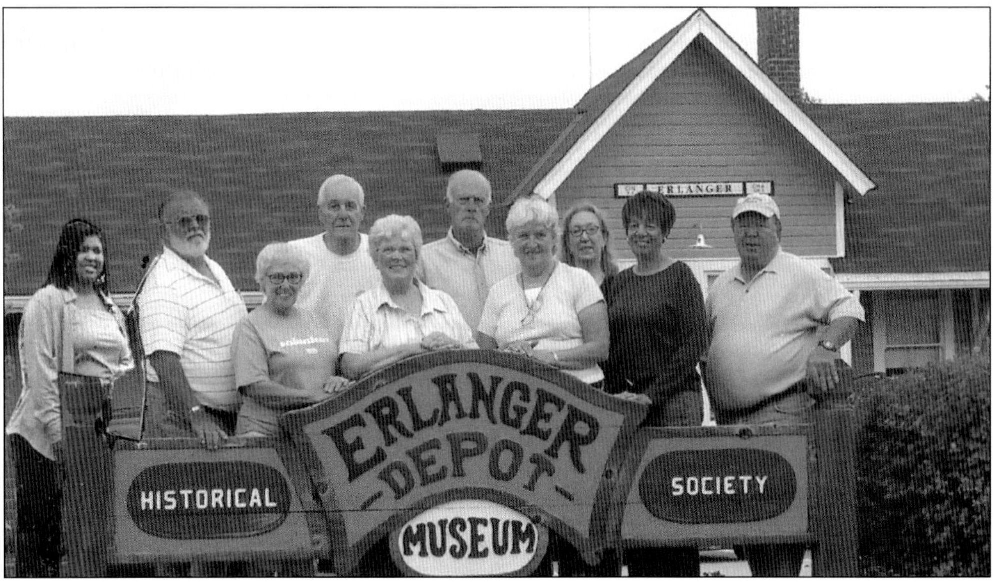

ARCADIA BOOK COMMITTEE. The book committee included, from left to right, Stacey Carter, Ed VonEye, Fay Whaley, Jack Scheben, Patricia Hahn, Terry Collis, Betty Roszmann, Lisa Schumann, Joyce Florence, and chairperson Paul J. Dusing. (Photograph by Paul Dusing.)

Contents

Acknowledgements		6
Introduction		7
1.	Institutions: Government, Groups, and Public Service	9
2.	Community: Churches, Schools, and Libraries	27
3.	Businesses: Restaurants, Shops, and Industry	65
4.	People and Events: Families, Citizens, Scenes, and Sports	85
5.	Transportation: Planes, Trains, and Automobiles	113

ACKNOWLEDGMENTS

The Elsmere and Erlanger Kentucky Historical Societies would like to thank the following for their help in compiling this book. We need to give credit especially to Eileen Kuhn, Kentucky History Services coordinator of the Mary Ann Mongan Library in Covington, Kentucky, for her help and cooperation. Our thanks go to principals David Palmore and Eric Sayler of the Erlanger Elsmere School System for allowing us to use their space to bring people together to share their photographs. Thanks also to all the folks who searched their scrapbooks, photo albums, attics, and basements to find their vintage photographs. All of the photographs, unless otherwise noted, are courtesy of Kenton County Library or the Erlanger Historical Society. We owe a debt of gratitude to the City of Erlanger and their information systems and telecommunication director, Rebecca Hopkins, and for all the help and patience we received from our editors at Arcadia Publishing, Luke Cunningham and Amy Perryman. Putting together a book is always the work of many people. We hope this pictorial history celebrates the history of the neighborhoods of Elsmere and Erlanger, will showcase the people unique to this area, and will bring back memories and that all will learn some new information about their heritage. The committee consists of Jack Scheben, Fay Whaley, Betty Roszmann, Lisa Schumann, Ed VonEye, Terry Collis, Joyce Florence, Stacey Carter, Patricia Hahn, and chairman Paul Dusing.

Introduction

Elsmere and Erlanger, Kentucky, are 13 miles southwest of Cincinnati, Ohio. The population of Elsmere is 8,139, and the population of Erlanger is 16,676. The cities are located in the Bluegrass Region in Kenton County, which was established in 1840. The communities of Erlanger and Elsmere (originally called South Erlanger), though close in proximity, were very distinct in character. Erlanger was predominately Protestant, with the Erlanger Union Church built to serve all Protestant denominations in 1888. Elsmere was more German Catholic, with St. Henry Church and school built in September 1888. Elsmere also had a large African American population served by the African Methodist Episcopal Church and the First Baptist Church, both started in the 1890s.

In May 1896, the area previously known as South Erlanger incorporated as the city of Elsmere, named after Elsmere Avenue in Norwood, Ohio. In the following year, 1897, the city of Erlanger incorporated and was named after the Baron Frederick Emile d'Erlanger, whose banking firm owned a majority of the company holding the lease for the railroad. The year after Kentucky became a state in 1792, the state legislature passed an act that called for the clearing of a wagon road from Frankfort to Cincinnati. This road closely followed the old buffalo road, which ran along the Dry Ridge and became known as the Georgetown Road. There was not a town between Covington and Georgetown. In 1813, Robert Johnson and John D. Watkins, owners of the land that would become Elsmere and Erlanger, divided their property into two equal tracts of 1,100 acres. Later that year, Johnson sold half of his tract to Bartlett Graves and the other half to John Stansifer. Bartlett Graves became the first permanent settler of what was to become Erlanger. Graves purchased the 550 acres from Robert Johnson for $1,375. Graves built the first home in the area. He first built a large log cabin, and then in 1819, he built a kiln; after several years of labor, Graves finished a large Colonial home on what is now Commonwealth Avenue, across from Erlanger Baptist Church. The home was called Walnut Grove, and Bartlett Graves lived there until his death. The house burned down about 1895. With the help of his large family and a number of slaves, Graves's working plantation produced everything necessary for a mid-19th-century family, including all their food and the material needed for clothing.

John Stansifer was a native of Germany, born in 1744. He first came as an indentured servant to Virginia, where he married Jemima Clore. They had 10 children before coming to Kentucky. The 550 acres of the Johnson tract that John Stansifer purchased became Elsmere. Stansifer's will was probated March 24, 1823, and his land was divided among his 10 children: Ephraim Stansifer, John Stansifer Jr., Frankey Stansifer Leathers, Lucey Stansifer Crain, Jemima Stansifer Yager, Simeon Stansifer, Abraham Stansifer, Polly Stansifer Bush, Sarah Stansifer Cleveland, and Patsy Stansifer Whitford. By 1850, John's family had sold all its interest in the property, known as South Erlanger at that time.

Along with stagecoaches, an ever-increasing number of wagons and more farmers using the Georgetown Road to drive livestock to market caused a desperate need for an improved road. Every male 16 years of age and over was required to perform maintenance on the roads according to Kentucky law. The road was so bad that it took two days to get from Florence to Cincinnati. In 1839, the 10 miles of new road from Covington through Erlanger and Elsmere was finished at a cost of $7,800 per mile, the most expensive road in Kentucky. Kentucky farmers delivered their livestock to the markets in Covington and Cincinnati. About 70,000 hogs in addition to 10,000 cows came up the turnpike through the cities each year. Huge droves of cattle, hogs, sheep, horses, mules, and turkeys were frequently seen on the turnpike along South Erlanger and Erlanger.

And then the railroad arrived. February 12, 1874, was one of the most important days in Erlanger and Elsmere's history as the trustees of the Cincinnati Southern Railroad announced that they would build a bridge over the Ohio River into Ludlow and that the railroad would follow the Lexington Pike to Florence. That meant the railroad was coming to Elsmere and Erlanger. The impact of the railroad on these communities cannot be overestimated. The railroad brought many interesting and industrious people to the area. This is when the Elsmere and Erlanger Syndicates were formed to entice buyers; free commuter transportation to Cincinnati was added as an incentive. What began as a small railroad community suddenly matured into a major suburb along the old Lexington Pike.

Cincinnati officials were shocked when the federal government in 1942 announced its intention to support the Boone County/Erlanger site for the area airport. The site was an excellent choice for Greater Cincinnati, located only 11 miles from Fountain Square. Each and every advancement at the airport brought growth in Northern Kentucky, much of it in Elsmere and Erlanger.

The Elsmere and Erlanger Historical Societies realize that while these two cities are separate, they are still one in their efforts to respect families, religions, schools, and other organizations to form the community they have become. Although many of the people and many of the homes and buildings are gone, this book helps to create a visual journey of what they did in times past to make the cities of Elsmere and Erlanger the great cities they are today.

One

Institutions
Government, Groups, and Public Service

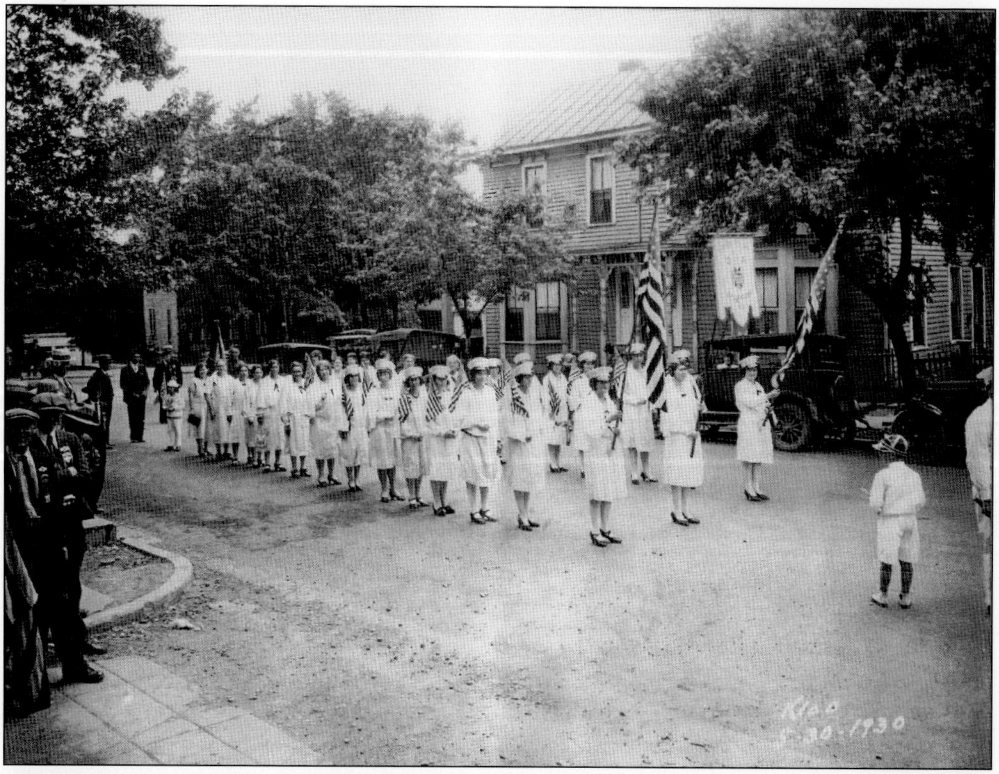

Daughters of America Parade. The Daughters of America marched in the 1930s parade. The photograph is of the corner of Dixie Highway and Commonwealth Avenue. The ladies are standing on Commonwealth Avenue. The building in the background is the Kohorst Hotel. It was formerly the Scheben Hotel and the Ficke Hotel. (Courtesy of Larry Lindemann.)

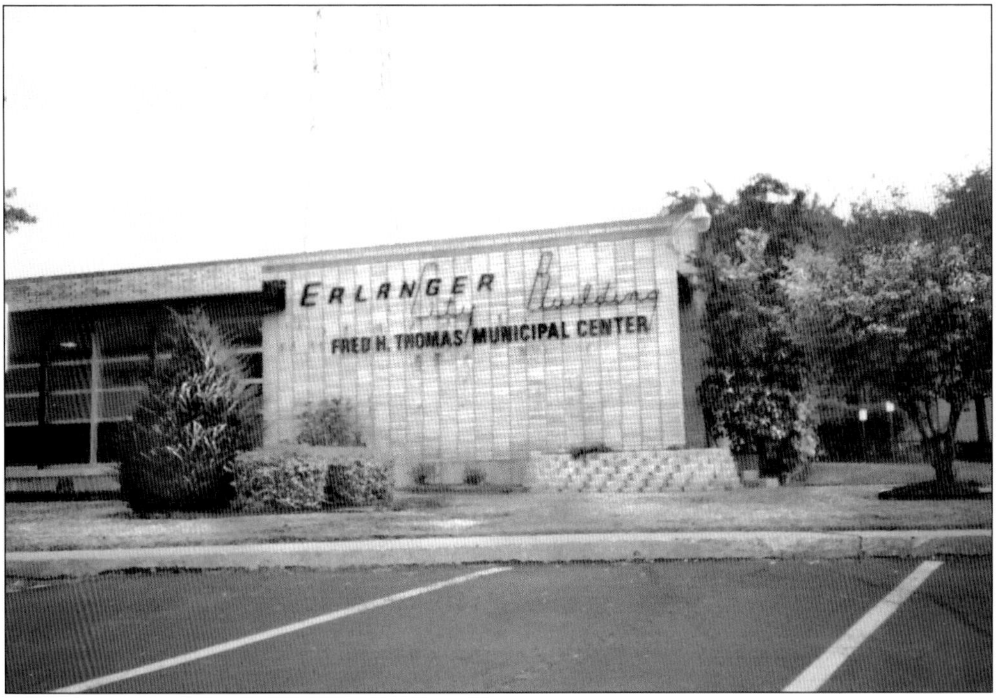

ERLANGER CITY BUILDING. Located at 505 Commonwealth Avenue, the city building was named in honor of Fred H. Thomas. Thomas served 12 years as mayor of Erlanger and more than 40 years in city government. Fred was Erlanger's seventh mayor. Mayor Thomas was named Northern Kentucky Outstanding Local Official in 1984 by the Northern Kentucky Area Development District.

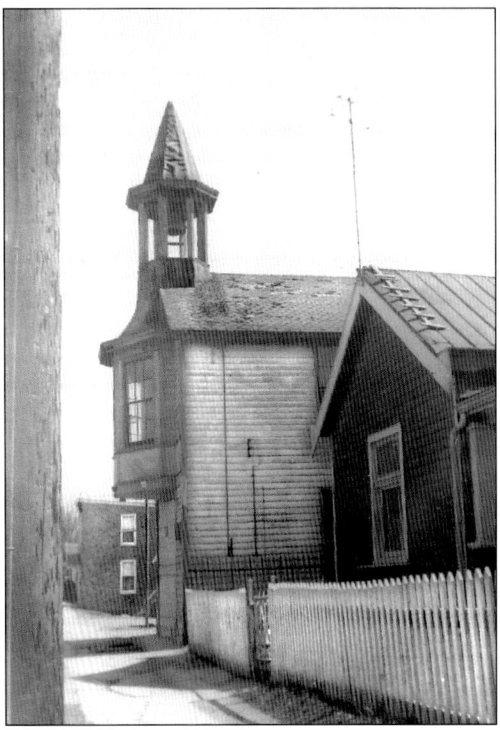

ELSMERE FIRE STATION. The first volunteer fire department was known as the Elsmere and Woodside Volunteer Fire Department and was created in 1899. It was staffed by George Rost as the fire chief and assistant Daniel Wilkins. This building was used as a combination fire department, city hall, and jail. (Courtesy of Betty Roszmann.)

FRED THOMAS. A graduate of Holmes High School in Covington, Kentucky, Thomas moved to Erlanger in 1943. After serving in the navy from 1943 to 1945, he returned to Erlanger. He served on city council from 1951 through 1981, when he was first elected mayor. He then served as mayor from 1981 through 1993 and retired at that time because of poor health.

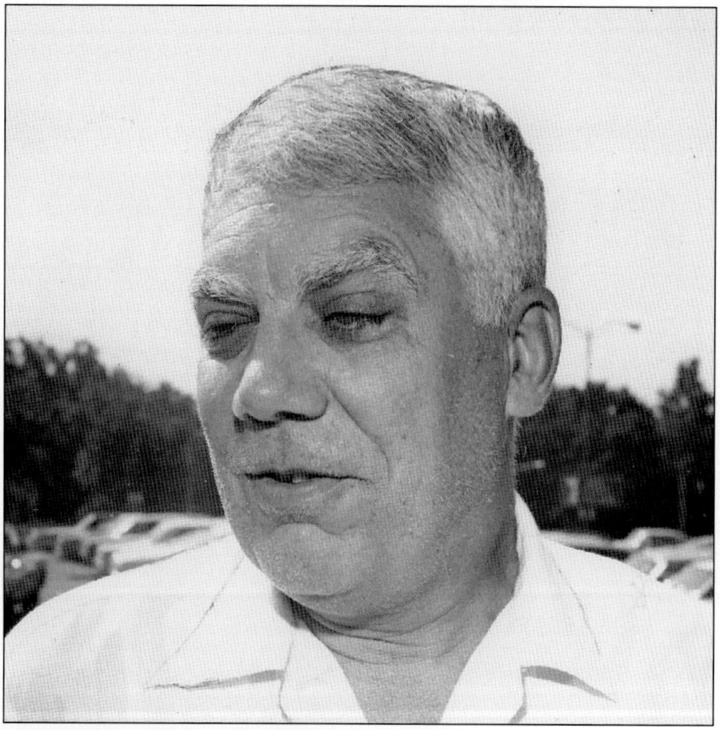

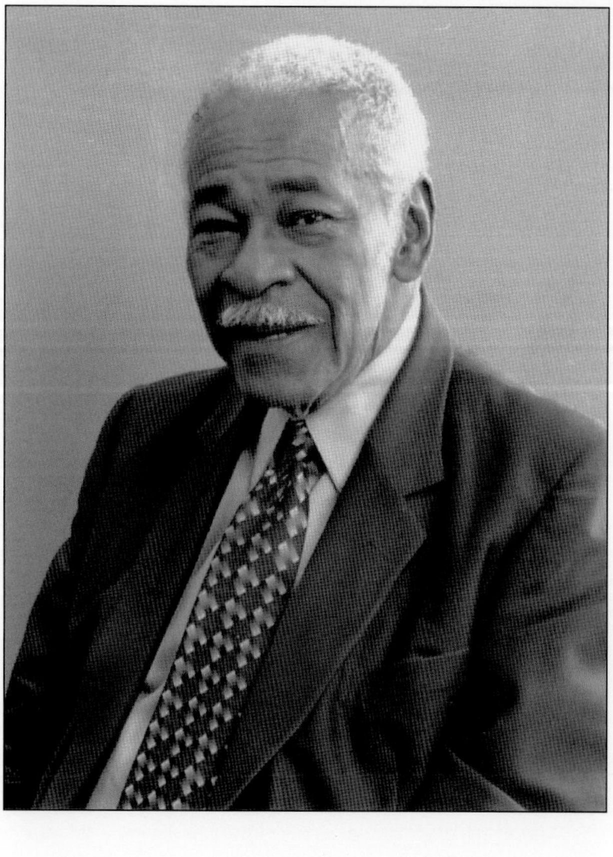

BILL BRADFORD. In 1974, Mayor Bradford was the first African American elected to city council in Elsmere. In 1998, he also became the first African American elected mayor in Northern Kentucky. The Bradford family has lived in the Elsmere area since the late 1800s. He and his family have been active members in the Barnes Temple AME Church in Elsmere. (Courtesy of Andy Curran.)

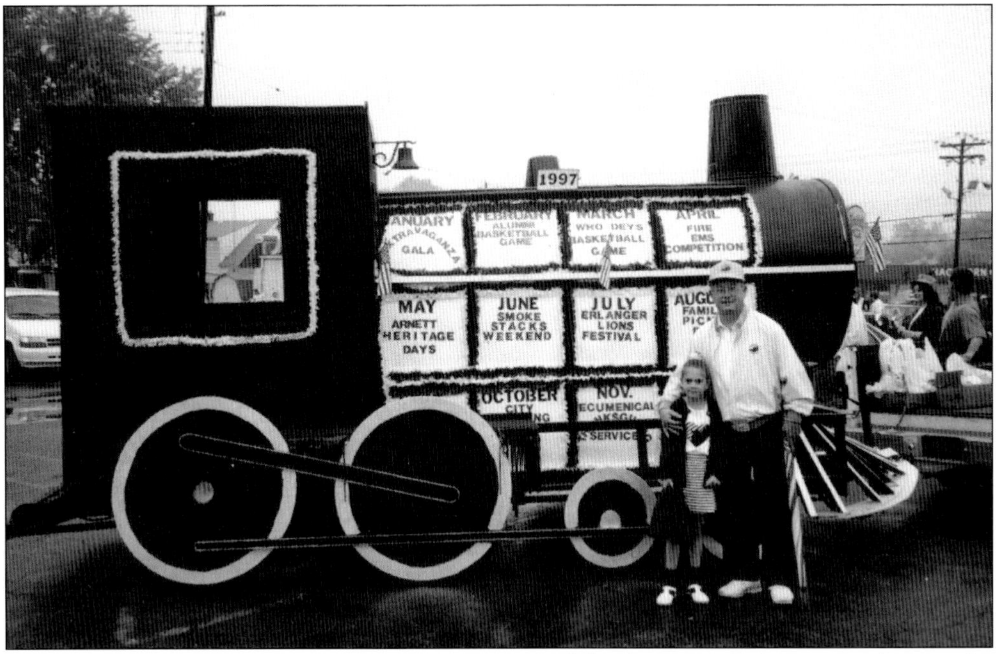

The 1997 Erlanger Centennial. This train was built by the City of Erlanger to advertise the events of the year-long celebration of the centennial. It was entered in all local parades in 1997. Paul Hahn, who served on Erlanger City Council at the time, and his granddaughter Katelyn Burke enjoyed a ride on the train in the Erlanger-Elsmere Memorial Day parade.

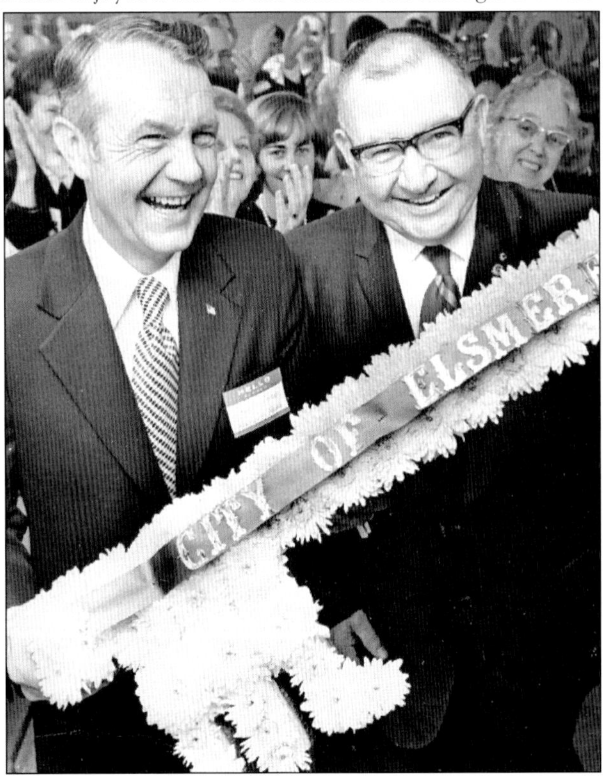

Wendell Ford and Joseph "Buck" Lucas. The Elsmere mayor presented Gov. Wendell Ford (left) with a floral key to the city of Elsmere. Joseph "Buck" Lucas was later elected as the sheriff of Kenton County. He started his law enforcement career with the Kentucky Highway Patrol, which later became the Kentucky State Police. He served on the Erlanger Police Department and the Kenton County Police Department. Buck passed away September 28, 1984.

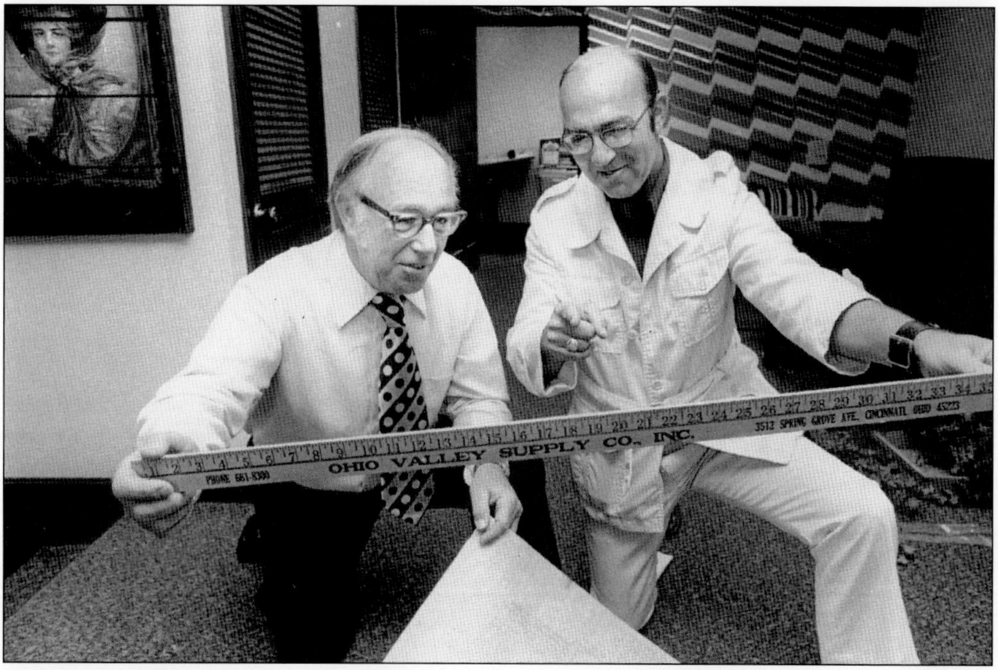

ELSMERE AND ERLANGER MAYORS. This 1975 photograph shows Elsmere mayor Al Wermeling (left) and Erlanger mayor Jim Ellis. Both men served on their respective city councils in the early 1970s. Al was elected mayor of Elsmere and served from 1974 until 1985 and again from 1990 until 1998. Jim Ellis served only one term as Erlanger mayor, from 1973 until 1976.

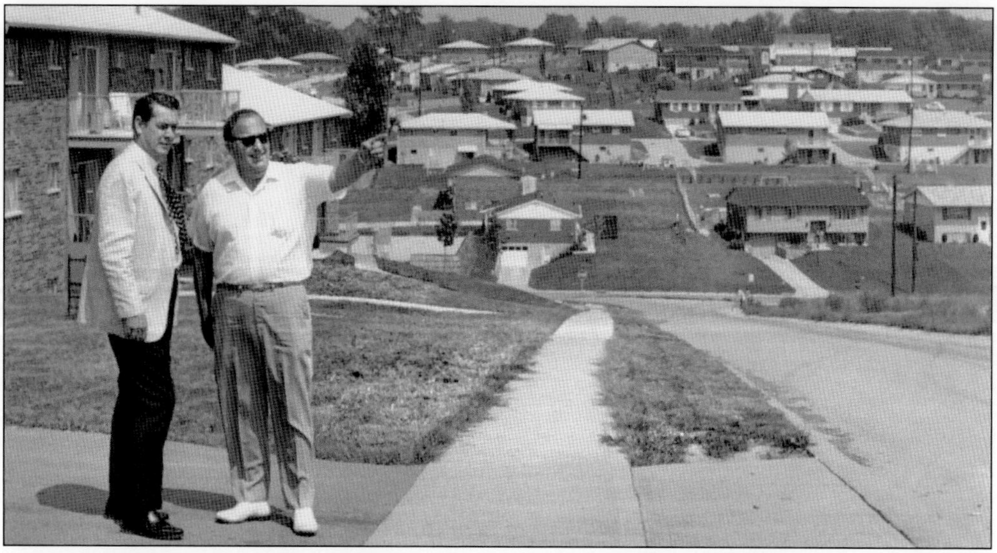

AUSTIN MANN AND CLYDE ROUSE. These two are pictured checking out development on Kimberly Drive in Erlanger. Austin Mann (left) was mayor of Erlanger in 1969. Mann served in World War II. He served on the Erlanger-Elsmere School Board in 1950, on city council in 1953, and as mayor in 1969. He also owned Austin Mann Realty. Mann died in 1992. Clyde Rouse taught English at Lloyd High School and served in the Air Corps in World War II. Rouse also served as city coordinator from 1951 to 1981 and was on the school board from 1981 to 1991. He died in 1991.

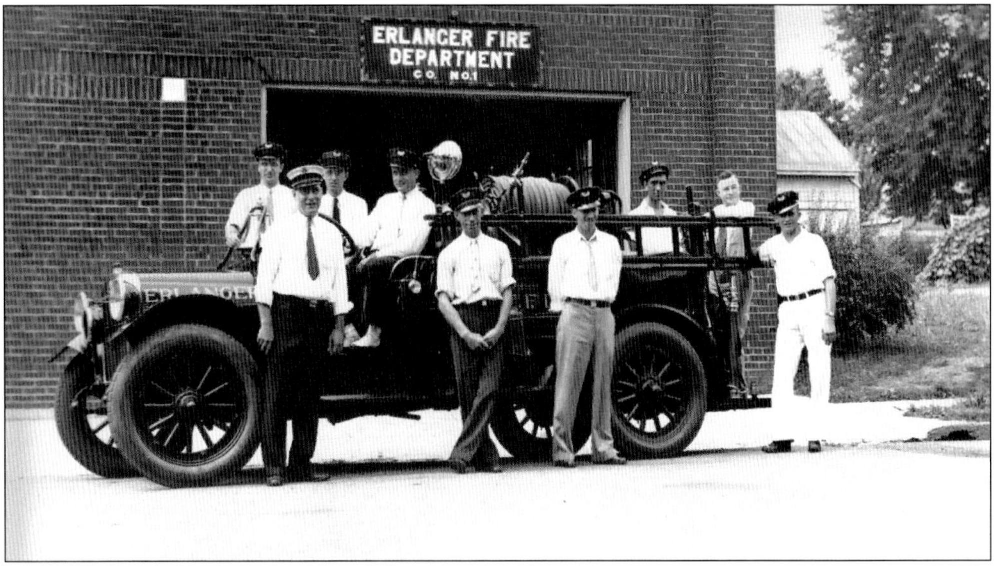

Erlanger Fire Department First Vehicle. This used fire truck was purchased in 1925 from the City of Covington by the local Veterans of Foreign Wars Post. It was housed in the Scheben Hardware Building next to the Erlanger Town Hall, located at the intersection of Dixie Highway and Erlanger Road.

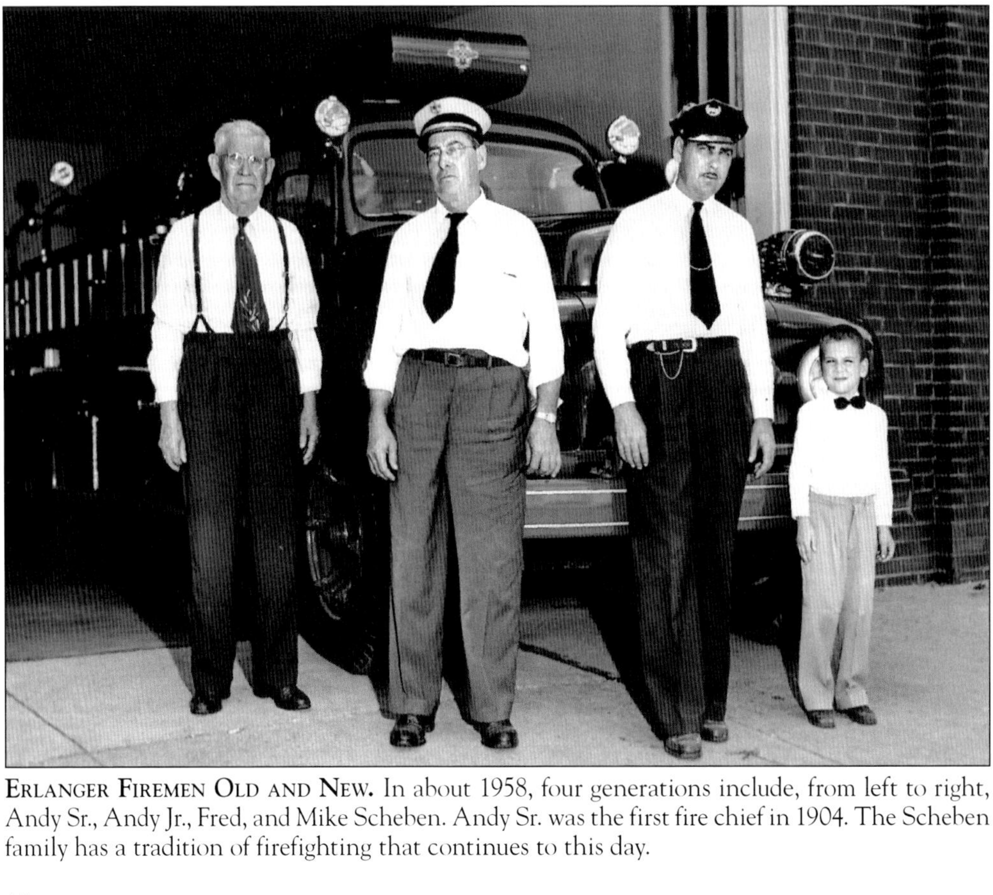

Erlanger Firemen Old and New. In about 1958, four generations include, from left to right, Andy Sr., Andy Jr., Fred, and Mike Scheben. Andy Sr. was the first fire chief in 1904. The Scheben family has a tradition of firefighting that continues to this day.

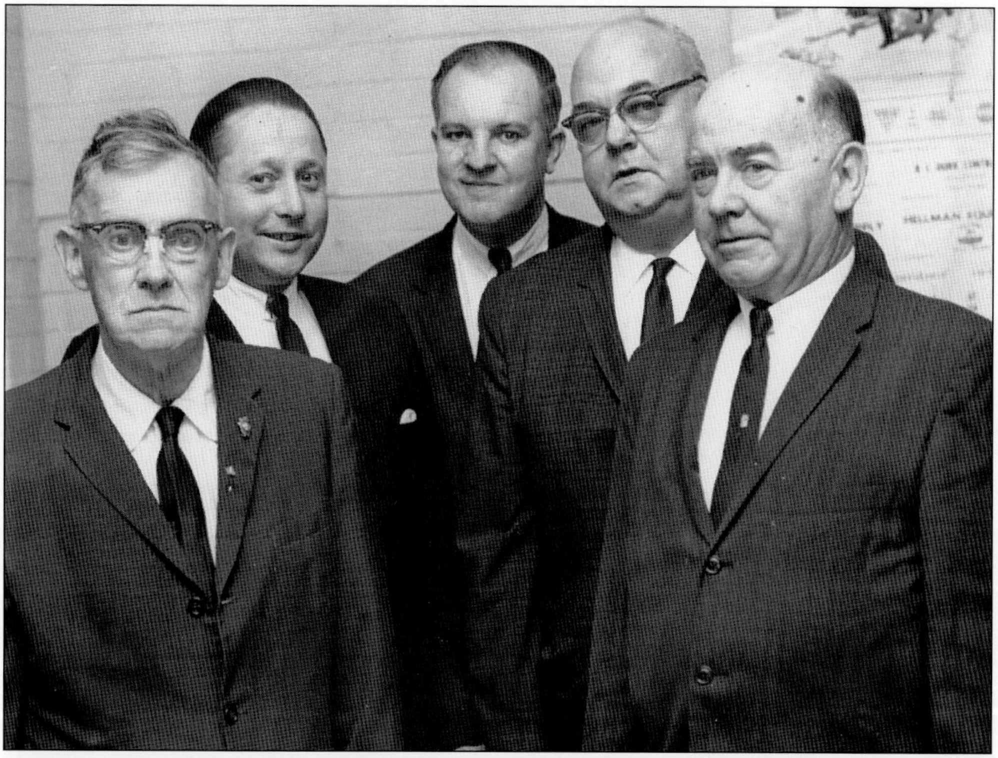

Northern Kentucky Firefighters Association. The organization was formed in 1934, and 12 cities joined. John Crowell of Elsmere and Andrew Scheben of Erlanger served on the 1934 executive board. In this 1967 photograph, John Crowell (far left) still served as an officer.

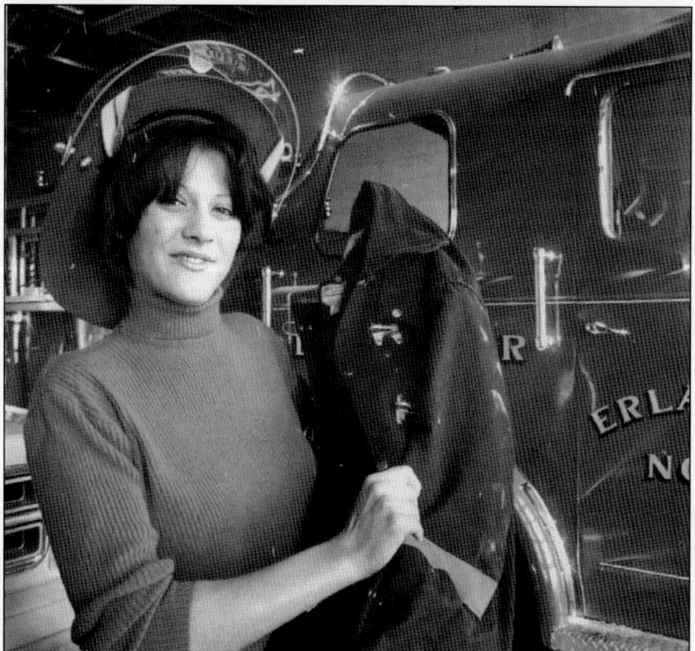

First Female Firefighter. Michele Westermeyer was the first female firefighter in the area. She joined the Erlanger Fire Department as a volunteer in 1977 and later moved on to Covington Fire Department, where she was retired as a captain in August 2005 after 26 years on the job.

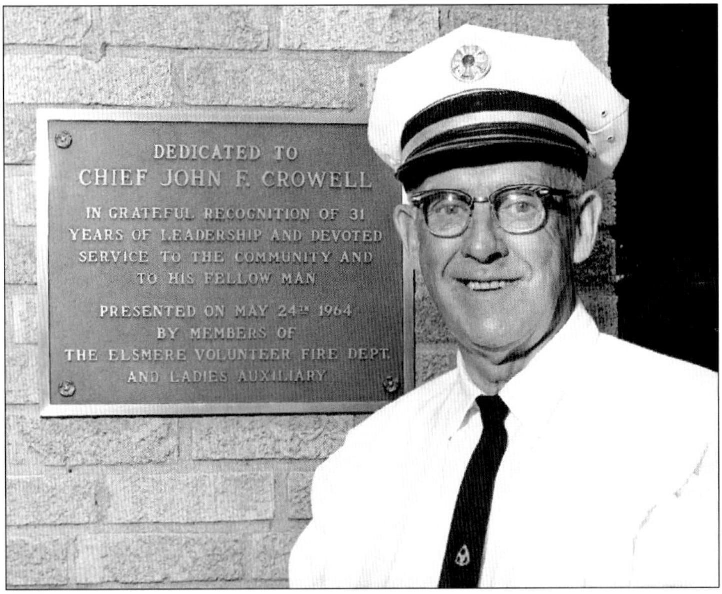

CHIEF JOHN F. CROWELL. The Elsmere Fire Department building was dedicated in 1964 to longtime fire chief John F. Crowell. He helped start many programs and procedures still used by area fire departments today. One of these is the successful "Move up" system, wherein fire companies move up (fill in) at other stations during multi-alarm incidents.

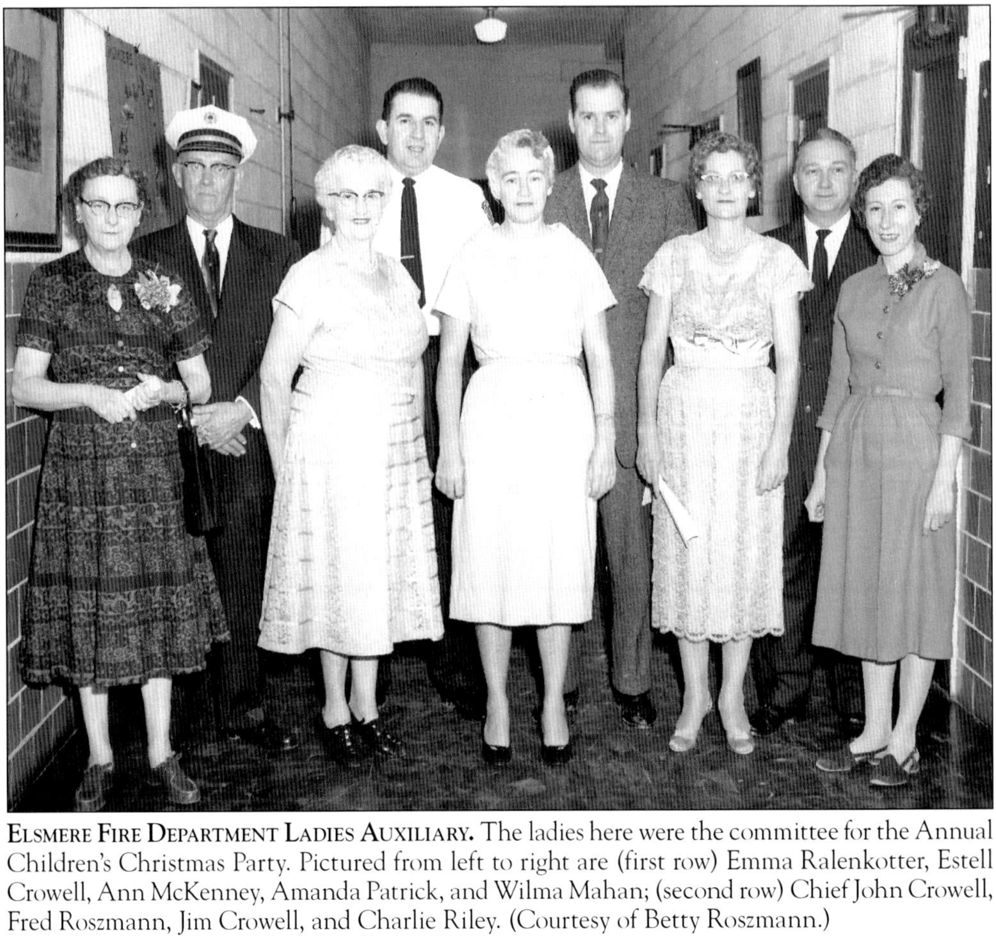

ELSMERE FIRE DEPARTMENT LADIES AUXILIARY. The ladies here were the committee for the Annual Children's Christmas Party. Pictured from left to right are (first row) Emma Ralenkotter, Estell Crowell, Ann McKenney, Amanda Patrick, and Wilma Mahan; (second row) Chief John Crowell, Fred Roszmann, Jim Crowell, and Charlie Riley. (Courtesy of Betty Roszmann.)

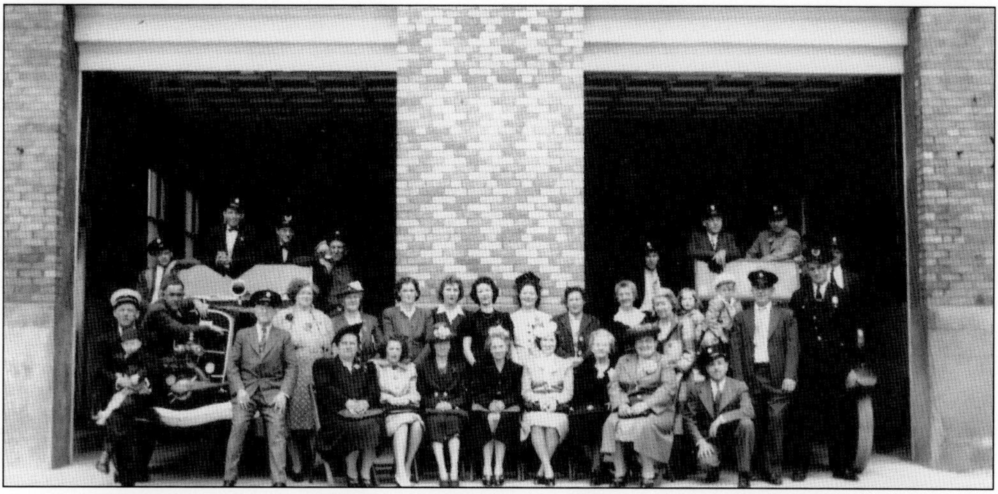

Elsmere Fire Department. This building was purchased November 10, 1942, for a new firehouse. This picture is a celebration of opening new fire bays. Note the open cab on the left pumper. The "old" truck on the right looks to have solid rubber tires. (Courtesy of Betty Roszmann.)

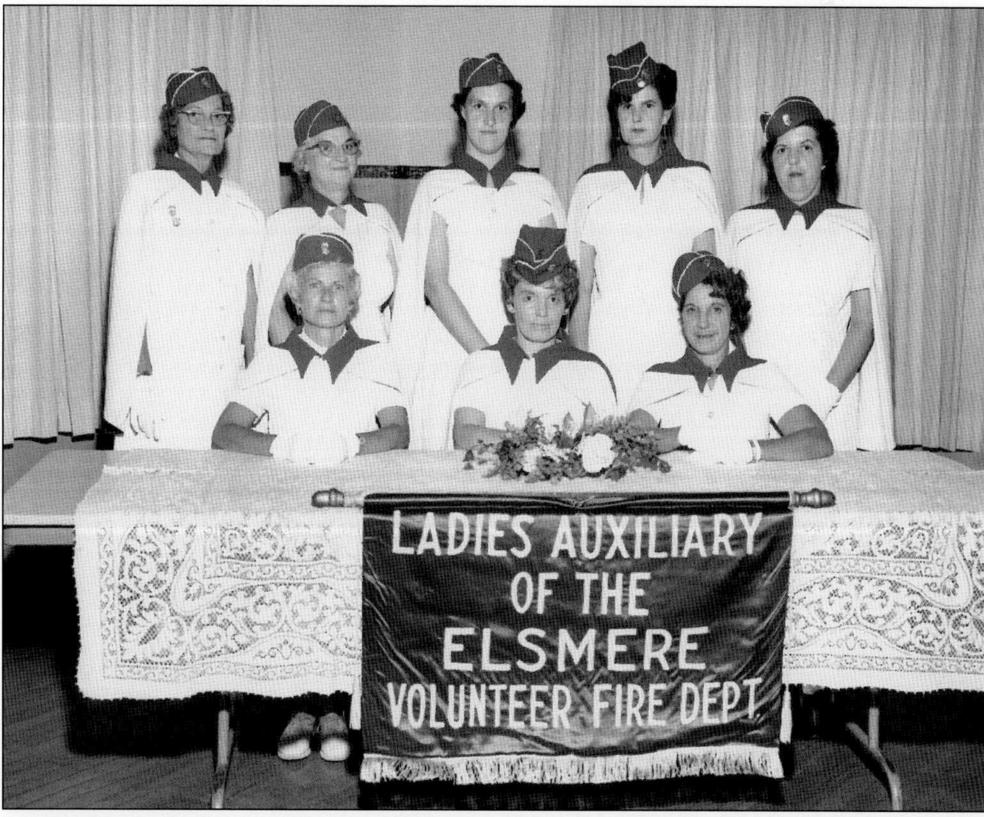

Ladies Auxiliary of the Elsmere Volunteer Fire Department. The Ladies Auxiliary was founded in 1933 by Mrs. Estell Crowell at the request of fire chief Walter Beil. This was the first auxiliary to a fire department in Kentucky. Officers are, from left to right, (first row) Carol Bowman, Shirley Serra, and Nelda Snow; (second row) Amanda Patrick, Betty Lucas, Betty Roszmann, Emily Clifton, and Betty Atha. (Courtesy of Betty Roszmann.)

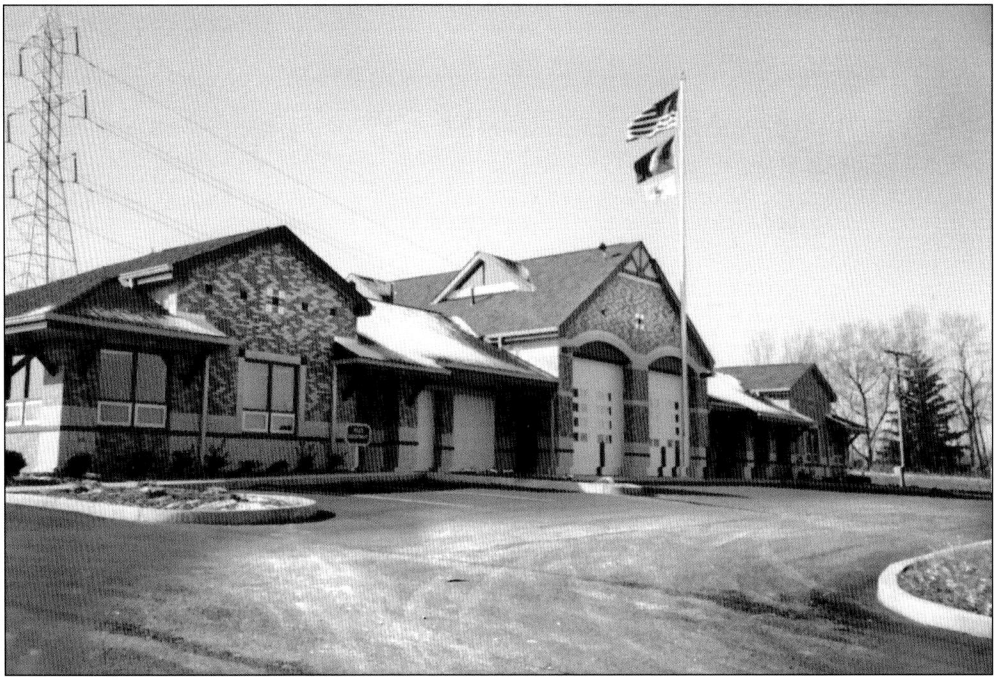

Erlanger Fire Station No. 3. In 1991, the Erlanger Fire Department opened a third firehouse to serve the rapidly expanding neighborhoods in the southern part of the city. The building was divided into three sections. On the left was an area occupied by the police department. The center consisted of two pull-through bays for fire vehicles and (on the right side) a community meeting area and a kitchen area for the firemen. Station No. 3 was dedicated and a plaque installed in honor of the Scheben family's long history of service and commitment to the Erlanger Fire Department.

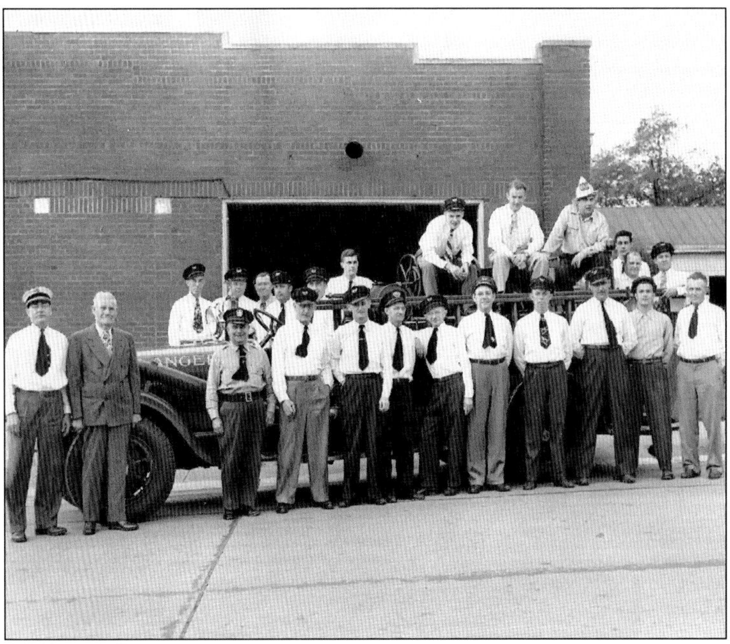

Erlanger Volunteer Fire Department. The vehicles pictured is a 1928 Studebaker 12-cylinder truck that was used as a fire truck. The photograph was taken in front of the Scheben Hardware Store, which served as the station house and was next door to the Erlanger town hall.

ELSMERE POLICE DEPARTMENT. Shown from left to right are Woodrow Snow, Harlan West, Tony Eades, Bill Hiler, Wendell Kegley, Robert Dvorak, and Frank Serra around 1975.

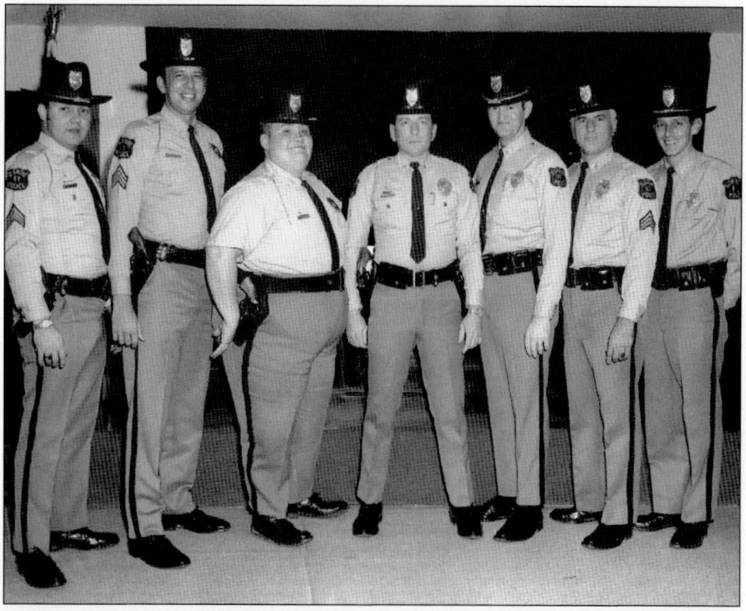

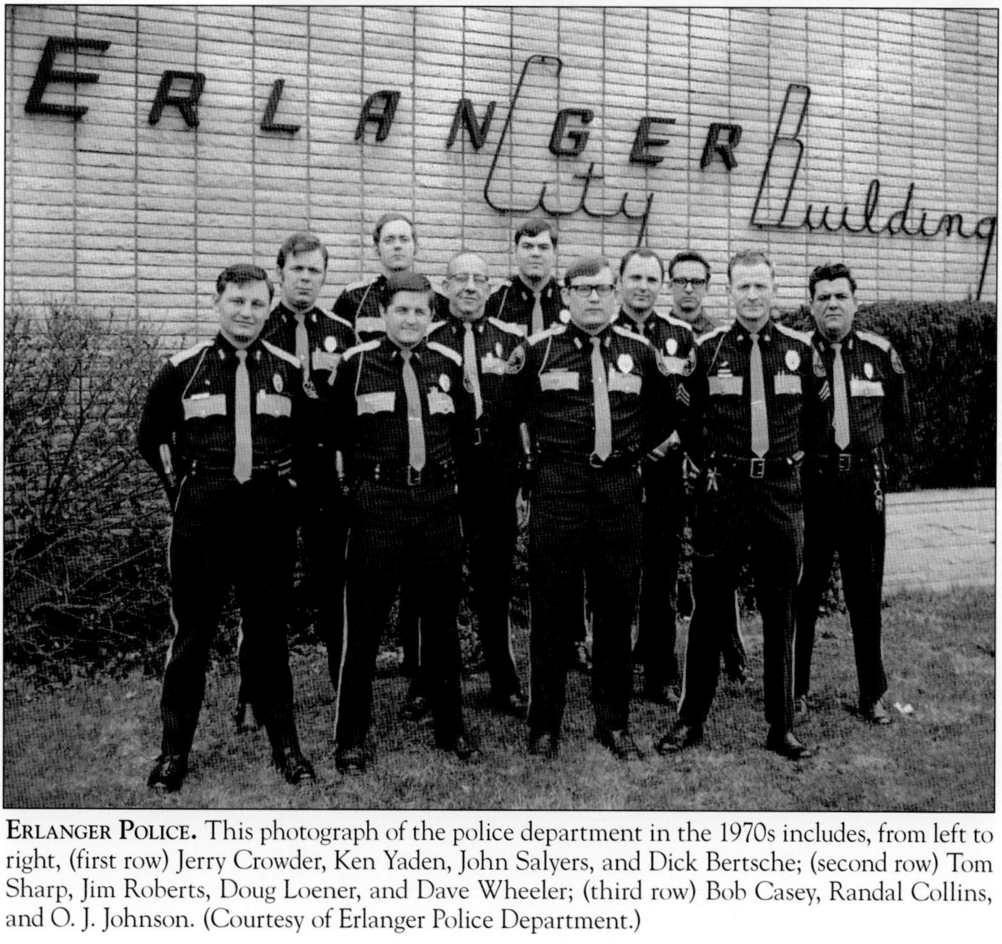

ERLANGER POLICE. This photograph of the police department in the 1970s includes, from left to right, (first row) Jerry Crowder, Ken Yaden, John Salyers, and Dick Bertsche; (second row) Tom Sharp, Jim Roberts, Doug Loener, and Dave Wheeler; (third row) Bob Casey, Randal Collins, and O. J. Johnson. (Courtesy of Erlanger Police Department.)

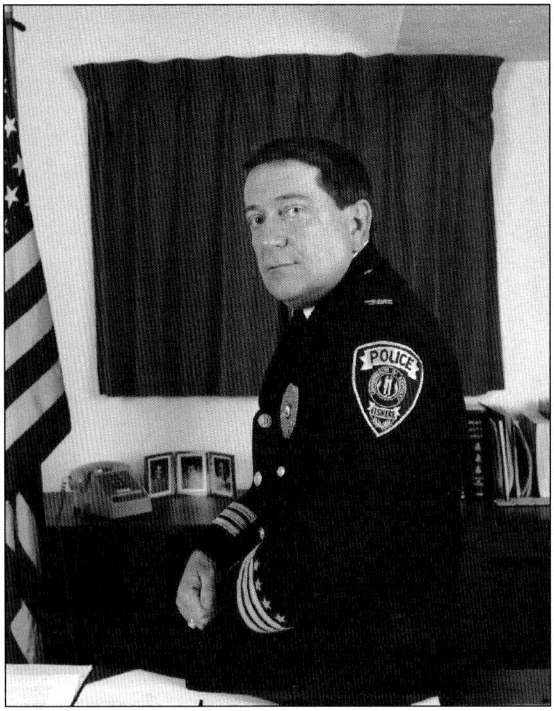

CHIEF BILL HILER. A true native son of the city of Elsmere, Hiler was born in Elsmere and graduated from Lloyd High School. He started his law enforcement career in Elsmere as a patrolman in 1963. In 1964, he went to work for the City of Erlanger, where he worked until 1969, at which time he went to work for the Florence Police Department. He returned to work for the City of Elsmere in 1970 and served as chief of police for 25 years before retiring in 1995. After retiring, he served in the Boone County judicial system for another nine years.

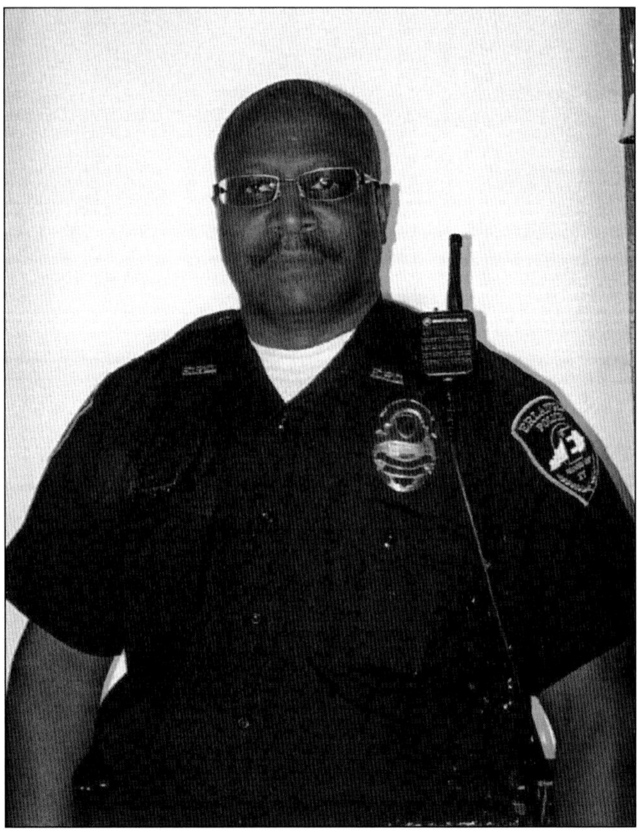

FIRST AFRICAN AMERICAN POLICEMEN. Officer Darryl Jouett was the first African American police officer in Erlanger when he was hired in July 1989. Prior to his position in Erlanger, he was in the air force and served as a military policeman for seven years. He received his 20-Year Pin for his service in Erlanger in August 2009. The first African American officer in Elsmere was Allen Thomas, who served from 1978 to 1980. (Photograph by Paul Dusing.)

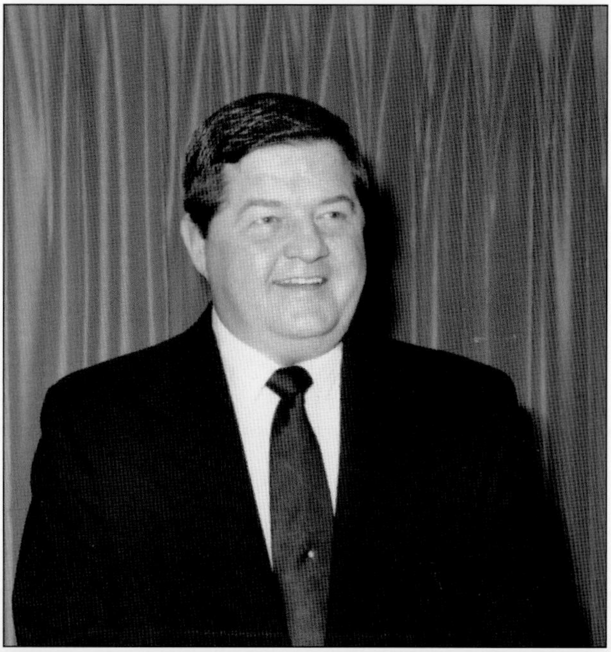

Ken Yaden, Erlanger Police Chief. Hired in August 1966, Yaden became assistant chief in 1973 and chief in April 1986. Ken became Erlanger's first retired police chief on October 31, 1990. He was the first Erlanger officer to attend FBI National Academy, U.S. Secret Service Protection School, U.S. ATF Bomb School, and the U.S. DEA Covert Agent Training School. Ken was the first full-time director of Northern Kentucky Drug Strike Force in 1975 and 1976. He also established the D.A.R.E. officer program in the Erlanger-Elsmere school system in 1989.

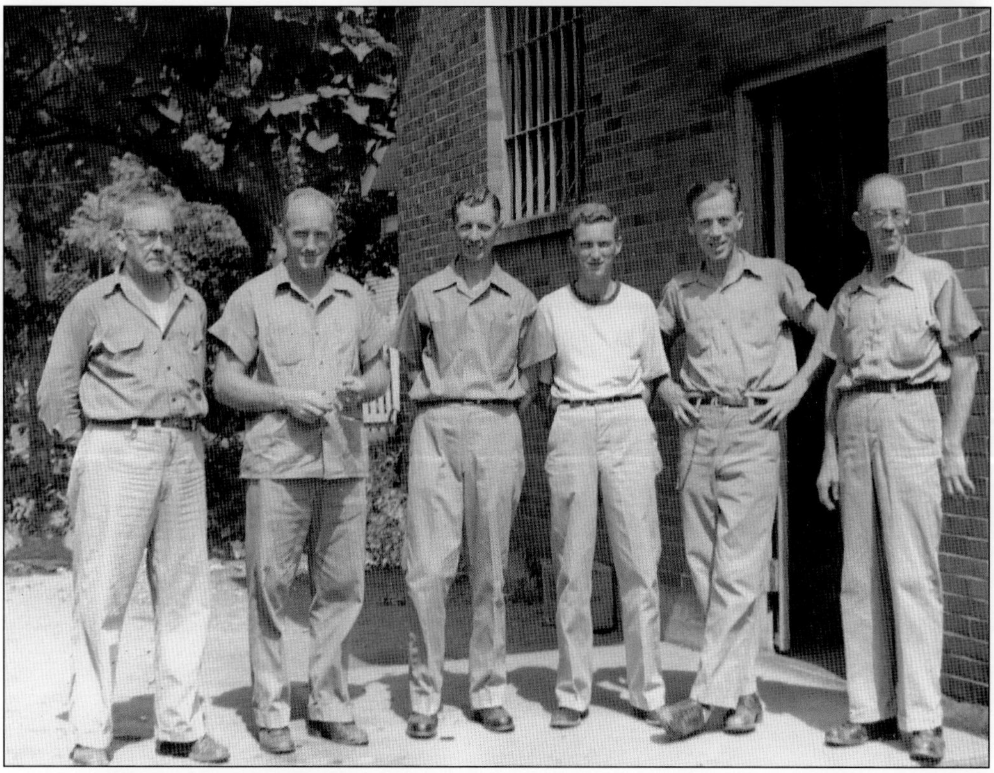

Erlanger-Elsmere Mailmen. Six of the men who delivered the mail in the 1950s are in front of the building that once stood at Graves and Dixie Highway. From left to right are Luke Ruarl, Bob Hilgeford, Joe Meece, Chester Retschulte, Dick Johnson, and Clyde Collis. (Courtesy of Terry Collis.)

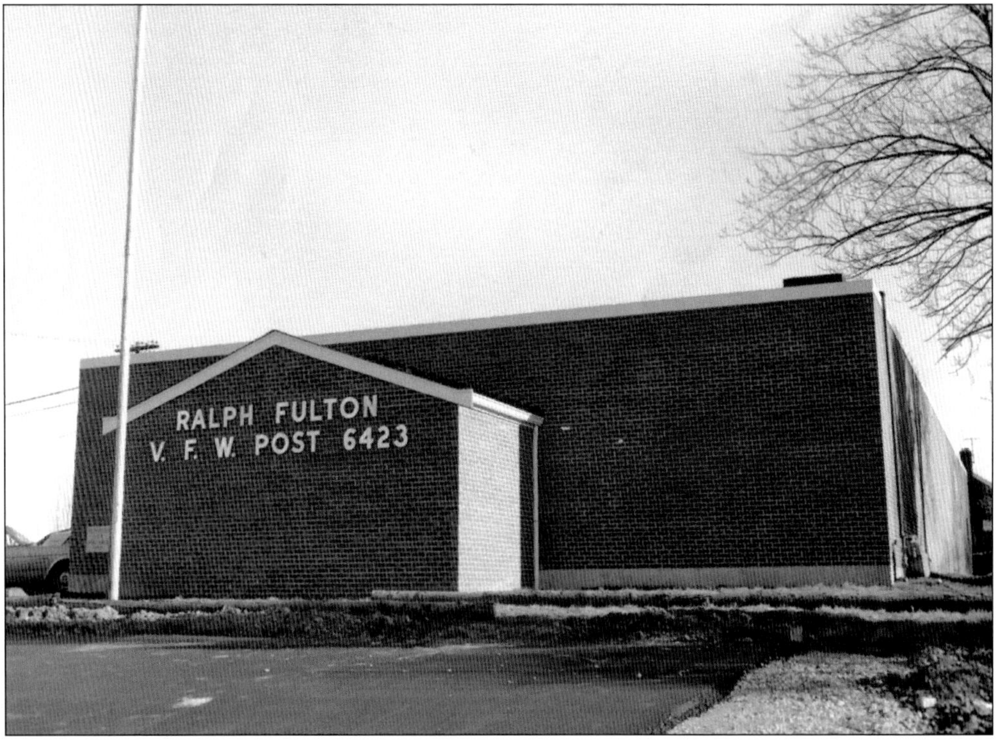

RALPH FULTON VETERANS OF FOREIGN WARS POST 6423. The building is located at 4435 Dixie Highway. The VFW was established in 1946. The post was named after Ralph Fulton, the first World War II casualty from Erlanger. This post is responsible for the annual Erlanger-Elsmere Memorial Day parade. Their motto is "Those fighting for freedom must never be forgotten."

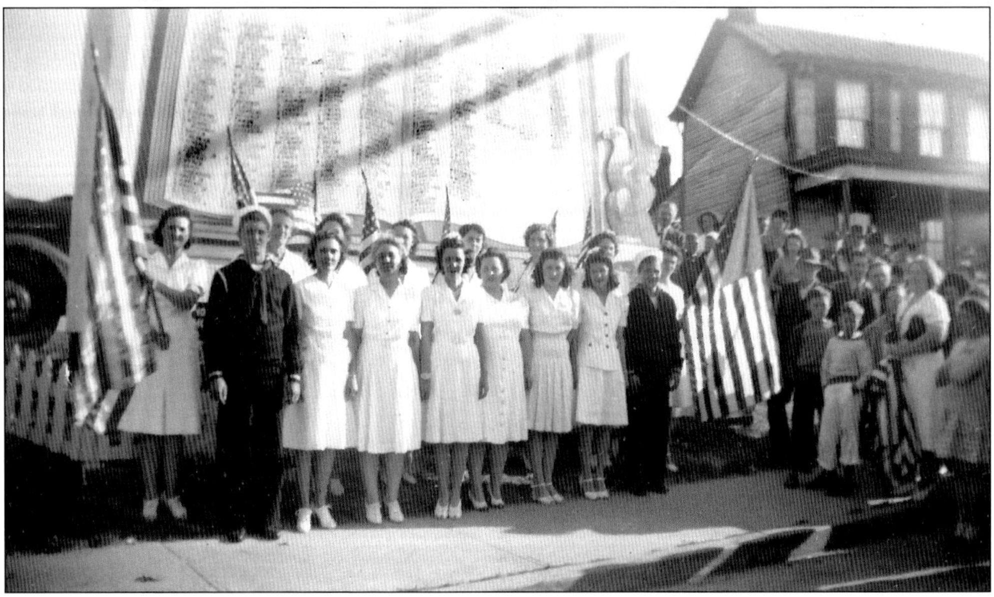

WORLD WAR II HONOR ROLL. This was the Service Men Honor Roll, listing Erlanger and Elsmere World War II servicemen, around 1945. It was located at the corner of Carlisle and Dixie Highway, where the Dollar Store now stands. (Courtesy of Larry Lindeman.)

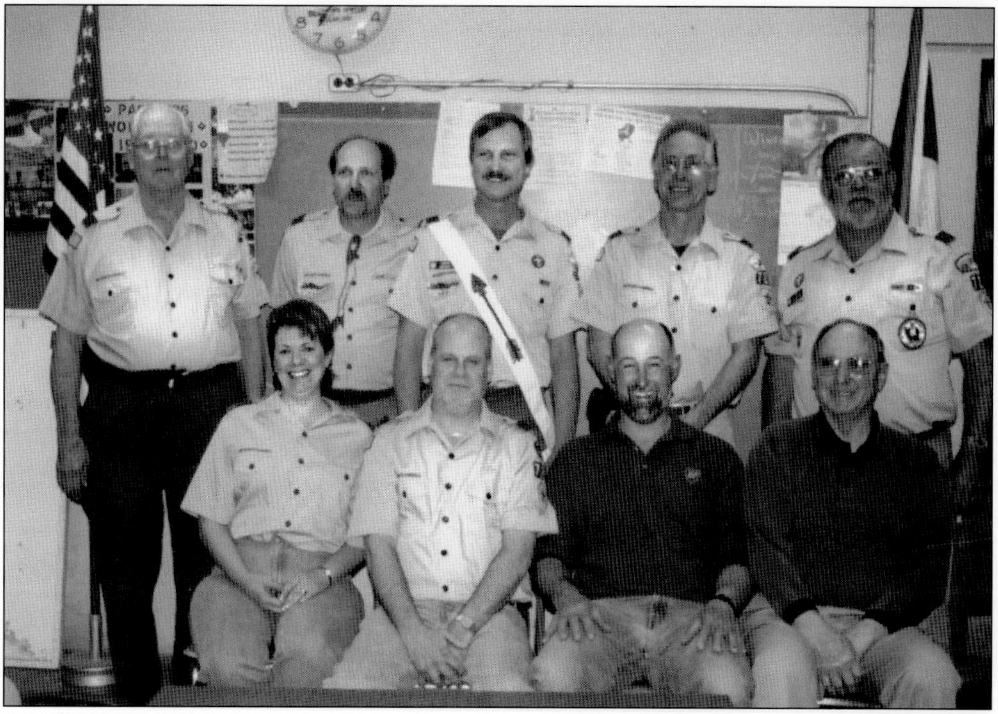

BOY SCOUTS OF AMERICA. Pictured above are past and present leaders of Scout Troop 726, sponsored by St. Henry Church, Elsmere, since 1951. They are, from left to right, (first row) Kelly Schuetz, Steven Schuetz, Pat Cahill, and Jim Eifert; (second row) Bob Tholemeier, Doug Eifert, Dave Eifert, Hartmut Parnitzke, and Ed Von Eye. (Courtesy of Ed Von Eye.)

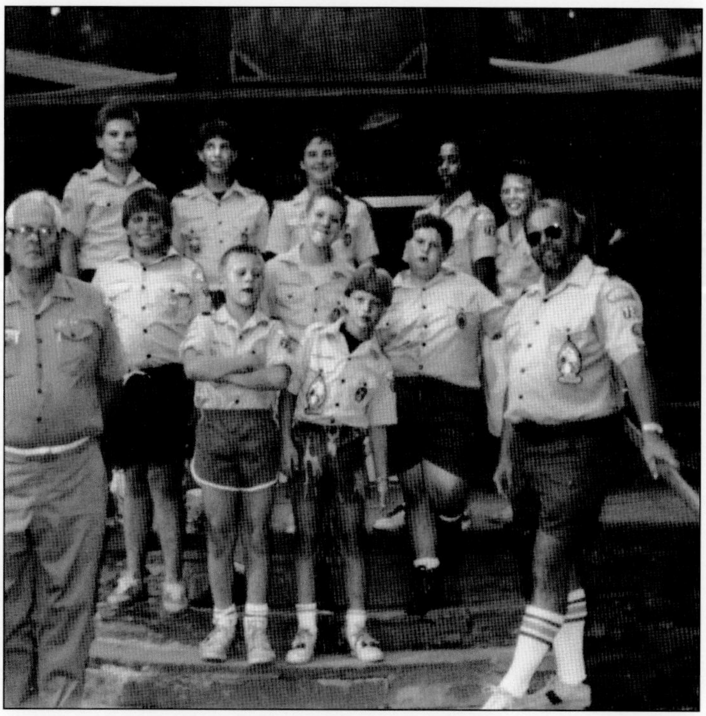

BOY SCOUT SUMMER CAMP, 1989. From left to right are (first row) Bob Tholemeier, John Green, Kevin Ballinger, and Ed Von Eye; (second row) Jason Richardson, Kevin Carothers, and Gary Huth; (third row) Kevin Sullivan, Danny Biedenharn, Tim Sullivan, Dwayne Norman, and Tom Von Eye. (Courtesy of Ed Von Eye.)

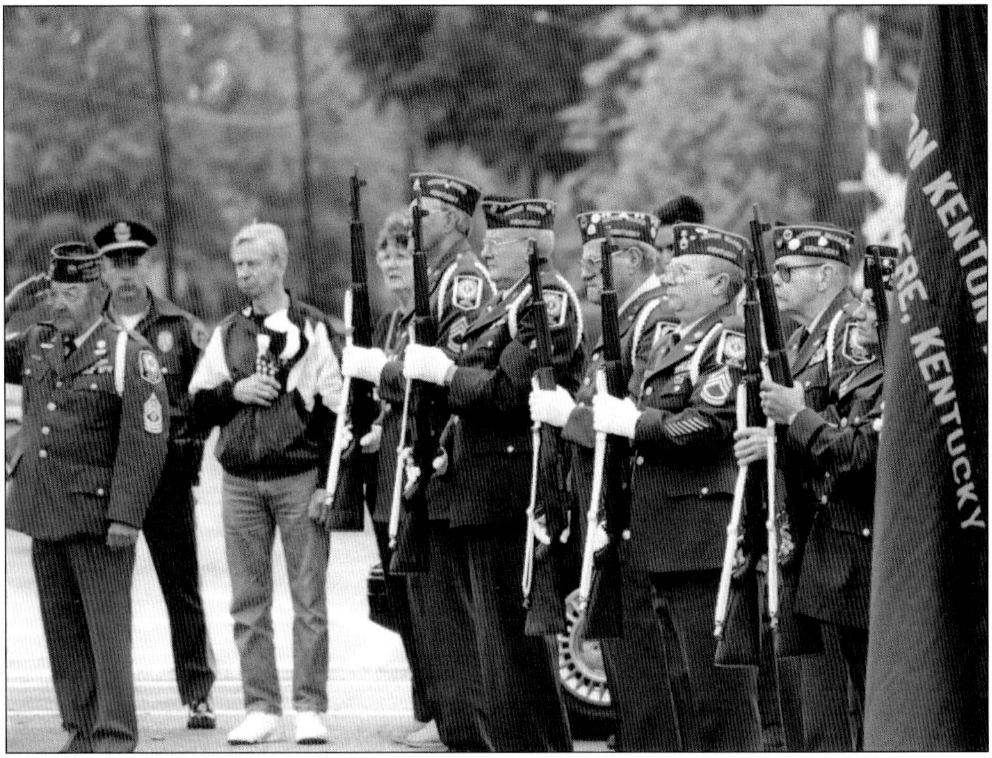

ELSMERE AMERICAN LEGION. The National American Legion was chartered by Congress in 1919 as a patriotic wartime veteran's organization. The Elsmere Simon Kenton Post No. 20 is located at 119 Garvey Avenue.

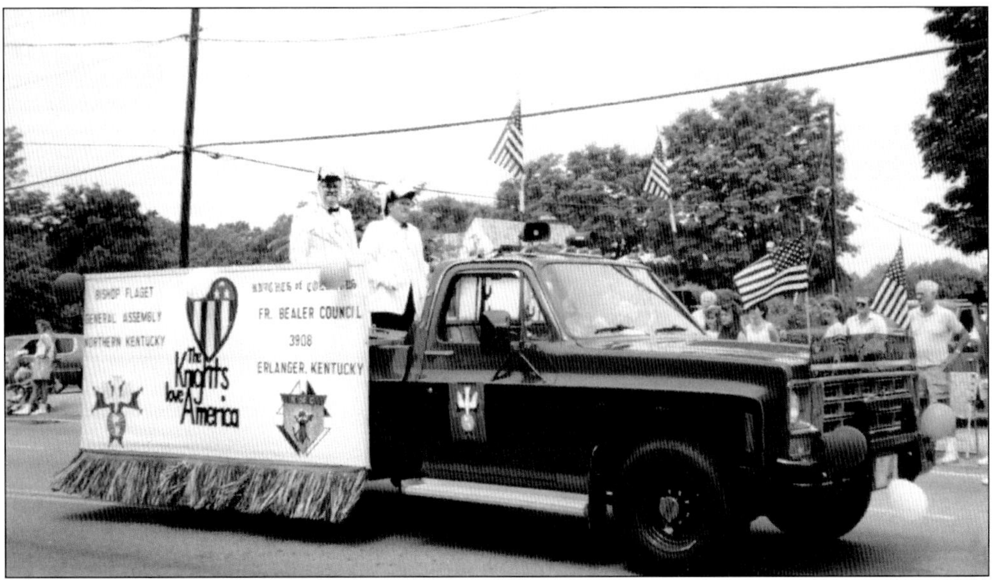

KNIGHTS OF COLUMBUS. Father Bealer Knights of Columbus Council No. 3908 has been an active organization in the Elsmere-Erlanger community since October 24, 1954. Photographed are Urban Lageman (left) and Bill Buerger representing the council in the annual Memorial Day parade. (Courtesy of Esther Lageman.)

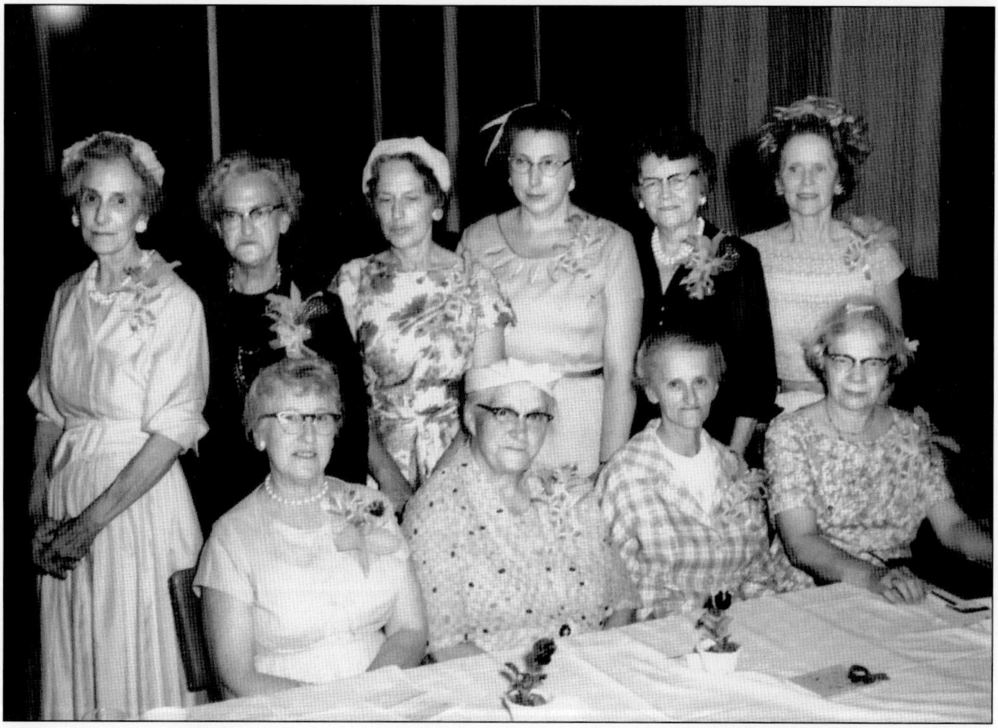

ERLANGER WOMEN'S CLUB. It would be impossible to list all the contributions made by the Erlanger Women's Club to the community during its 82 years of existence. The organization established the first library in 1914. They conducted musicals at the Railroad Park to raise funds. In the 1930s, the club formed the first symphony committee in Kentucky. The club donated 190 trees to beautify the community and purchased playground equipment for local parks. In the 1970s, they held arts and crafts shows in the Railroad Park and even brought the steam engine *The Best Friend of Charleston* to the celebration. In 1996, the club disbanded, but the community is a better place because of their work throughout the decades.

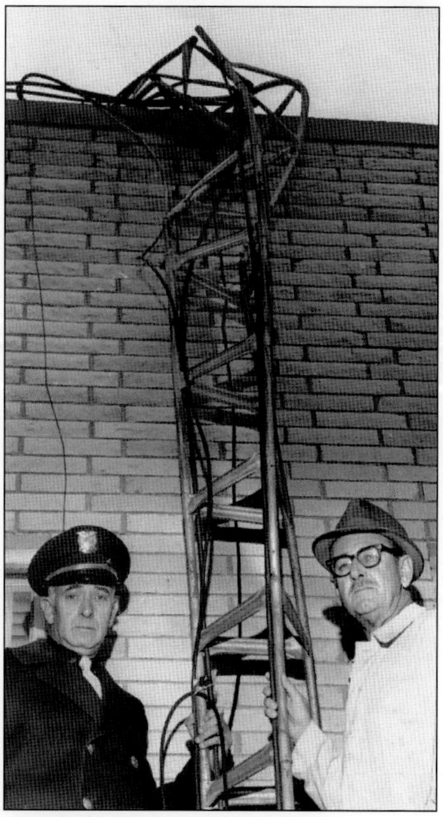

STORM DAMAGE TO ANTENNA. Chief John W. Rust (left) served the City of Erlanger as police chief from 1966 until his death in 1973, and Leon "Shake" Ryle, City of Erlanger building inspector and public works director for over 25 years, retired in 1985. They are inspecting the police radio dispatching antenna damaged in 1971 by lightning. "Shake" received his nickname because in his youth, his friends thought he looked like Shakespeare.

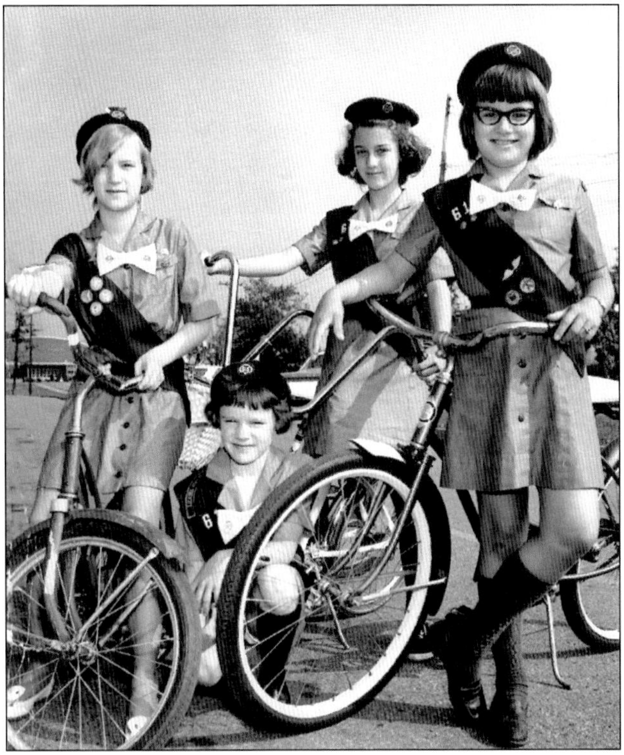

Girl Scouts. The Licking Valley Girl Scouts Council started in Erlanger in 1918. Girl Scouting provides safe places to play, exercise, and socialize, critical for ensuring that girls develop healthy habits and relationships. Pictured here after receiving their healthy living badges in 1969 are, from left to right, Frankie Jo Richie, Kathy May, Debbie Gers, and Kim Hiles.

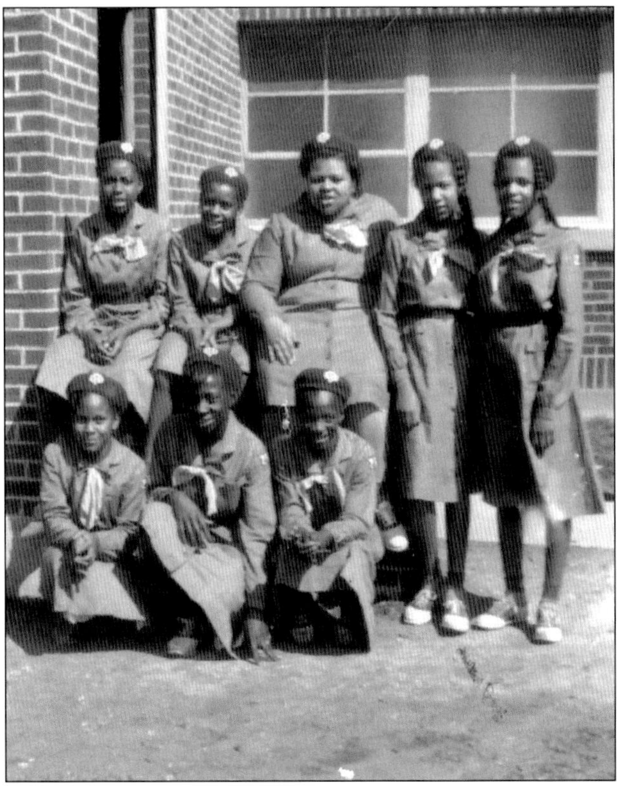

Girl Scout Troop in Elsmere. This troop was organized at Wilkins Heights School in 1954 under the leadership of Wilma Porterfield and Ann Sleet, both longtime residents of Elsmere. Pictured from left to right are (first row) Carol Dixon, Joyce Luke, and Bernice Luke; (second row) Martha Pinkelton, Jenny Gaines, Rosella Weaver, Eleanor Porterfield, and Eloise Porterfield. (Courtesy of Nancy and Rosella Weaver.)

Two

Community

Churches, Schools, and Libraries

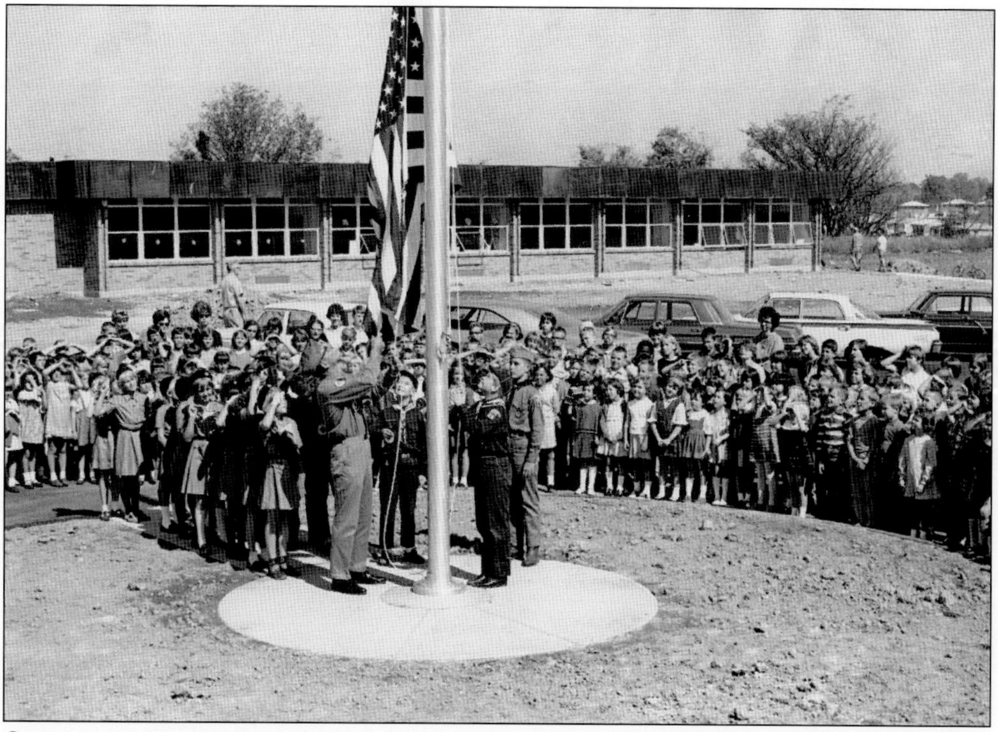

Opening of Arnett Elementary. The school is located at 3552 Kimberly Drive in Elsmere, Kentucky. It opened in 1967, and this was the flag-raising ceremony with the Boy and Girl Scouts acting as honor guard while the student body salutes the flag.

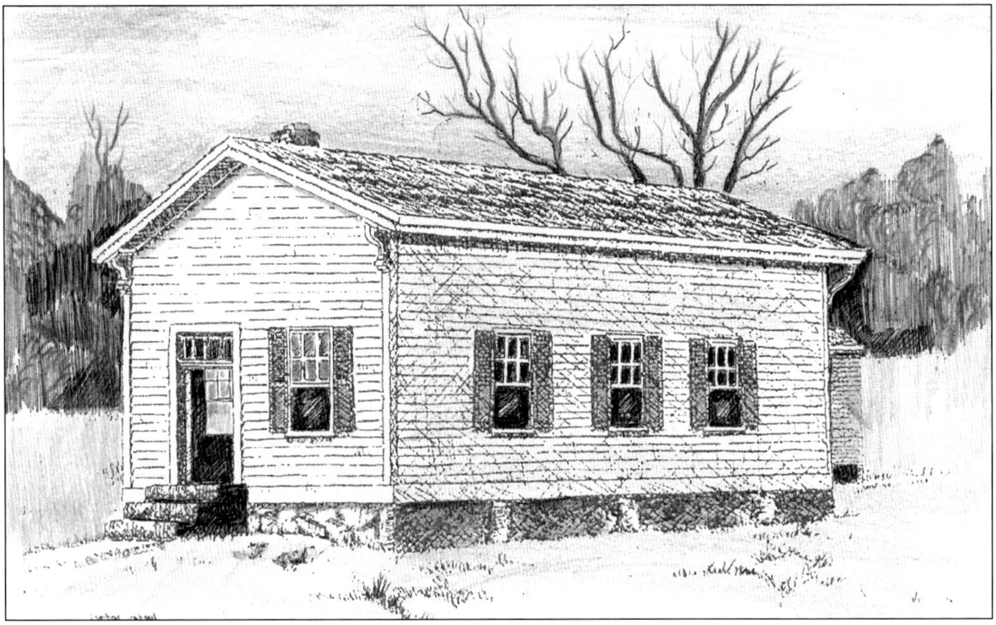

Dunbar School. In 1888, Thomas and Fannie Green, Mat Slaughter, and George Whitlock sponsored fund-raisers to build a school for the large African American community in Elsmere and Erlanger. The school was first built on Dixie Highway in 1896. Edward Anderson from Cynthiana was hired for grades one through eight. The school burned down and was rebuilt in Elsmere at 437 Spring Street. It was named the Dunbar School and stands today as a home.

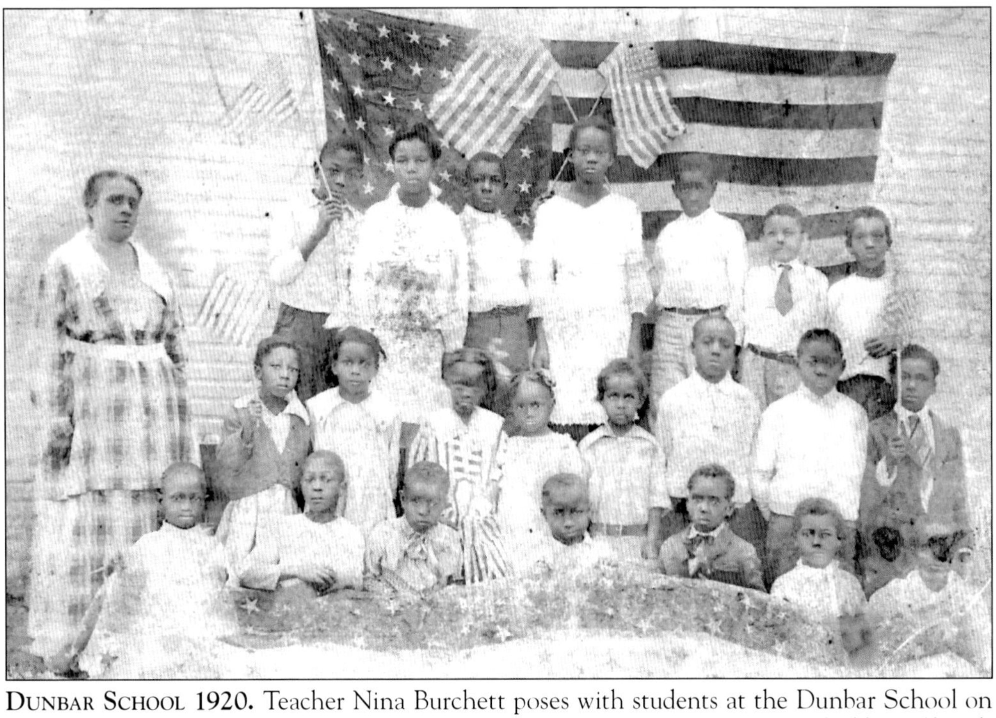

Dunbar School 1920. Teacher Nina Burchett poses with students at the Dunbar School on Spring Street. In the third row are Wilma Carneal (second from left) and Mary Blackburn (fourth from left). (Courtesy of Eleanor King.)

TEACHER AT THE DUNBAR SCHOOL. Wilma Carneal Porterfield graduated from the eighth grade at Dunbar School. After receiving her Bachelors of Arts degree from Wilberforce University, she returned to Elsmere and taught grades four through eight at the Dunbar School (1941 and 1948) and at Wilkins Heights School (1948–1951). In addition to teaching, Wilma was an active member at Barnes Temple Church. Wilma's sister, Cora Carneal Porterfield, also taught at the Dunbar School. (Courtesy of Joyce Florence.)

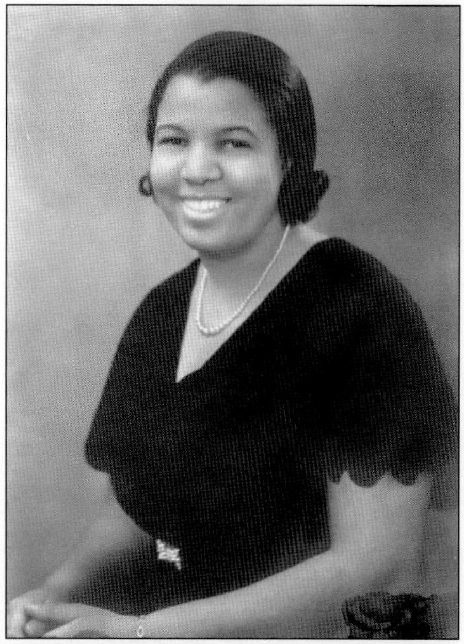

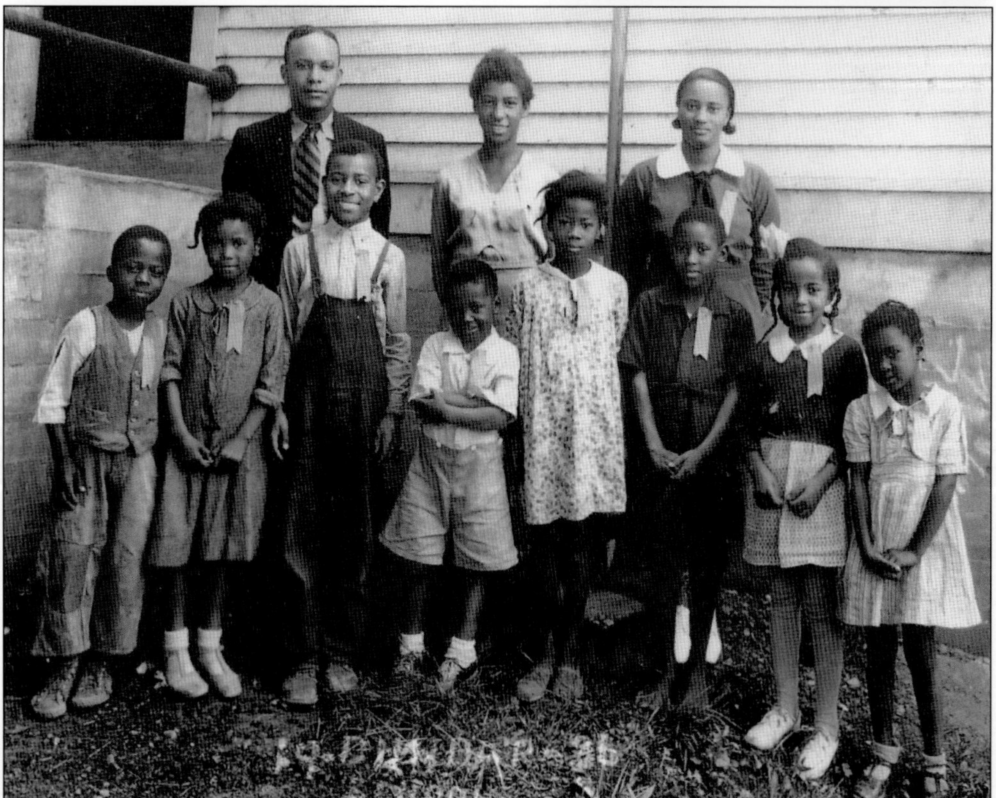

DUNBAR SCHOOL STUDENTS, 1936. Thomas Lewis, teacher at Dunbar School in Elsmere (1934–1941), is shown with a group of students who received blue ribbons for good hygiene from the school nurse, Mrs. Emma Jackson, pictured standing at back right. (Courtesy of Bill and Linda Lewis.)

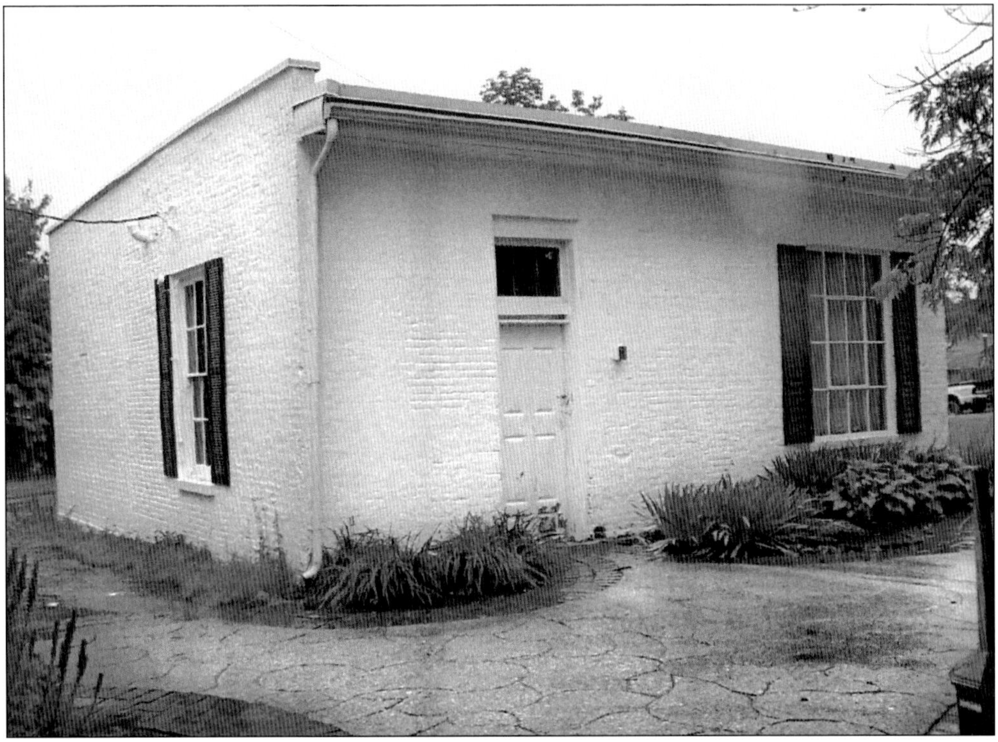

SMOKEHOUSE BEHIND FOREST LAWN. The Erlanger and Elsmere area had numerous private schools during the 1800s, including one located in old slave quarters behind the Stevenson home in the late 1860s taught by a Miss Billings. This one was located in the smokehouse behind the Manley residence, now Forest Lawn Cemetery. It still stands today. Lottie Williams was the teacher. Another school was built on Dixie Highway across from Grave's Pond and called Locust Grove Academy. It still stands. (Photograph by Paul Dusing.)

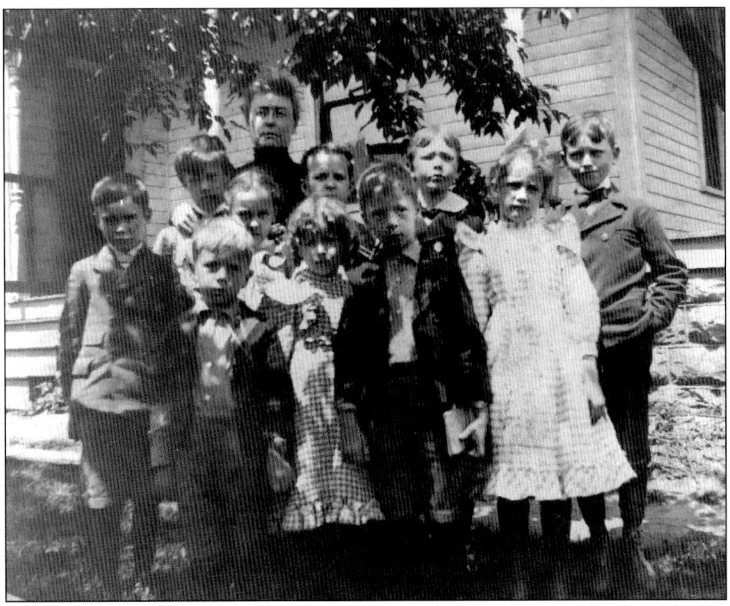

MISS GEORGIA KIRTLEY'S PRIVATE SCHOOL. This is another private school that was run by Georgia Kirtley in the old Hilker house at 109 Erlanger Road. Pictured with Georgia Kirtley are, from left to right, (first row) Floyd Ryle, Robert Slater, Mary Helen Buckner, Harry Slater, and Mary Alice Stevenson; (second row) James Blick, May Blick, Louise Buckner, Almar Buckner, and Tom Buckner.

ST. HENRY SCHOOL. In 1893, a small school was added next to St. Henry's Church. The children were first taught by R. Renikens, Peter Berberich, Otto Fritz, and Belle Pratt. In 1899, Fr. B. J. Kolbe engaged the Sisters of St. Benedict to take charge of the school, located at the corner of Garvey and Shaw Avenues.

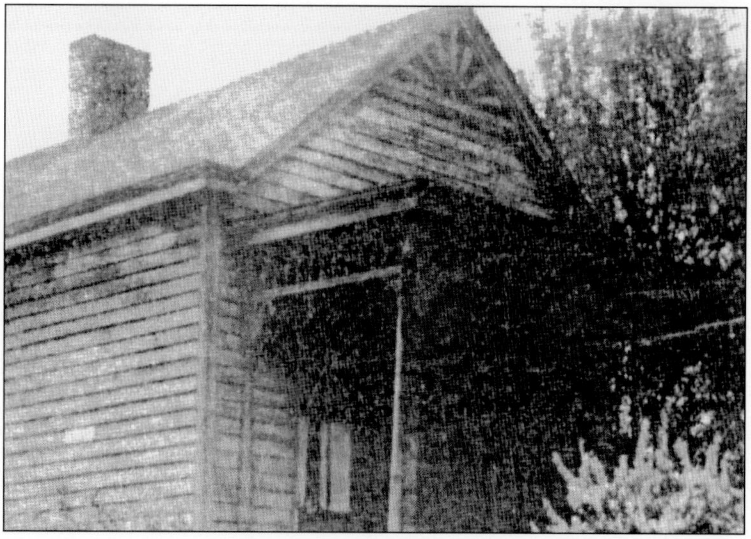

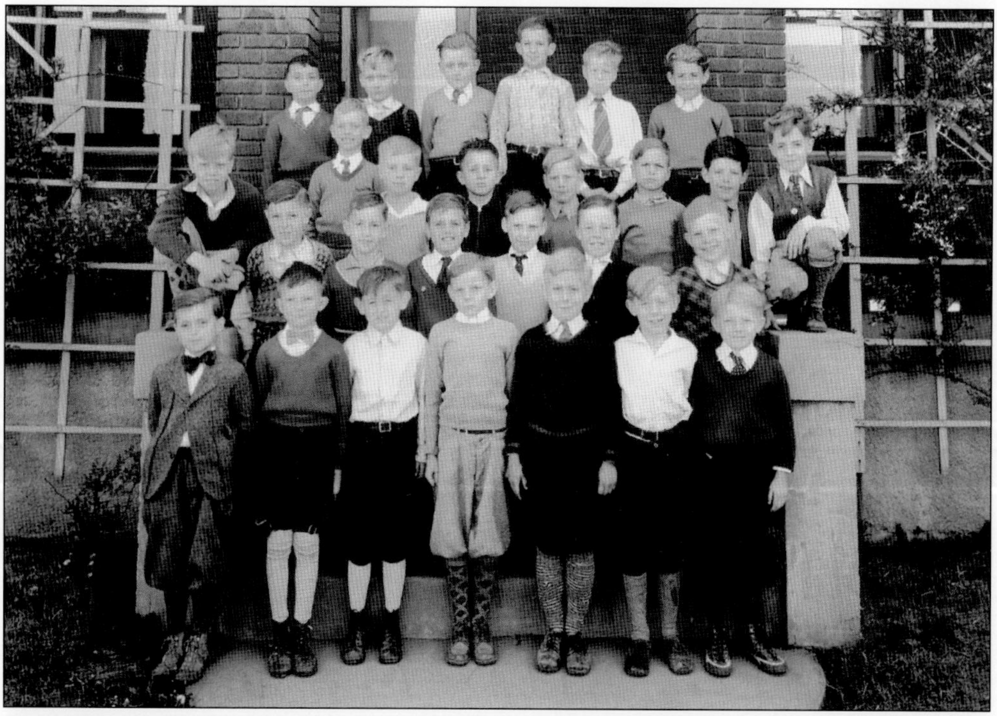

THE 1935 CLASS OF ST. HENRY SCHOOL: from left to right stand (first row) Paul Steffen, Sylvester Bolte, George Kreidler, David Laidlo, Harry Nussbaum, Art Bly, and Donald Wilmhoff; (second row) Richard Hegge (kneeling on wall), Donald Snow, Bill Ruehl, Roland Brendel, Joe Schwartz, Tom Trumble, and unidentified; (third row) Gus Wessling, Elmer Stiene, James Michels, J. Berkemeier, ? Harmes, Harold Denzer, and Ronald Rosing; (fourth row) Ambrose Bender, Bob Thaman, Bob Schweinefuss, ? Reinders, Bernard Tobergte, and Bob Hoffman. (Courtesy of Joe and Marcie Schwartz.)

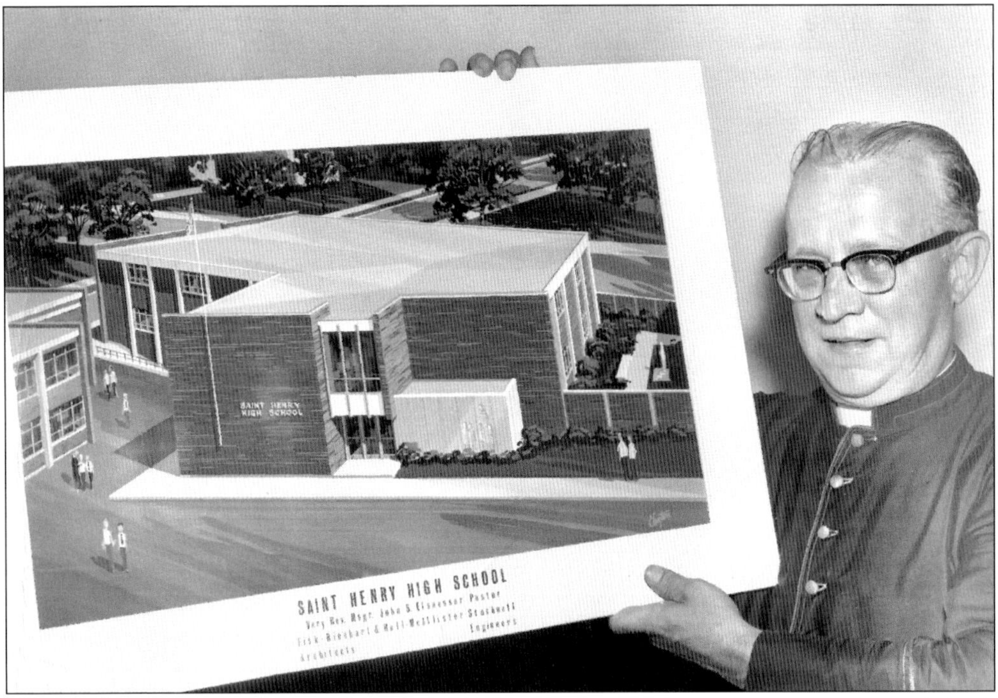

St. Henry High School. Msgr. John Elsaesser holds a photograph of the new St. Henry School, which opened December 6, 1967. Monsignor Elsaesser served as pastor of St. Henry Church from 1964 until 1981.

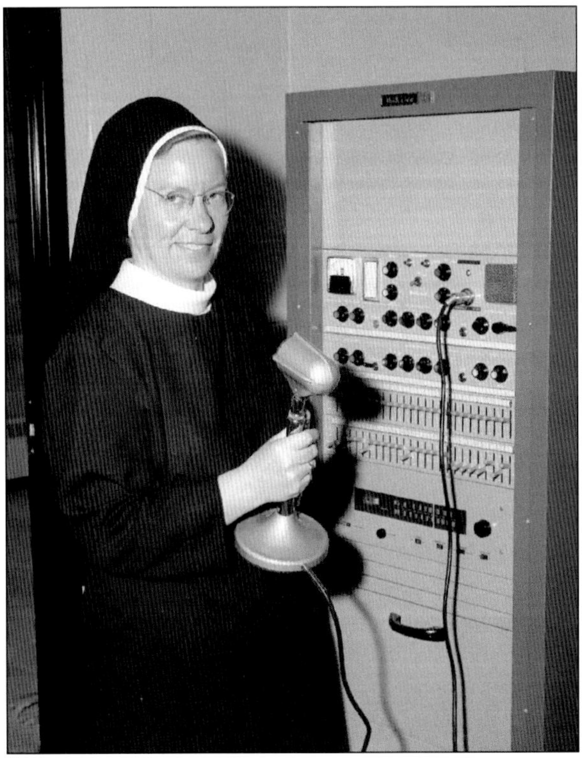

Sr. Joseph Marie O.S.B. (Order of St. Benedict). Sister Joseph Marie was principal of St. Henry High School from 1963 until 1973. She recalls the move to the new high school. Snow was everywhere, but 90 percent of the students showed up to help with the move. In two days, all the school furniture and equipment was transferred to the new building by the student body. Sister Blanche, in her boots and large cloak, sat in the old library directing the students while Sister Mildred stayed in the new library managing things at that end.

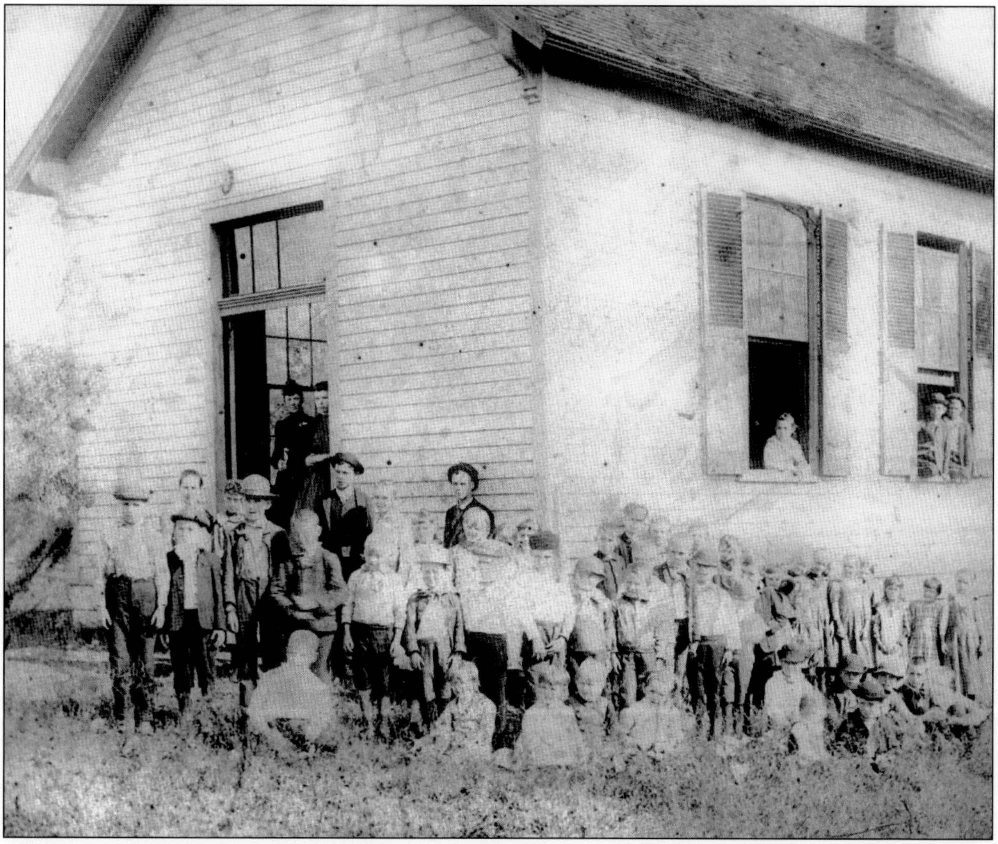

First District School. The building at 46 Erlanger Road was the location of the first district school in 1888. It served the area between Dry Creek and Turkeyfoot Road, from the Boone County line to Tupman Road, and included Elsmere. The charter was obtained from the county school superintendent, Mr. S. H. Kennedy, by three citizens: Ed Garvey, Jack Codey, and Alonzo Victor. Originally it was a frame house, as seen in the above photograph. In 1891, it was moved back 25 feet and two brick rooms were added. The photograph below shows the school as it appears today, used as a home.

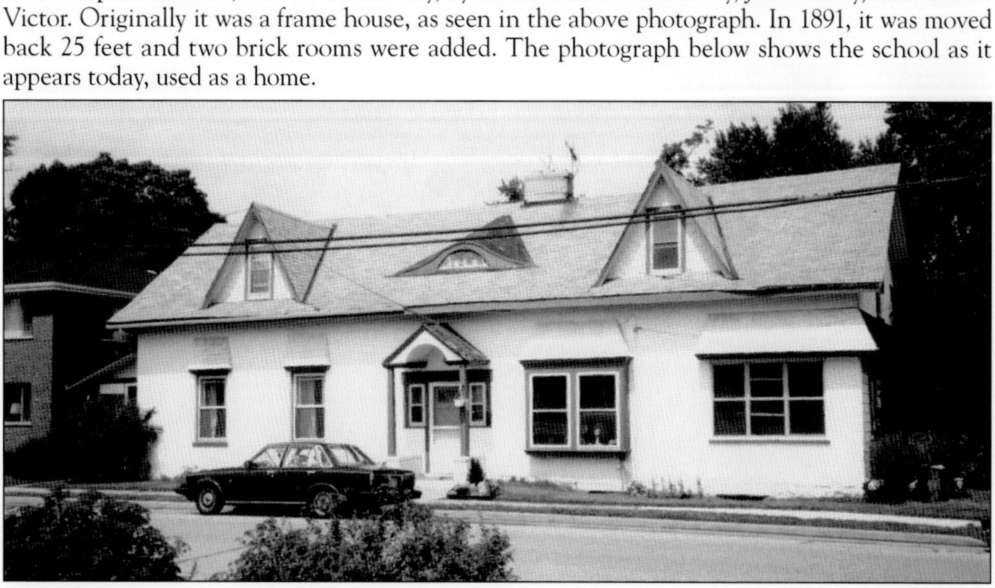

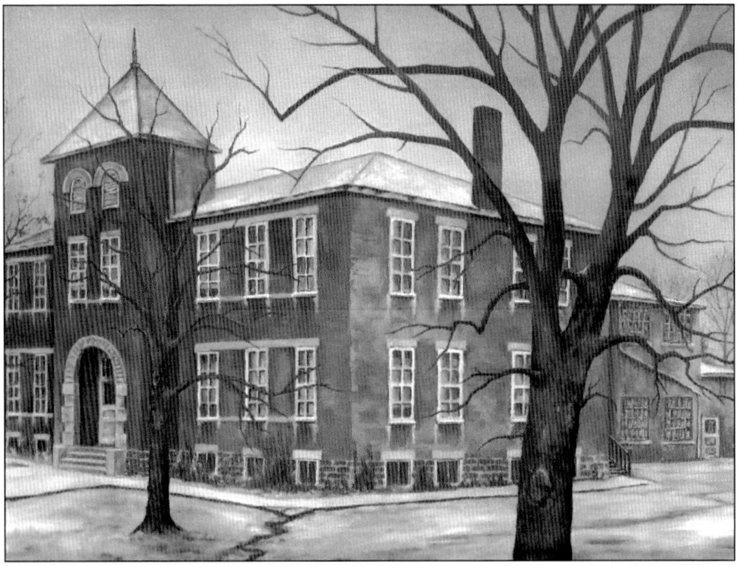

LOCUST STREET SCHOOL. The school was erected in 1907 for grades 1 through 12. The first graduates of Erlanger High School received diplomas in 1912. Three rooms and an auditorium were added in 1924. As the local population increased, a new high school was built in 1928. However, Locust Street School continued to operate as an elementary school until 1956.

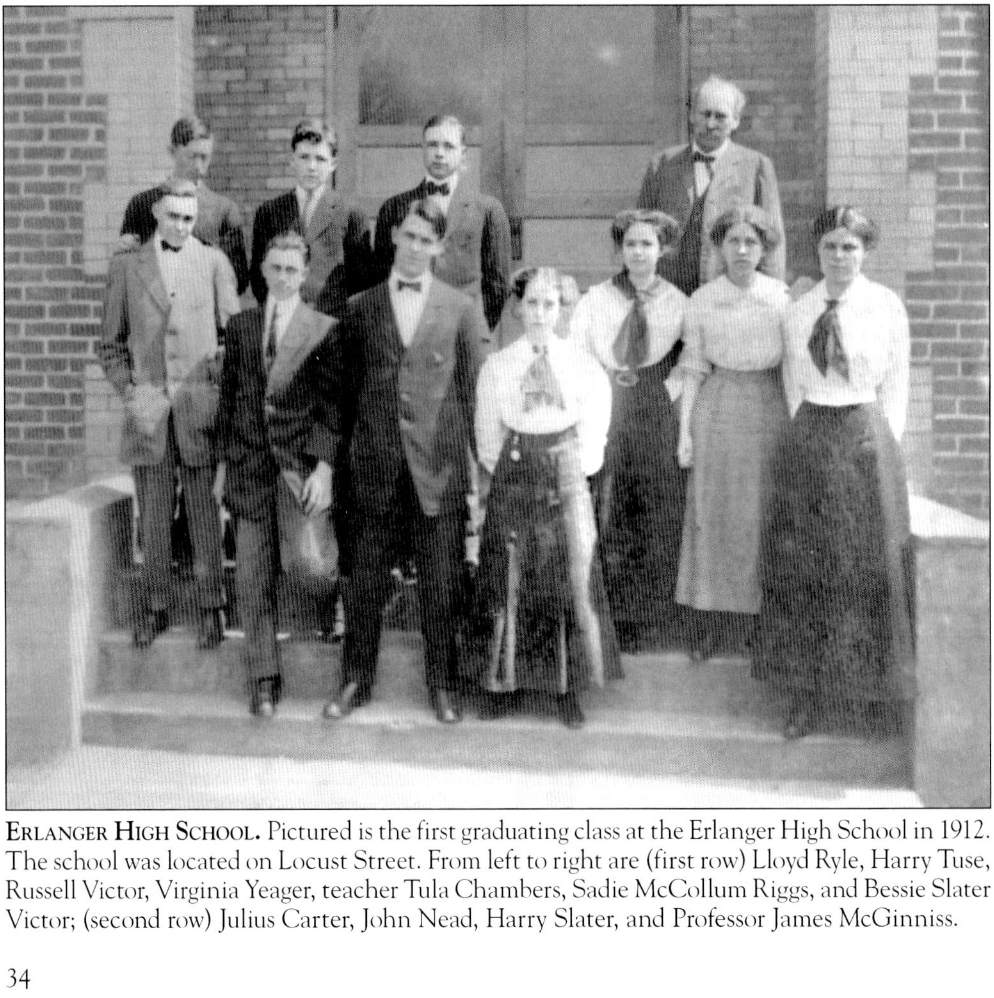

ERLANGER HIGH SCHOOL. Pictured is the first graduating class at the Erlanger High School in 1912. The school was located on Locust Street. From left to right are (first row) Lloyd Ryle, Harry Tuse, Russell Victor, Virginia Yeager, teacher Tula Chambers, Sadie McCollum Riggs, and Bessie Slater Victor; (second row) Julius Carter, John Nead, Harry Slater, and Professor James McGinniss.

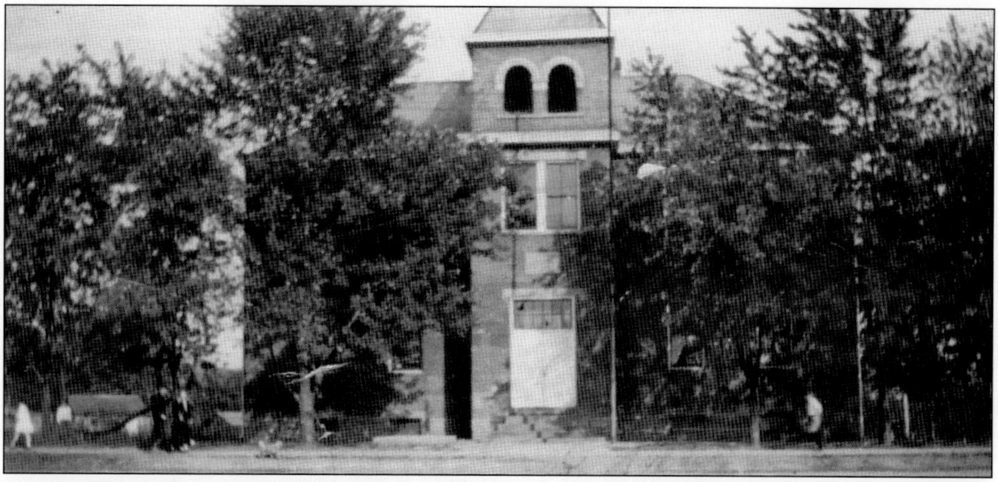

ELSMERE SCHOOL. In 1899, Elsmere built a brick school on Central Row. Grades one through six were conducted at this school. In 1924, enrollment was 233 pupils and seven teachers. A new school was built in 1942. An addition was built in 1957. In 1971, the school's name was changed to Dorothy Howell Elementary.

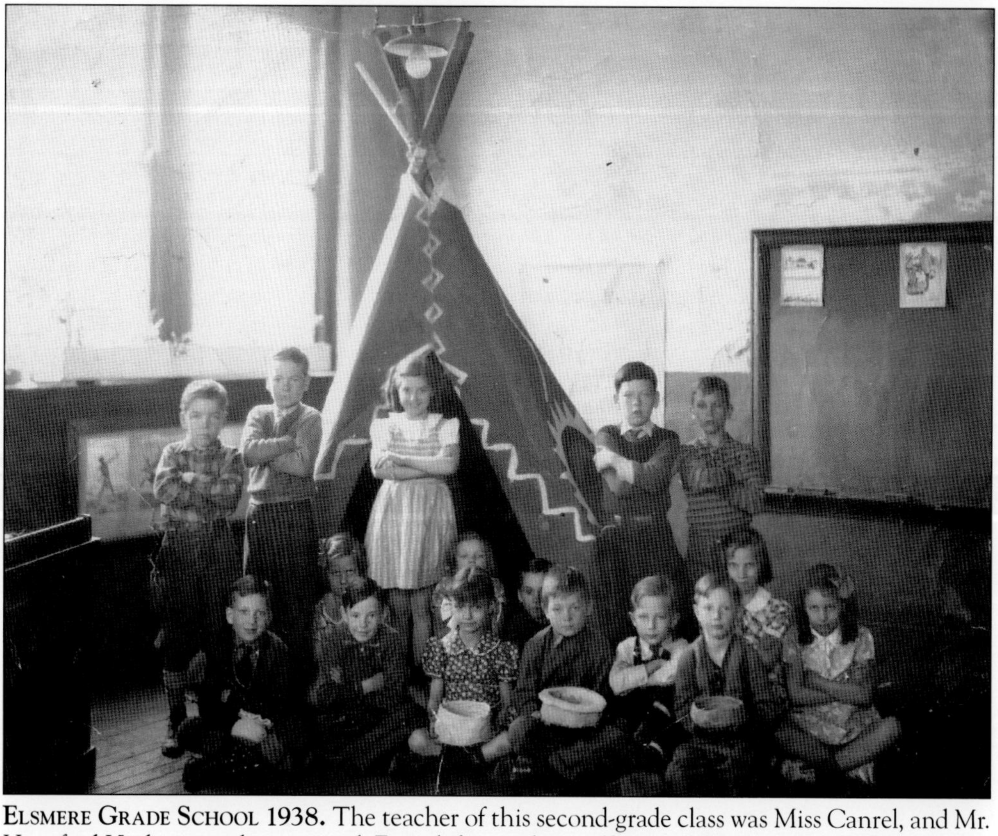

ELSMERE GRADE SCHOOL 1938. The teacher of this second-grade class was Miss Canrel, and Mr. Hansford Harlow was the principal. From left to right are (first row) Philip ?, "Babe" Bushelman, Nedy "Betty" Bob, Clay Schultz, Alvey Baxter, Dicke Morehead, and Claraby Tomas; (second row) unidentified, Neda Duvaul, James Martin, and Betty Ann Zitt; (third row) Gene Riley, Irven Davis, Carolyn Crowell, Chelsey Tomas, and H. Martin. (Courtesy of Irven Davis.)

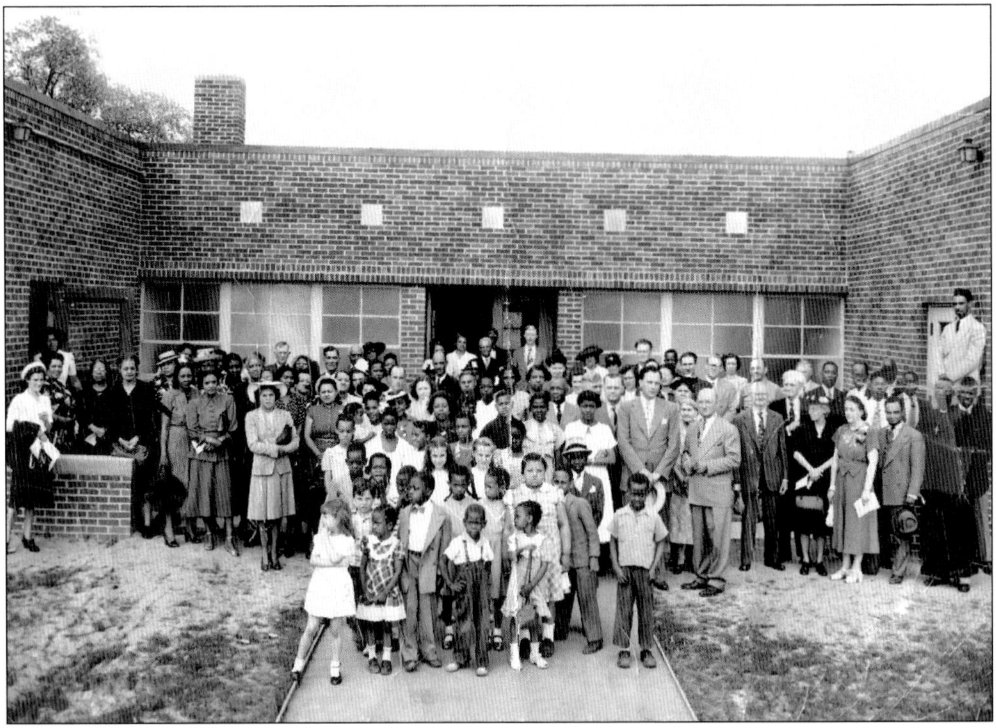

Wilkins Heights Dedication. The school was built in 1948 and dedicated in May 1949. Speakers included PTA president Lutie Rice, Newport Public Schools superintendent A. D. Owens, and Rev. Charles Wesley of Byrd Street Baptist Church. Rosella Porterfield and many others helped persuade the school board to build a new school on property purchased from Sebron and Sue Lee Wilkins, citing the dilapidated condition of Dunbar. (Courtesy of Stacey Carter.)

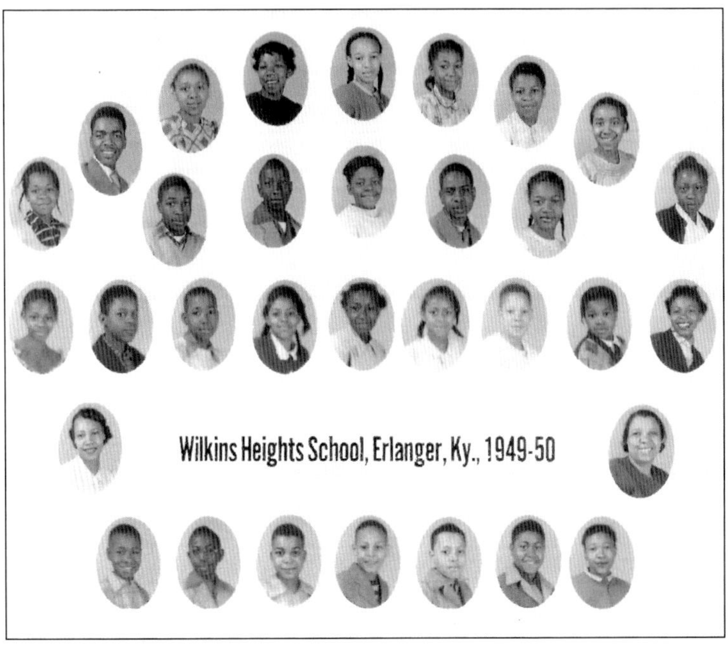

Wilkins Heights School, 1949–1950. These are students in grades four through eight at Wilkins Heights School with teacher Wilma (Carneal) Porterfield. (Courtesy of Bobbie Lou Bonner.)

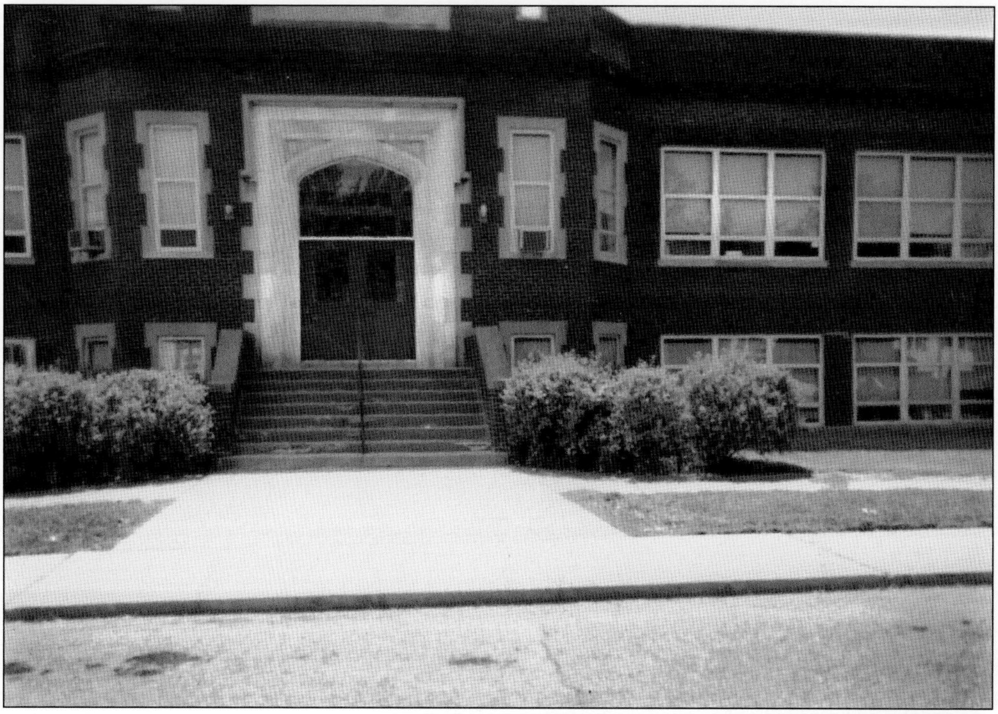

Lloyd Memorial High School. This school was named after John Uri Lloyd, well-known author, pharmacist, and professor. The first classes began about 1928 and continued there until 1956, when a new school was opened on the old Erlanger fairgrounds. John U. Lloyd donated money for the establishment of the Lloyd Medal, given to an outstanding student each year, usually a graduating senior. In 1971, the school changed the name of the old building to James Tichenor School. Today it is known as the Harold and Evelyn Ensor Annex. The photograph on the right shows John Uri Lloyd, for whom Lloyd Memorial High School is named. (Both courtesy of John Uri Lloyd Library.)

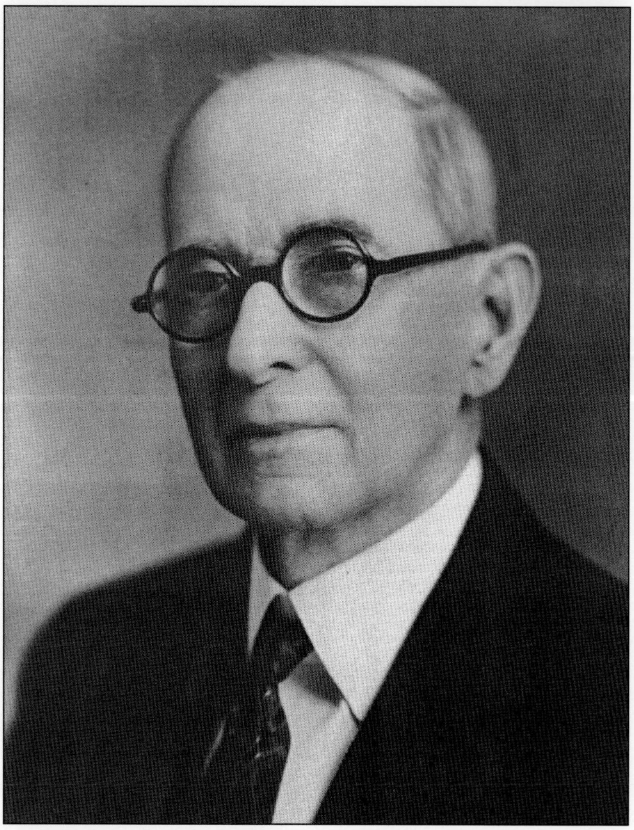

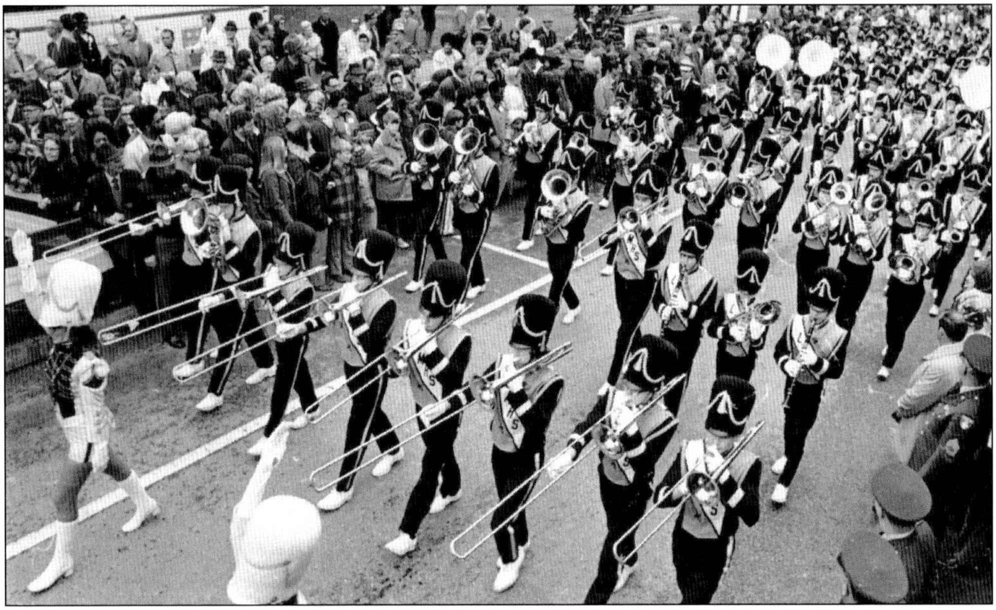

Lloyd Memorial High School Marching Band. The band is shown in Frankfort, Kentucky. Under the direction of Mr. Charles Hill, the band won many honors and competitions.

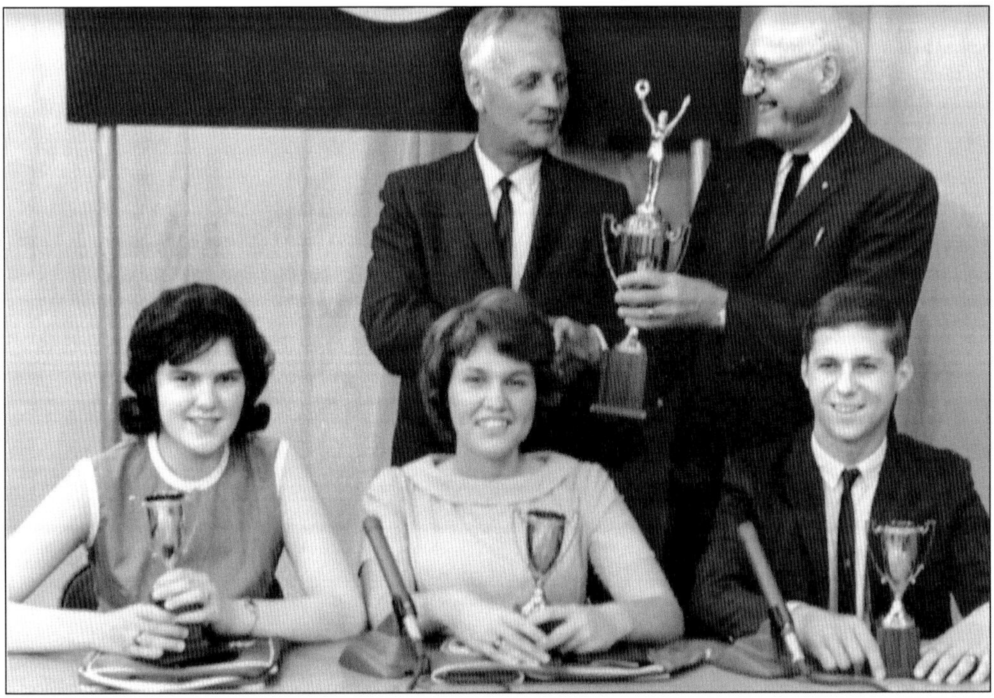

Lloyd Memorial High School's Academic Team. They won the Greater Cincinnati Championship in June 1965. The quiz show was broadcast on WLW-T and sponsored by Cincinnati Gas and Electric. The team won a trip to California as well as various books and encyclopedias for the school. Pictured from left to right are (first row) team members Karen Hopkins, Sandy Riegler, and Jim Moss; (second row) Cincinnati Gas and Electric vice president Jerry Hurtler and team coach C. M. Patrick, the dean of students and world history teacher.

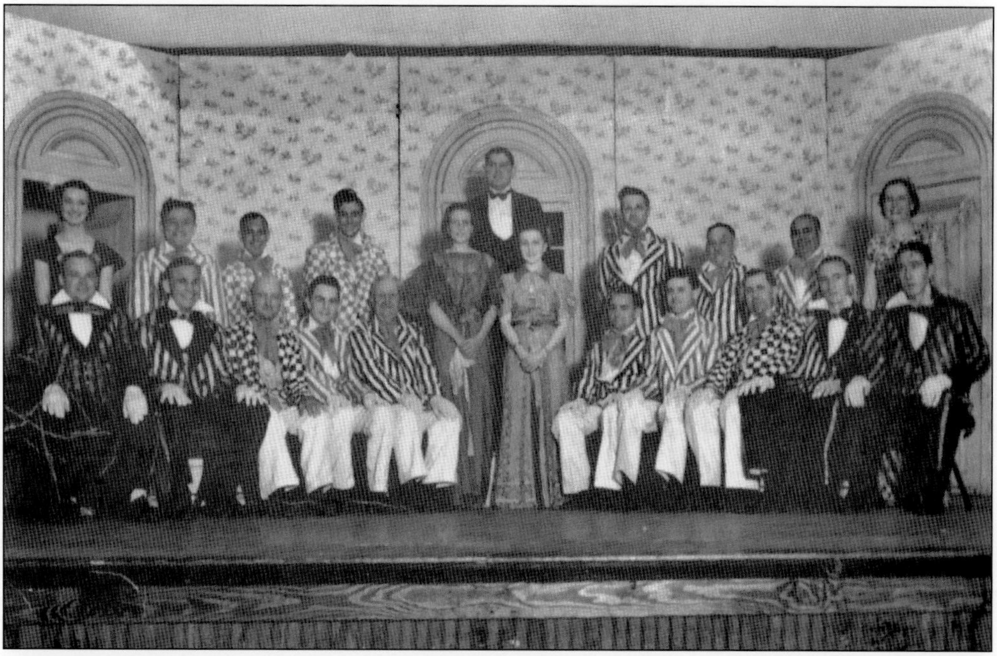

Lloyd Minstrel Show. Minstrel shows and "womanless weddings" were popular ways of raising money for a football field at the new high school. In 1928, some of the minstrels were, from left to right, (seated) Gurney Mitchell, Harold Pardom, Edgar Arnett, Whit Ashcraft, Courtney Walton, Joe Hogan, unidentified, Pat Day, Herbert B. Smith, and Dick Evans; (standing) Lida Catherine Keeney Martin, Harry Riggs, Morris Y. Thomas, Bob Miller, Elizabeth West Harrison, R. D. Martin, Betty Kay Gurney Bush, Al Beschman, "Pop" Domaschko, Chick Taylor, and Lillian Faber.

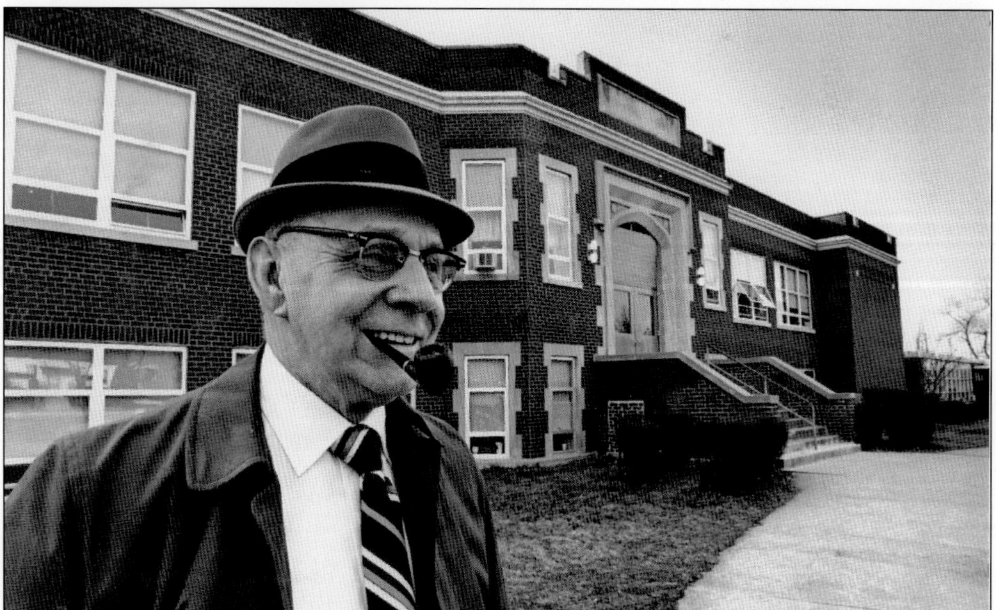

James I. Tichenor. James Tichenor started in 1941 as a basketball coach and math and science teacher at Lloyd High School. From 1961 to 1971, he served as assistant superintendent of the Erlanger-Elsmere School System. After he retired, the middle school was named after him.

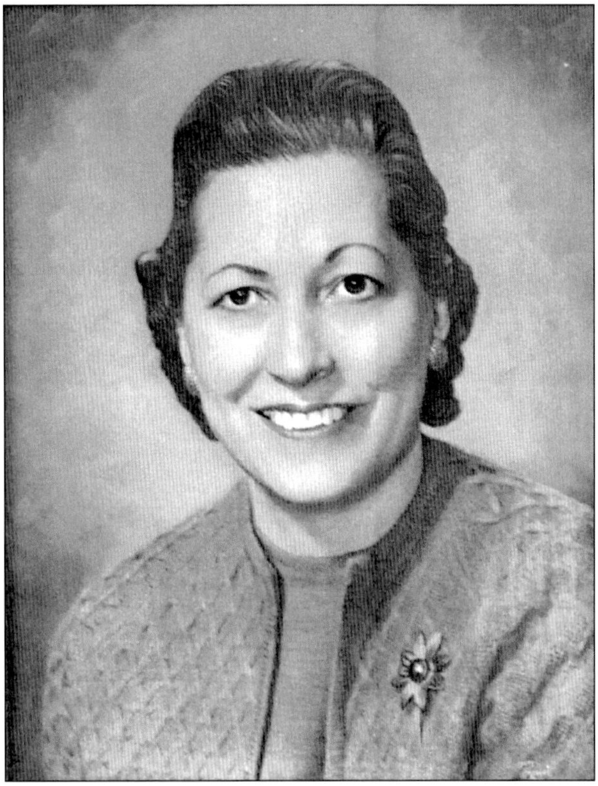

DOROTHY HOWELL. Dorothy Howell was born Dorothy Adams. After marrying Charles T. Howell, she became a teacher at Elsmere School in 1942. She was the principal between 1947 and 1975. Dorothy Howell died in 1977. Elsmere School was named Dorothy Howell Elementary in her honor in 1971. (Photograph by Paul Dusing.)

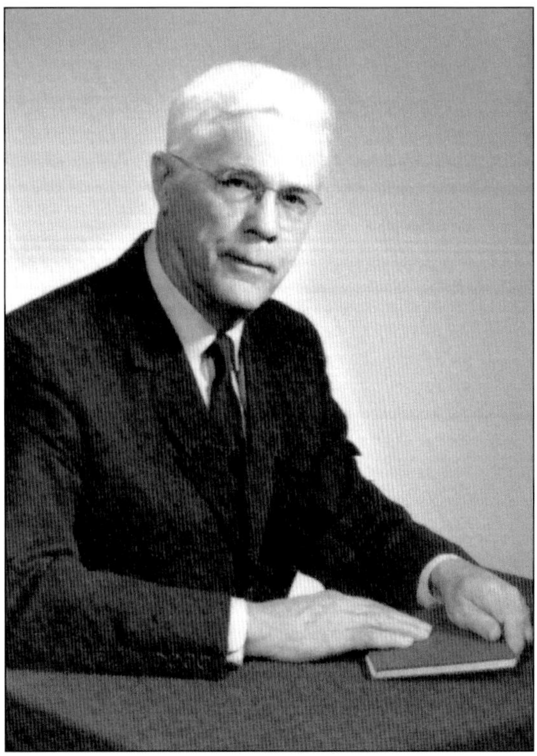

ARTHUR J. LINDEMAN. The Erlanger-Elsmere School Board approved the construction of two elementary schools in 1971. One building was on Erlanger Road and was named for Arthur J. Lindeman, who was a longtime school board member and supporter of education.

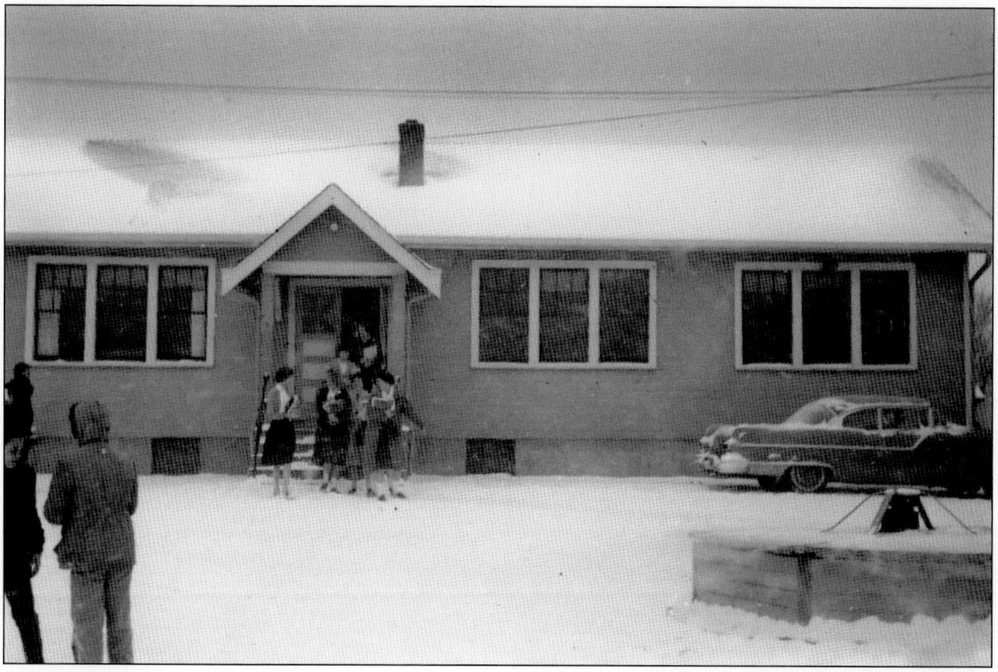

St. Henry Grade School. In 1929, with the St. Henry congregation growing and the number of schoolchildren increasing, Fr. George C. Bealer built a two-room wood-frame schoolhouse. Father Kolbe, pastor in 1933, added two more rooms to the school building. This building was demolished after the new high school was built in 1967.

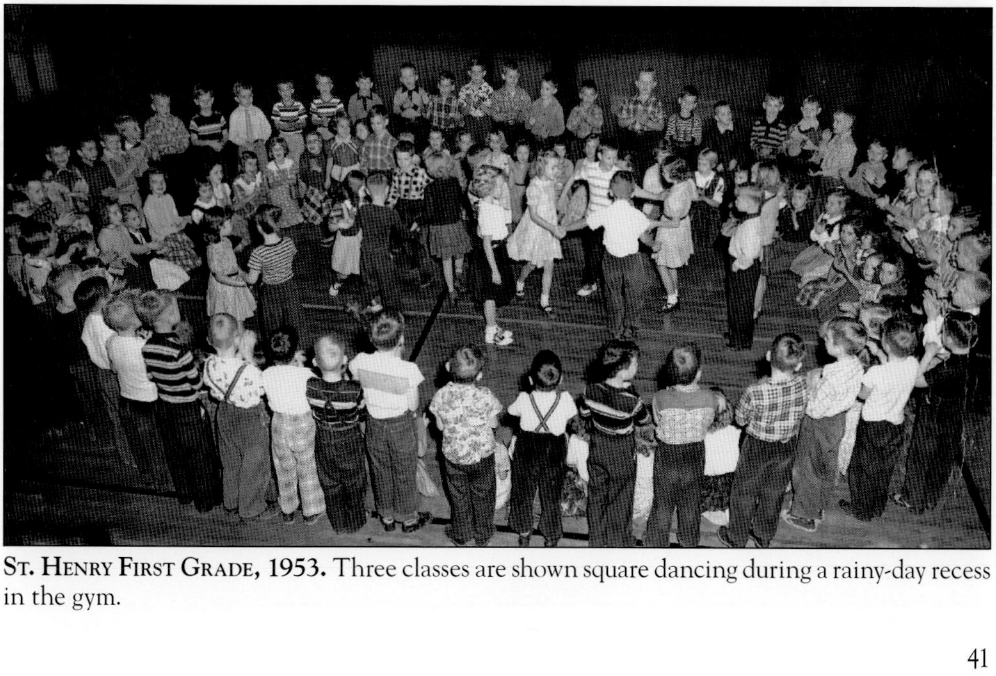

St. Henry First Grade, 1953. Three classes are shown square dancing during a rainy-day recess in the gym.

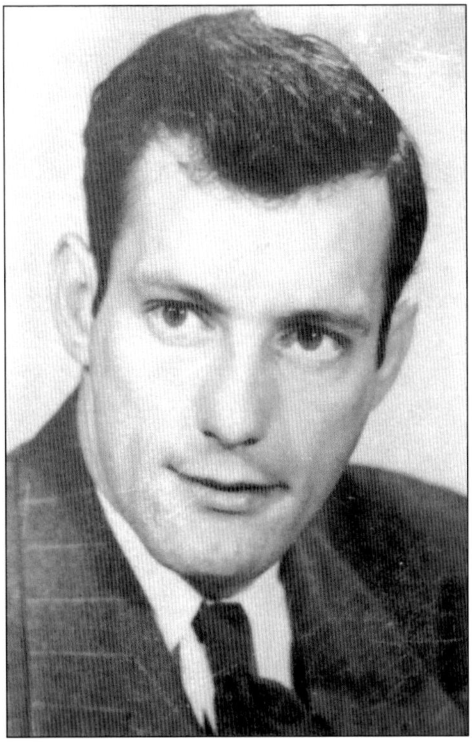

John W. Miles. Miles attended Erlanger-Elsmere schools from the first grade. He then attended Centre College and came to Erlanger-Elsmere to teach and coach. He became principal and then, in 1971, was selected as superintendent. He retired in 1982 and passed away in 1996.

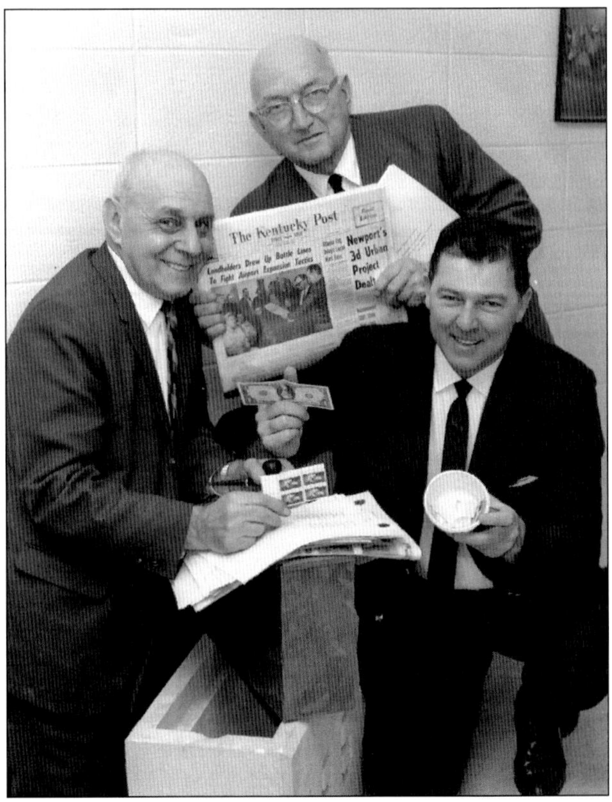

Arnett Elementary Dedication 1967. Originally called Stephenson Elementary, Arnett Elementary was named in honor of the former and longest-serving superintendent in Erlanger-Elsmere Schools, Edgar Arnett. He is pictured in the back, holding a copy of the *Kentucky Post* to be placed in the cornerstone. On the left is Supt. James Tichenor. Ray Weaver, first principal of Arnett Elementary, is seen on the right. Additions were made to the school in 1969 and 1972.

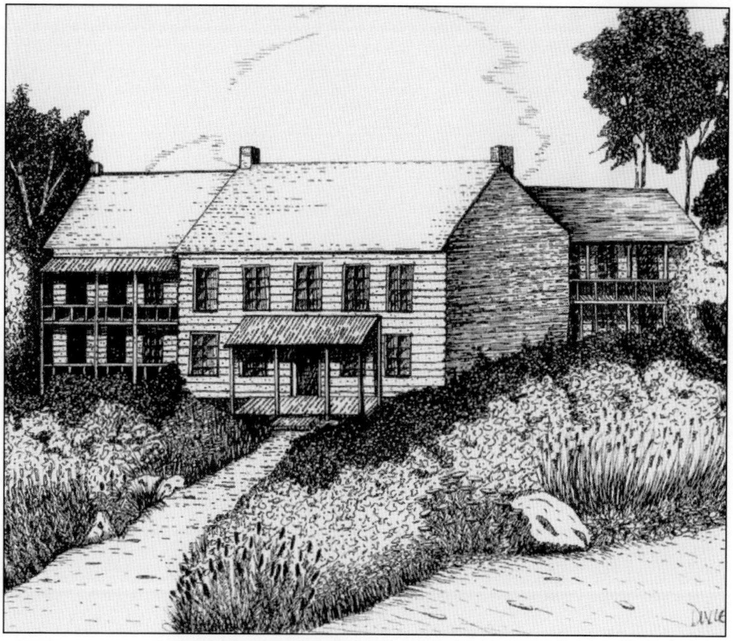

Bartlett Graves Log House. Graves was the first citizen of Erlanger. He first paid taxes on the land in 1808. He was high sheriff of Campbell County and a man of means. He built a new brick home within five years of bringing his family to Erlanger. The home was located on Commonwealth Avenue near the Erlanger Baptist Church. The home, called Walnut Grove, burned down in 1895. (Courtesy of Dixie Stevens.)

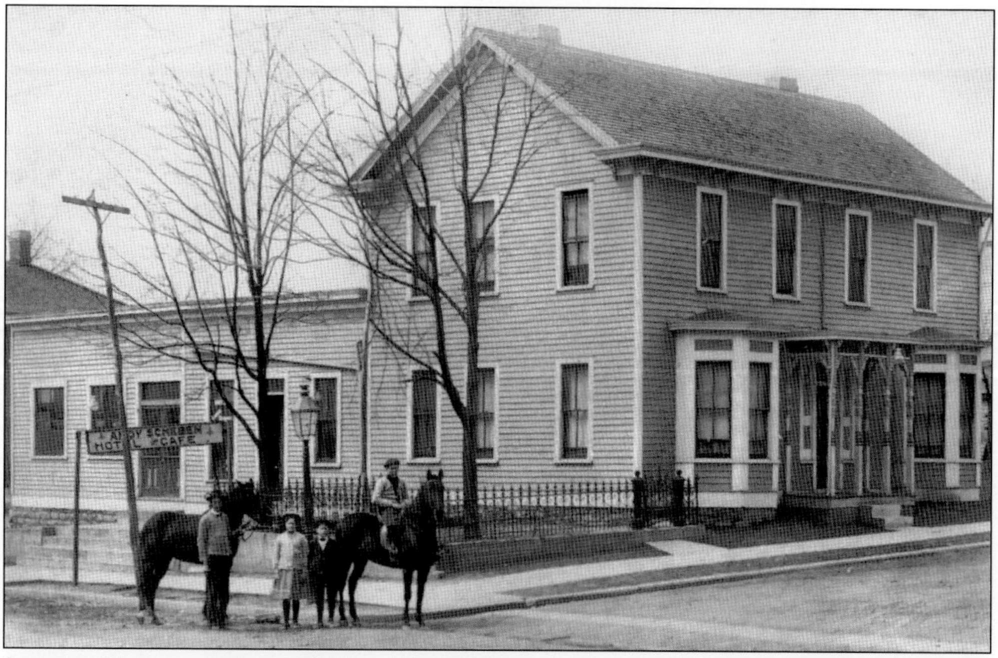

Scheben Hotel and Café. The hotel, located at Commonwealth and Dixie Highway, was built by the Ficke family in the 1880s. It was purchased by Andy Scheben around 1890. The property included a 17-room hotel, a restaurant with a bar, and two bowling lanes. Hotel patrons were brought to the hotel from the railroad depot by buggy. This photograph was taken about 1905. From left to right are Lonnie Fenny, Gertrude Scheben, Fred "Fritz" Scheben, and Andy Scheben Jr.

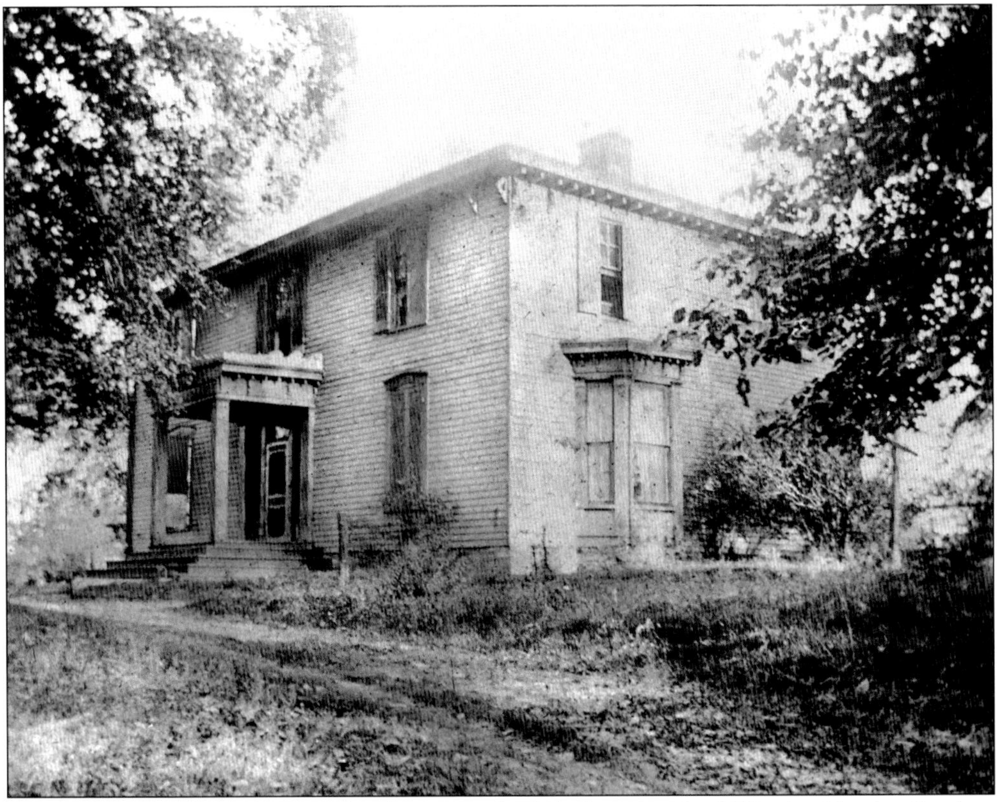

THE BEECHES-FRENCH HOME. This home was built before the Civil War by Charles Stephen French, brother of Mary Elizabeth French Timberlake and son of Judge Richard French. The house was later owned by Dr. Charles Judkins, organizer of the Erlanger Land Syndicate, and in 1915 by Edwin T. Gale and his family. During the 1915 tornado, the house was nearly destroyed. It was located where the Erlanger Post Office is located in 2009.

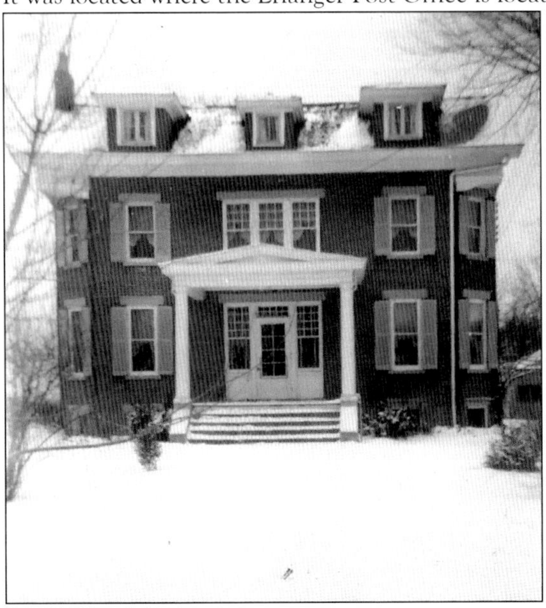

HARRY CARL HOME. The Carl home was located on Dixie Highway at Price Avenue. The family was very community minded. Mrs. Margaret Carl was active in the Woman's Club and Library Project. Harry Carl was on the school board for many years. They were the originators of Dixie Dew Products. Delicious candies were made in the garage of the home.

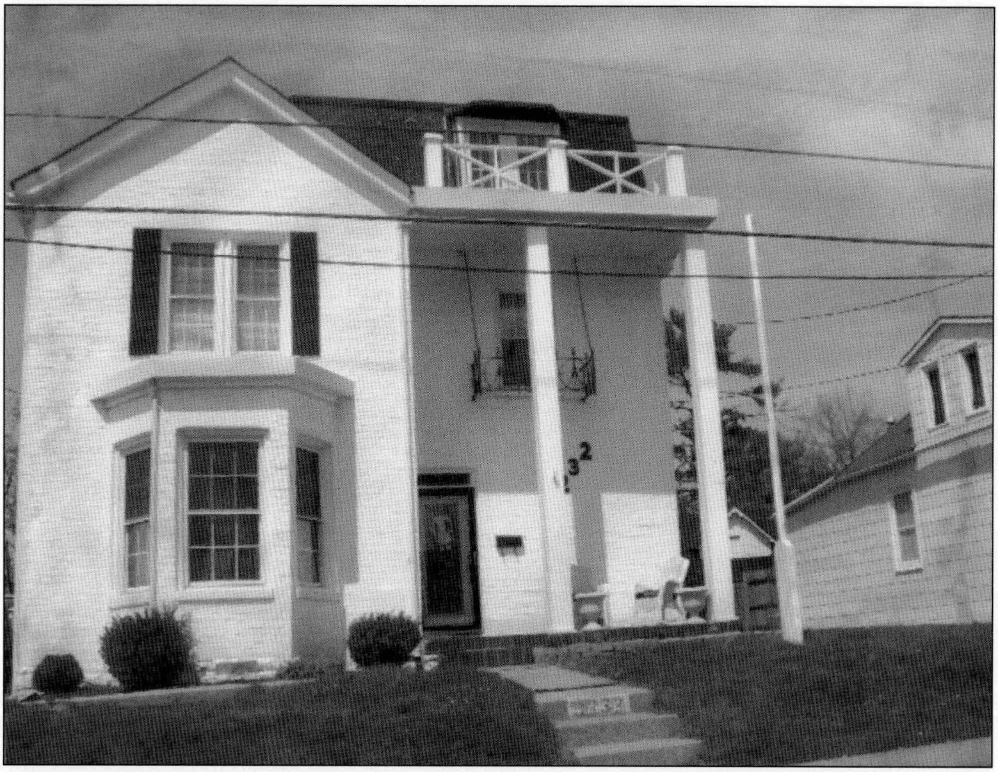

WAGINGER HOMESTEAD. John Waginger came to America in the late 1890s and built this beautiful home at 3232 Riggs Avenue. John sent money to his relatives, the Domaschkos, in Europe. In 1906, they came to Erlanger. Relatives often talk about the German parties that were held in the backyard with Pop Domaschko playing the accordion.

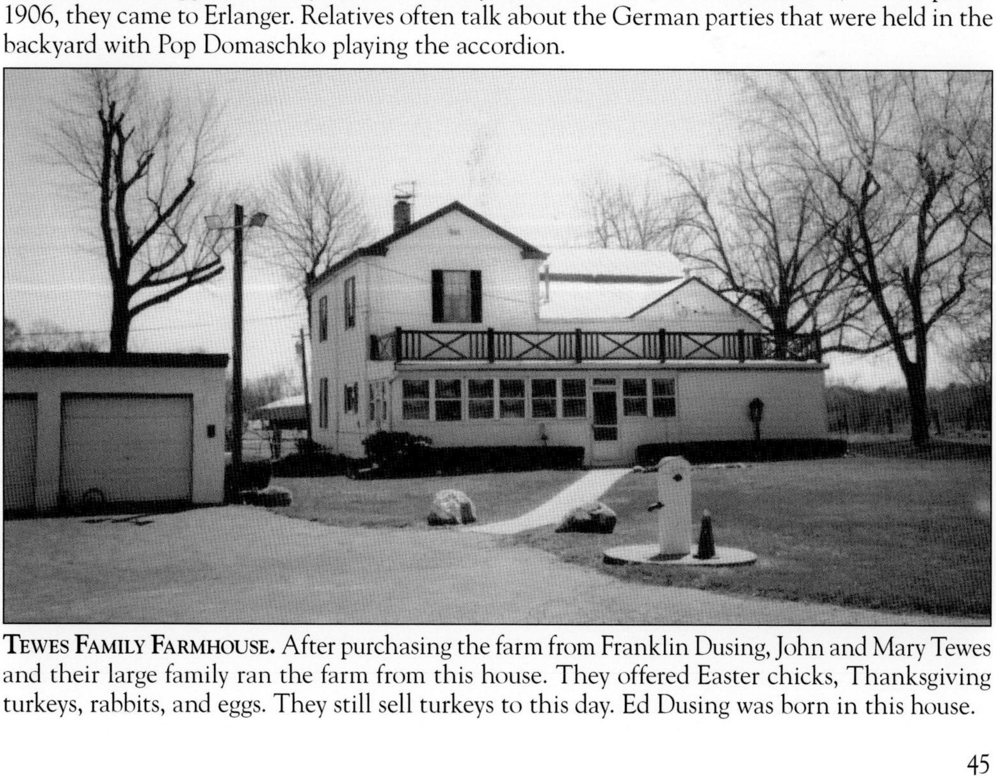

TEWES FAMILY FARMHOUSE. After purchasing the farm from Franklin Dusing, John and Mary Tewes and their large family ran the farm from this house. They offered Easter chicks, Thanksgiving turkeys, rabbits, and eggs. They still sell turkeys to this day. Ed Dusing was born in this house.

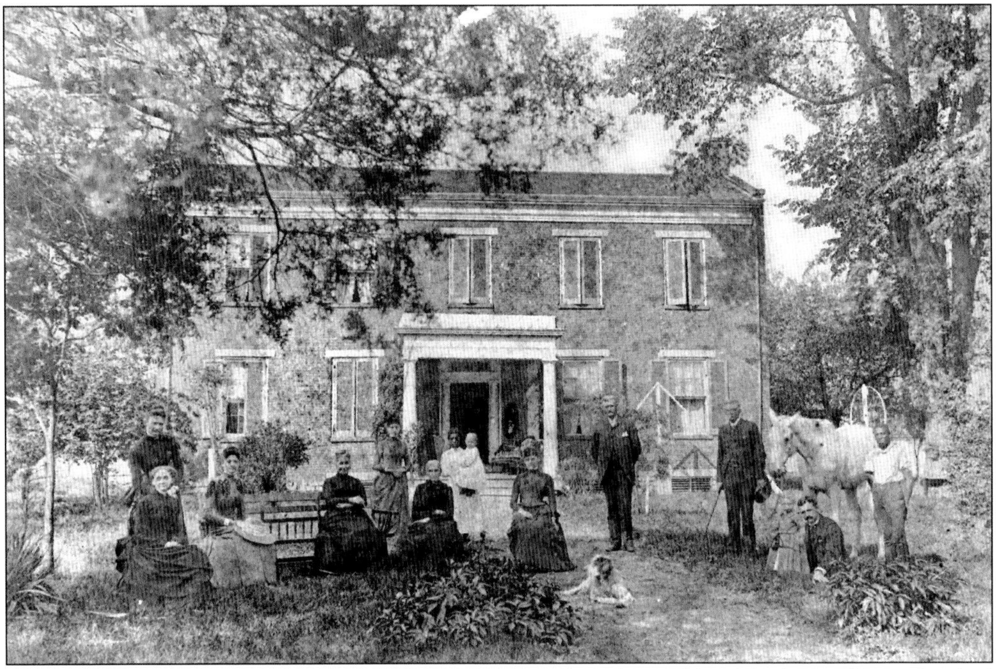

Rose Gate-Buckner Home. This is an 1880 photograph of the Hubbard Taylor and Lucy Sanford Buckner family at their home, Rose Gate, at Turkeyfoot Road and Dudley Pike in Erlanger. The Buckners were married in 1848 and had five children. Hubbard Taylor Buckner, who was widely known as a horseman, is standing to the left of the horse, and his son Hubbard George Buckner is seated next to the little girl. The rest of the Buckner children—Alexander Sanford, Lucy, Alice, and Sophia—are pictured here with their families, but their placements are unknown. Hubbard Taylor Buckner sold this property, which became Forest Lawn Cemetery, to Caleb S. Manly.

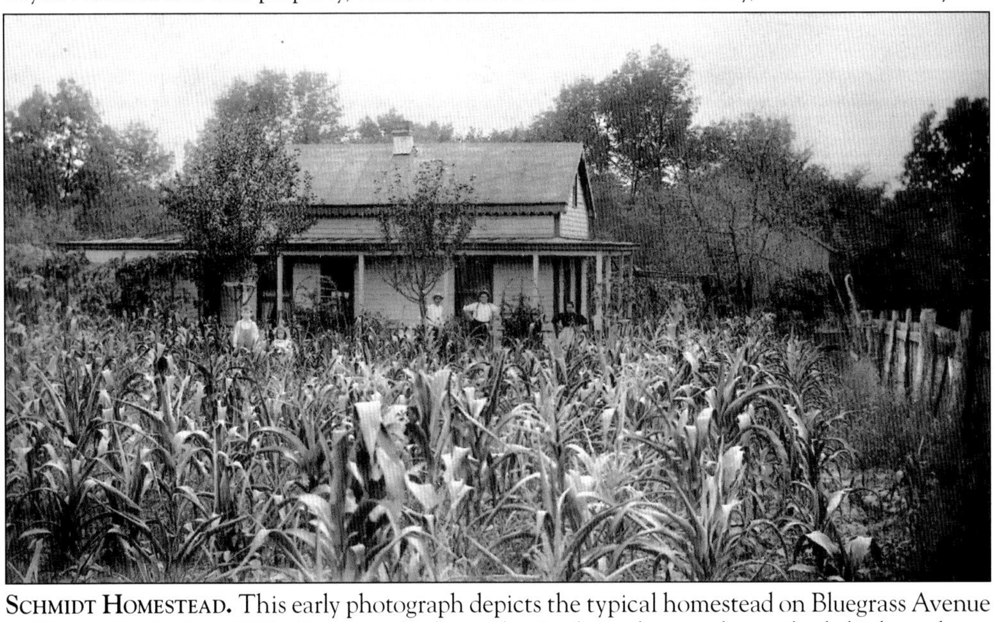

Schmidt Homestead. This early photograph depicts the typical homestead on Bluegrass Avenue in Elsmere in the late 1890s. Everyone had a garden in those days, and some had chickens, hogs, and cattle to feed the family. (Courtesy of Betty Roszmann.)

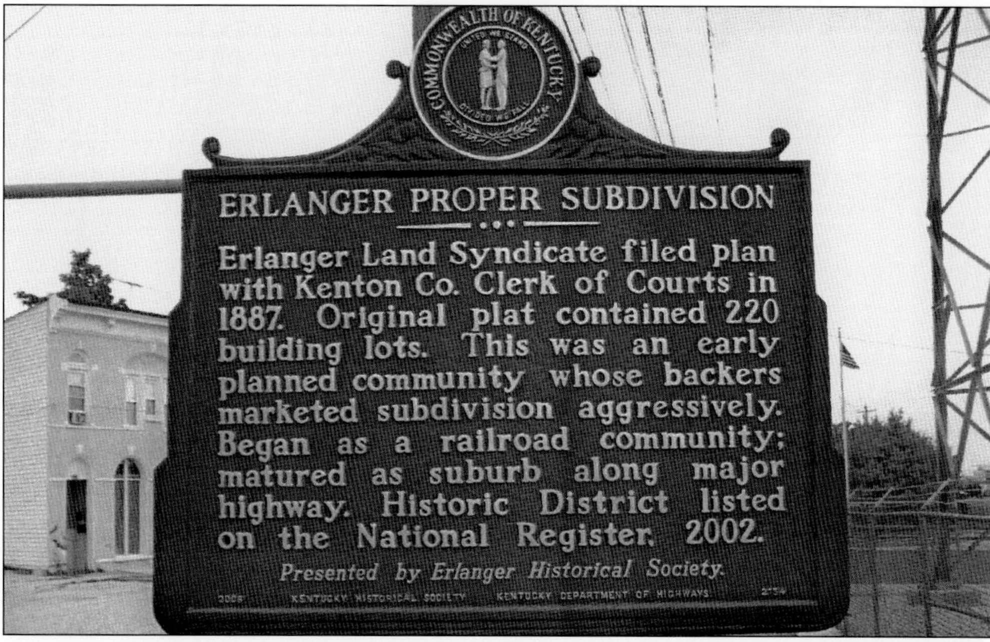

Kentucky Highway Marker No. 2154. In 2002, the National Register of Historic Places, through the Department of the Interior, recognized Erlanger's unique area and historic railroad depot. On September 19, 2004, the Erlanger Historical Society was the recipient of the Kentucky Highway Marker. The photograph below is of a home built by the Erlanger Land Syndicate. It is about 100 years old and is located at 7 Locust Street. Originally there were about 220 lots in one of the first subdivisions in the state of Kentucky, then the syndicate built five show homes with property. A special commuter train was run, with free fare and lunch, from Cincinnati and Covington for prospective buyers. As many as 20 railroad cars came to visit the area on Sunday afternoons. (Photographs by Paul Dusing.)

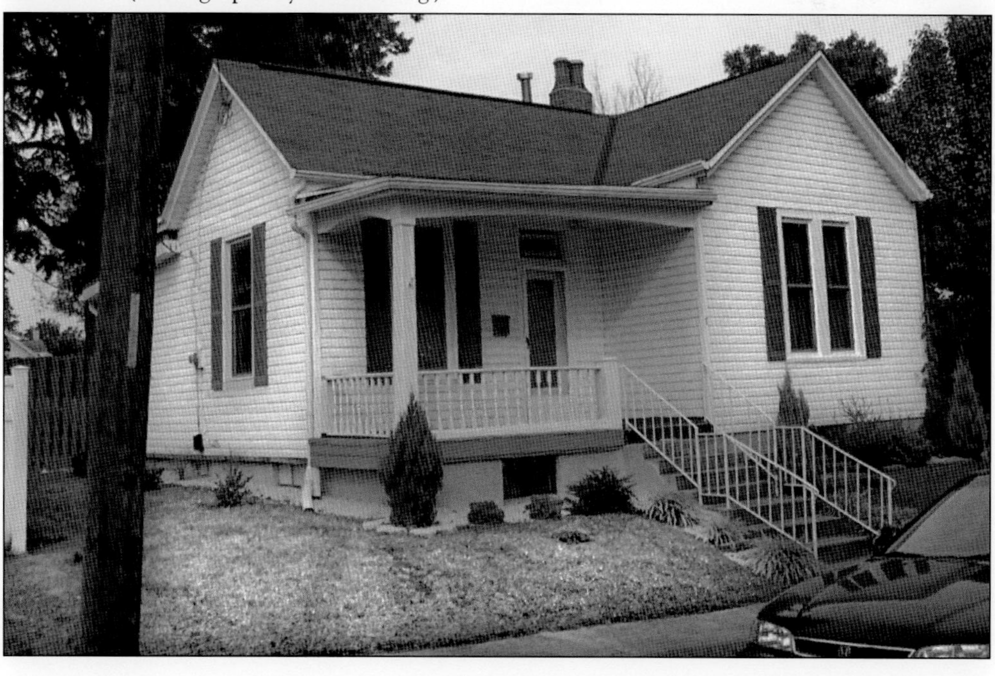

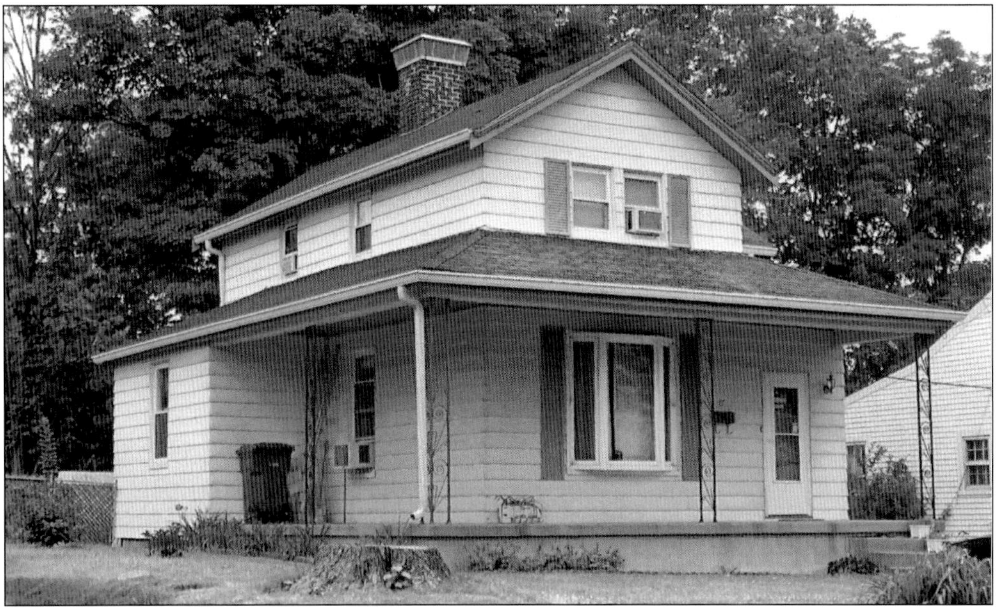

Erlanger Proper Subdivision Homes. The above photograph shows the home at 17 Locust Street. Dr. Charles P. Judkins and James Pendleton Garvey approached Cincinnati business associates to invest in the development of the land around the Erlanger train station. Charles Shipp, Baron d'Erlanger's lieutenant, then running the railroad, promised to offer commuter service to Cincinnati and to build railroad shops near the community. The group of investors became known as the Erlanger Land Syndicate. Most of the homes were similar in design and featured ornate exterior woodwork. The home at 26 Center Street (below) maintains the character of the original syndicate homes and includes some of the original stained glass. For over 50 years, this home has been occupied by the Gray family.

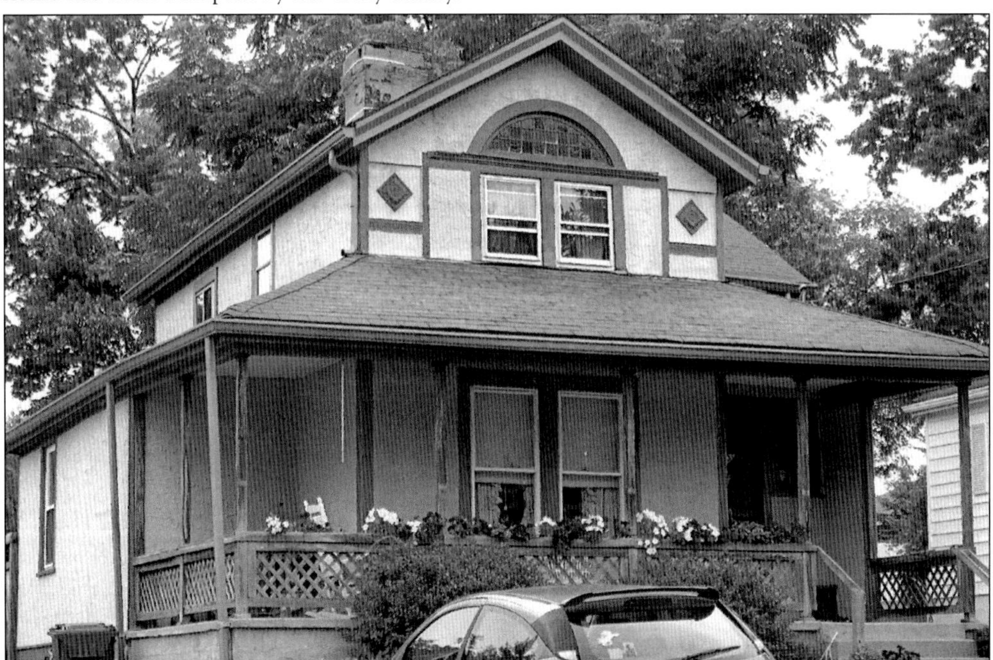

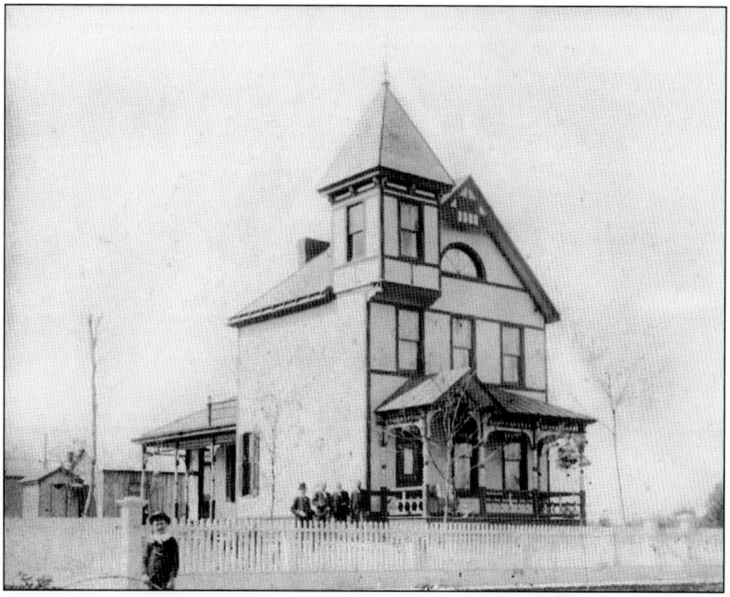

Huerkamp Home. Matthew Huerkamp, one of the first trustees of the city of Erlanger in 1897, lived in this house at 319 Erlanger Road. State highway commissioner and state legislator O. M. Rogers purchased the home in 1910. Katharine Rogers enjoyed entertaining and held many parties in the home. The family lived here until 1956. The home is now owned by attorney Randy Blankenship's family.

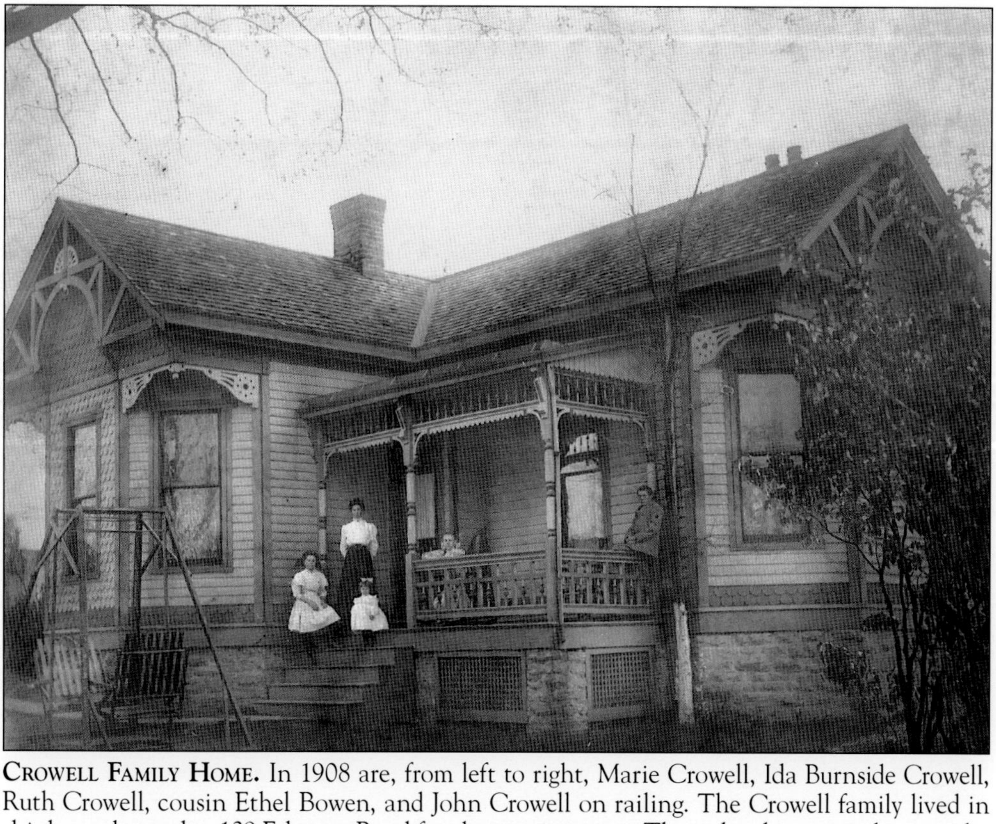

Crowell Family Home. In 1908 are, from left to right, Marie Crowell, Ida Burnside Crowell, Ruth Crowell, cousin Ethel Bowen, and John Crowell on railing. The Crowell family lived in this home located at 139 Erlanger Road for about seven years. Three daughters were born in the home, and Ruth Crowell contracted polio while living there.

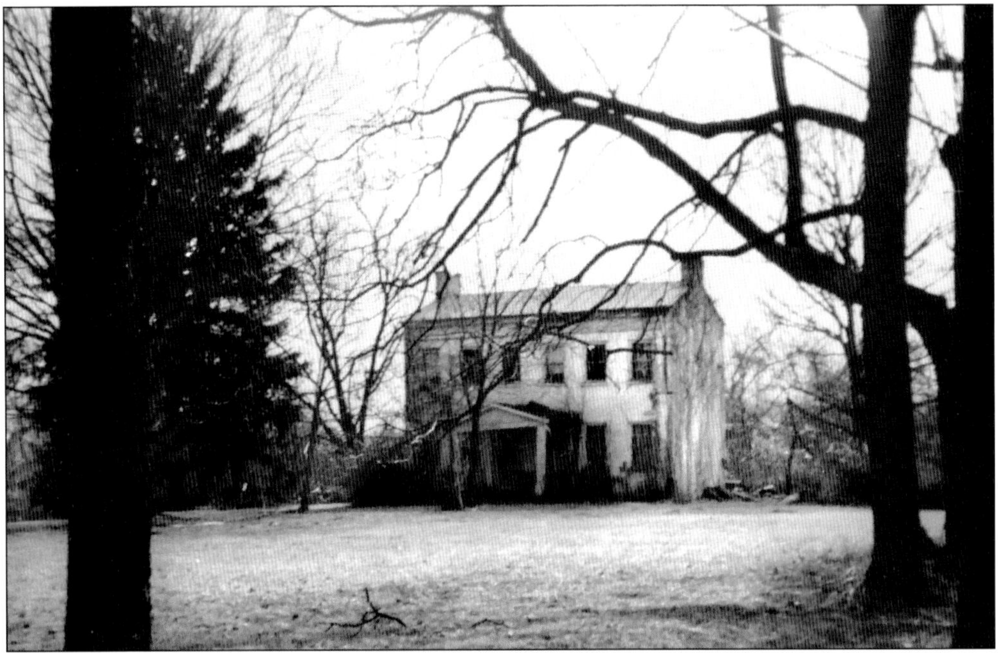

Baxter Harrison Property. This home and the adjacent Buffington Springs Hotel were built in the late 1890s. People of the eastern part of the United States came by train to bathe and relax in the waters of the three springs. In 1950, this caretaker's house was destroyed and the three active springs were capped with zinc lids. The hotel was destroyed by fire, and only one of the bathhouses remains.

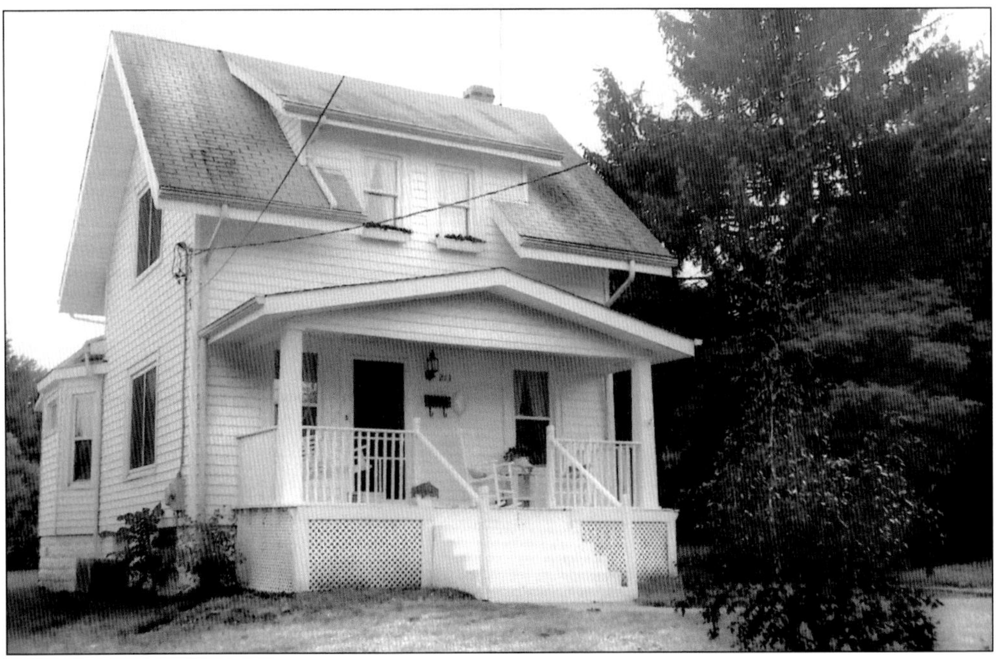

A 1936 Sears and Roebuck Home. This one-and-a-half-story, wood-frame structure is the first Sears and Roebuck home built in Erlanger. Located at 213 Erlanger Road, it has seen many families come and go over the years and is still maintained and occupied.

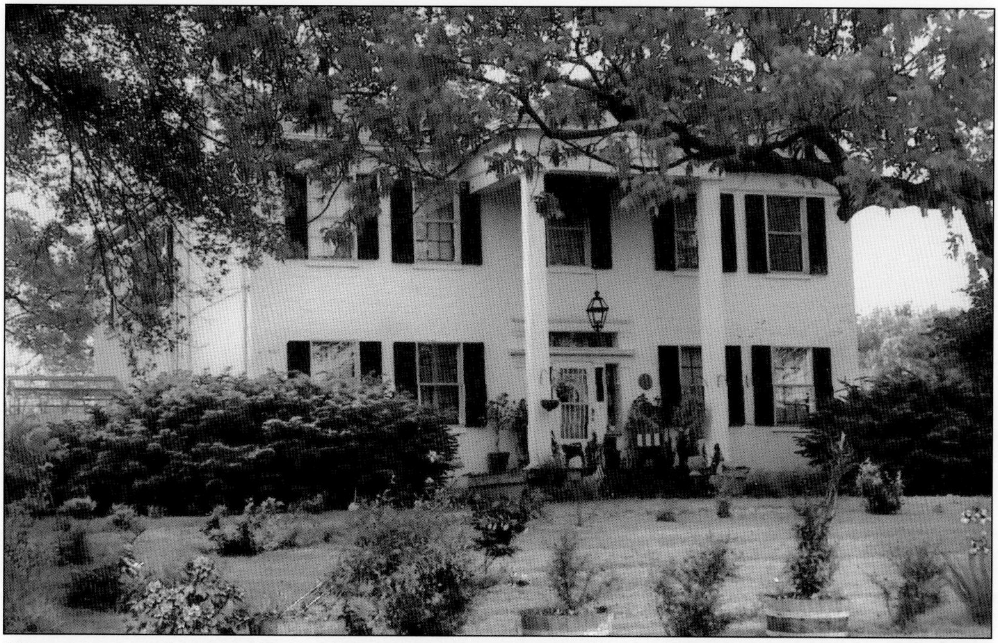

ZEDEKIAH AND LAVINIA TATE HOME. Crescent Springs Road was called Trapp Branch in 1868 when the 118 acres were purchased. The Tates' daughters—Maude Tate, who married John Schmidt, and Frances Tate, who married Albert S. Senour—built twin homes on the land. In 1948, Dr. George R. Coe lived in one of the homes. In 1959, many acres of the land were sold to the highway department for the construction of I-275.

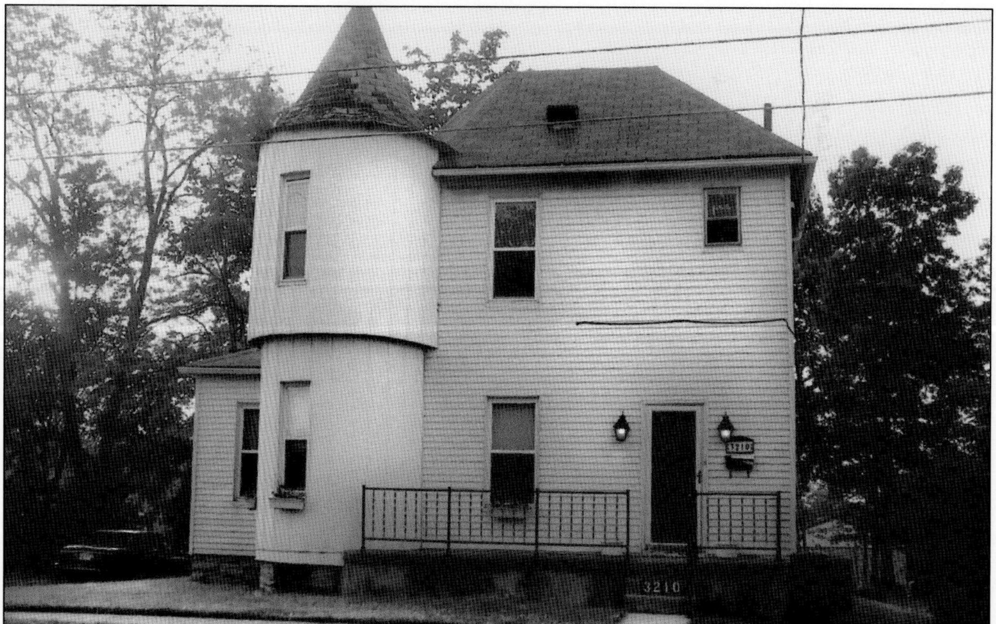

MOLONEY HOME. This late-1880s house is located at 3210 Riggs Avenue in Erlanger. From 1915 through 1935, John and Agnes Moloney raised their family here: John Jr., Ed "Bubs", Mary Helen, Abner, Agnes "Tootie", and Jimmy. The children attended Lloyd High School, where the boys played football. John Jr. became Covington's mayor in the 1950s. (Courtesy of Barbara Moloney Moore.)

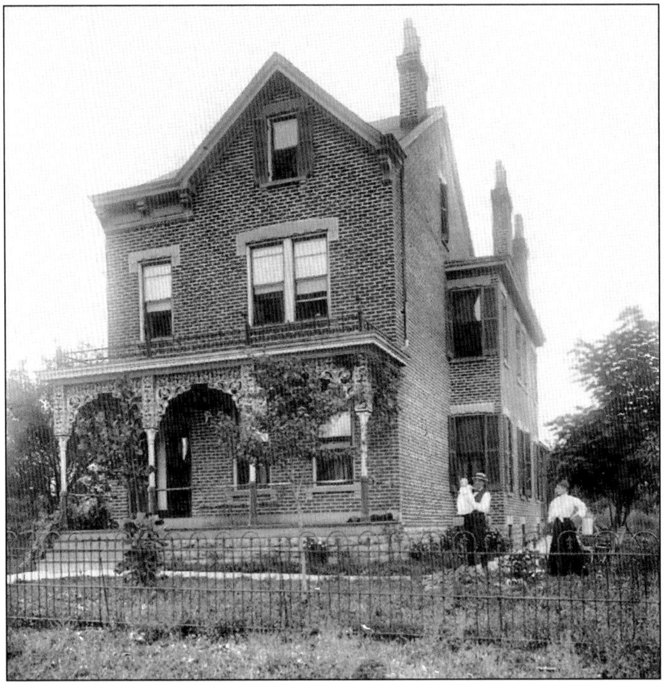

Linn and Nancy Gurney Home. The Gurneys came from Maysville and built this home at 480 Erlanger Road in 1875. They had four sons and five daughters and remained lifelong citizens of Erlanger. One of their granddaughters, Betty K. Gurney Bush, was a charter member of the Erlanger Historical Society.

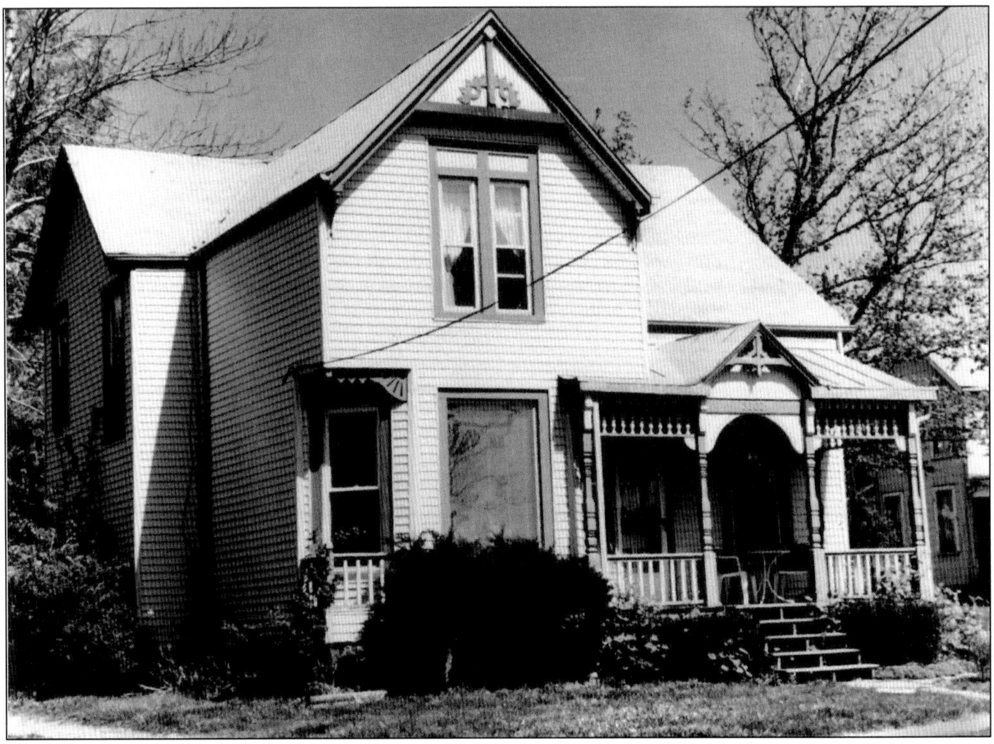

Railroad Station Manager's House. This Crescent Avenue home was built by the Southern Railroad for the station manager. From 1910 until 1930, the Redmund Kelly family lived in the home because Redmund was the station manager. He had three brothers, and all of them worked for the Southern Railroad. Dr. James Kelly, local pediatrician, was Redmund's grandson.

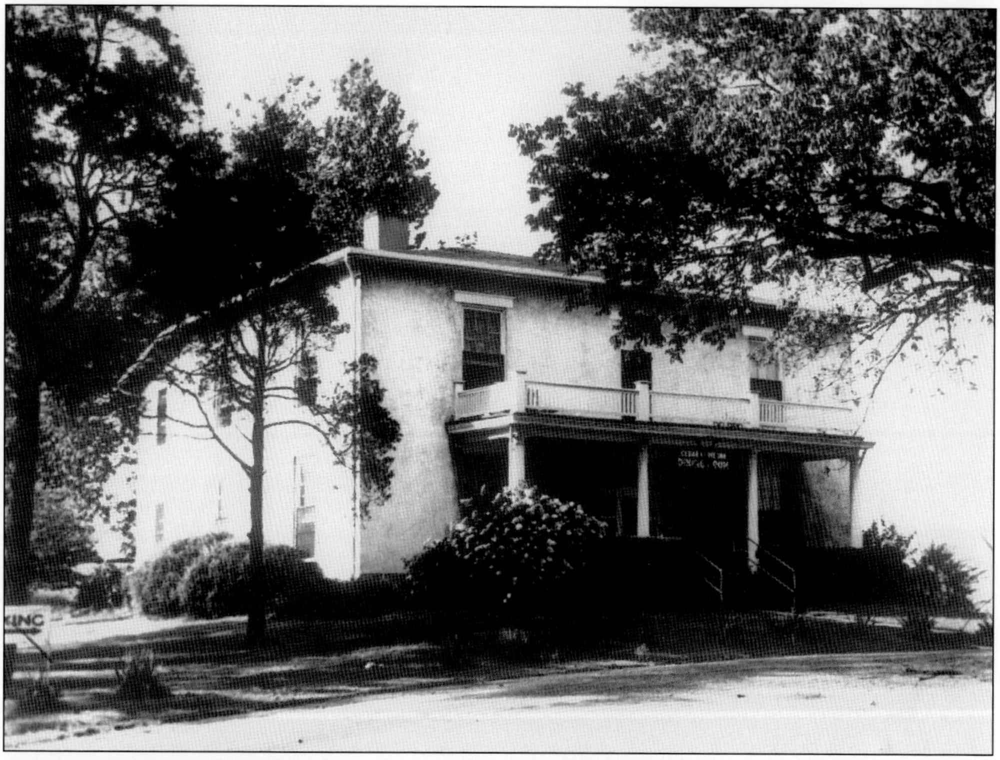

CEDAR GROVE INN. The restaurant was part of the "Gourmet Strip" at the corner of Forest Avenue and Dixie Highway. The restaurant, now a private residence, was one of the oldest standing homes in Erlanger. A fire closed Cedar Grove Inn in 1948. The First Church of God occupied the home for some time, and on January 20, 1959, Frisch's Restaurant opened in front of the old Cedar Grove Inn.

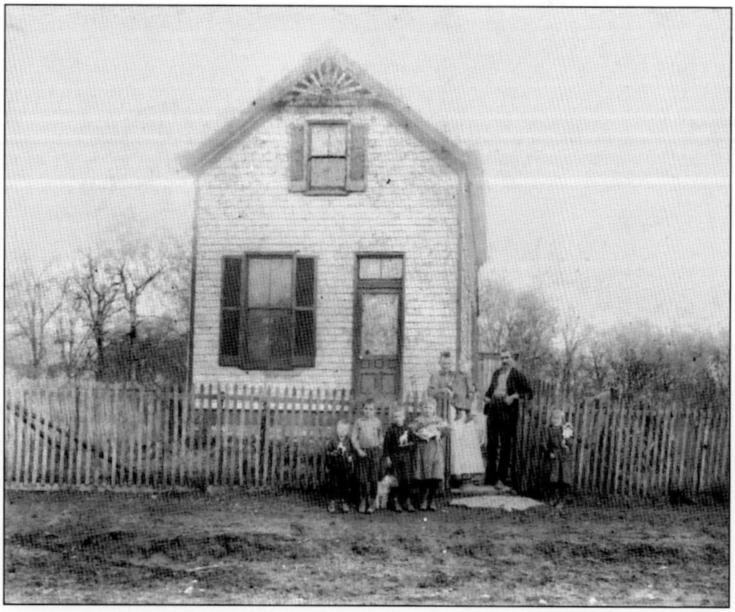

DAUWE HOME. A 1915 tornado struck the Erlanger and Elsmere area and many homes were destroyed. The Dauwe home on Garvey Avenue was totally destroyed. In Erlanger, the second story of the Stevenson home was torn off and the debris landed about a half a mile away near the Beeches home on Dixie Highway. Rumor has it that the bathtub from the Stevenson home was part of that debris.

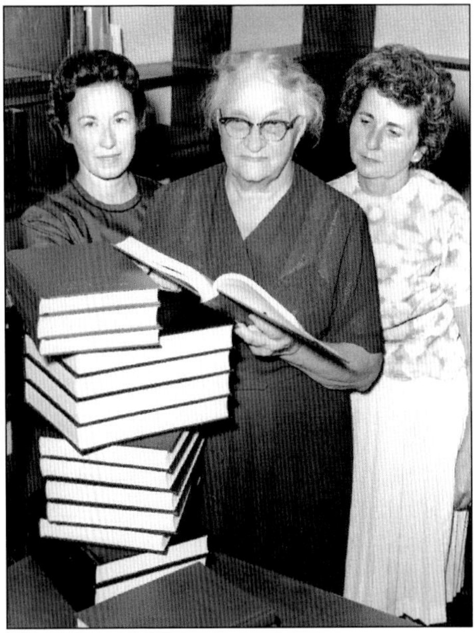

Volunteers at the Erlanger Library. Pictured from left to right are Mrs. Dottie Day, Mrs. Mary Alice Stevenson Taylor, and Mrs. Eleanor Buring. Mrs. Taylor was the longtime librarian, as was her mother, Katherine Earl Stevenson. The library at 97 Bartlett Avenue was dedicated in May 1957 to Mrs. Taylor.

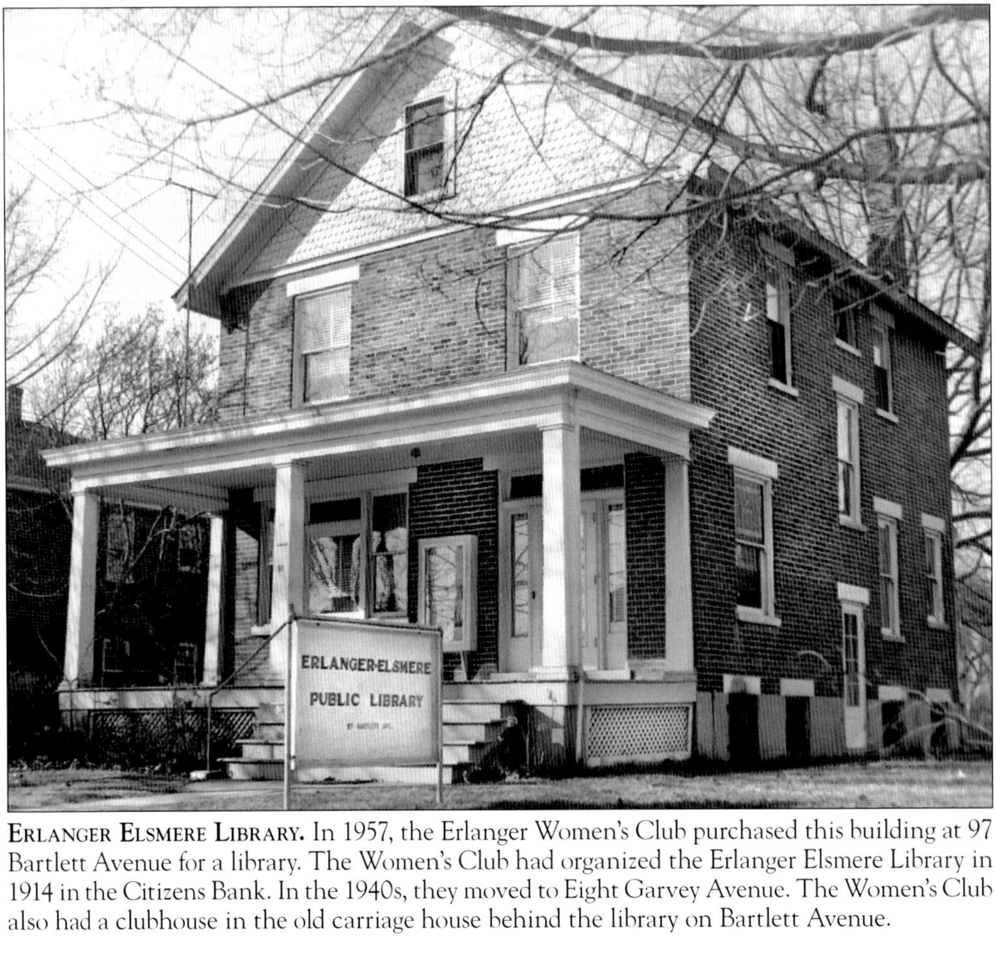

Erlanger Elsmere Library. In 1957, the Erlanger Women's Club purchased this building at 97 Bartlett Avenue for a library. The Women's Club had organized the Erlanger Elsmere Library in 1914 in the Citizens Bank. In the 1940s, they moved to Eight Garvey Avenue. The Women's Club also had a clubhouse in the old carriage house behind the library on Bartlett Avenue.

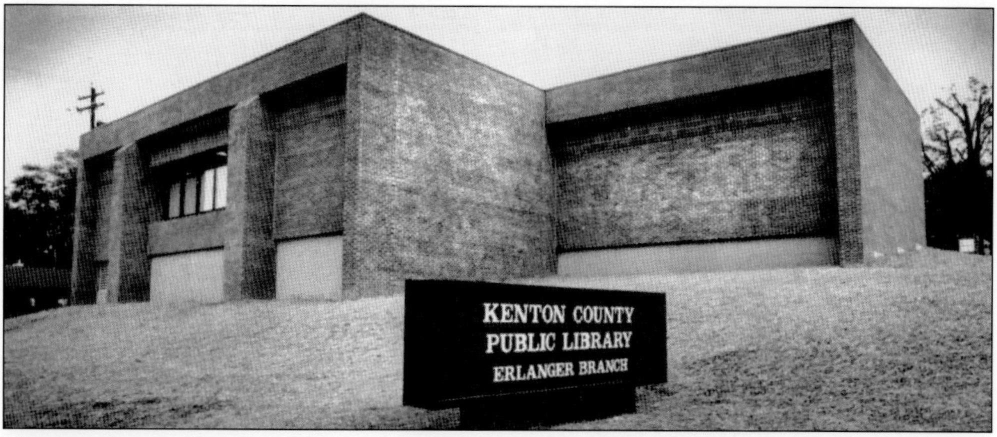

Kenton County Library, Erlanger Branch. This was the first Erlanger Library not owned and operated by the Erlanger Woman's Club. In the late 1960s, the Erlanger Woman's Club was approached by the Covington Public Library regarding the establishment of a county library system. The club agreed to support the project provided Erlanger would receive a new library with a full-time librarian. The result was this beautiful new library in 1978.

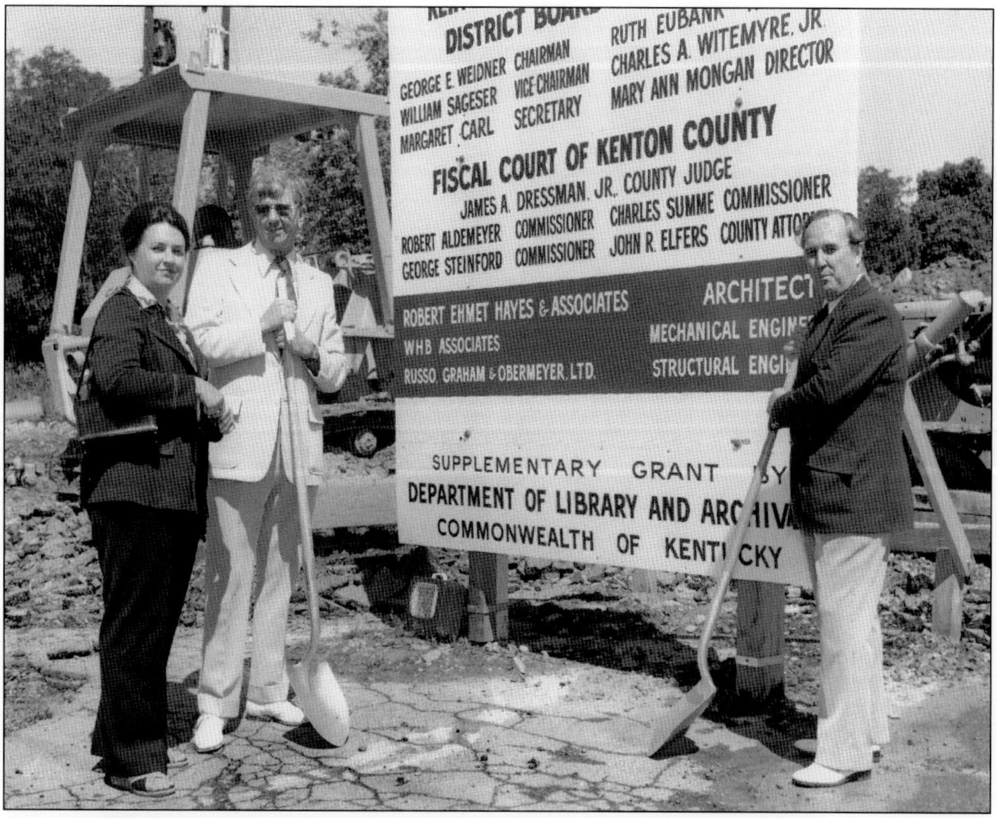

Ground Breaking. The new Erlanger Branch Library at 3130 Dixie Highway opened to the public in September 1978. This was the ground-breaking ceremony. Pictured from left to right are Ellen Hellard, George Weidner, and county judge-executive James Dressman.

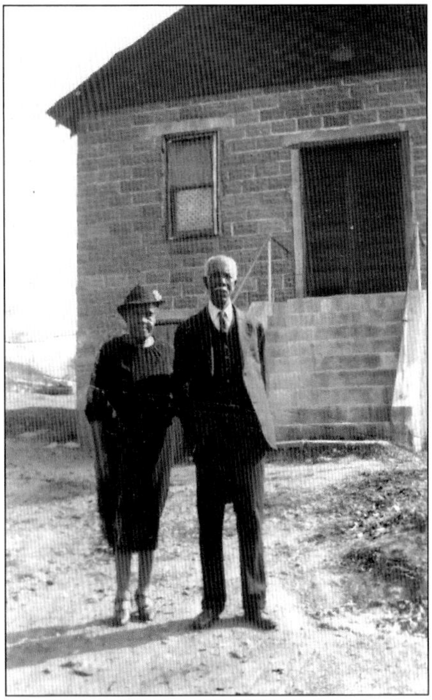

BARNES TEMPLE AFRICAN METHODIST EPISCOPAL CHURCH. The AME church was organized in 1896 by Rev. Daniel Ellison, and services were held at the Woodside Depot. The Barnes Temple Church is shown in the photograph with two of the charter members, William and Mary Carneal. It was built in 1935 at the present Fox Street location on land donated in 1905 by Lula "Lilly" Carneal. Rev. H. L. Barnes was pastor at that time. (Courtesy of Joyce Florence.)

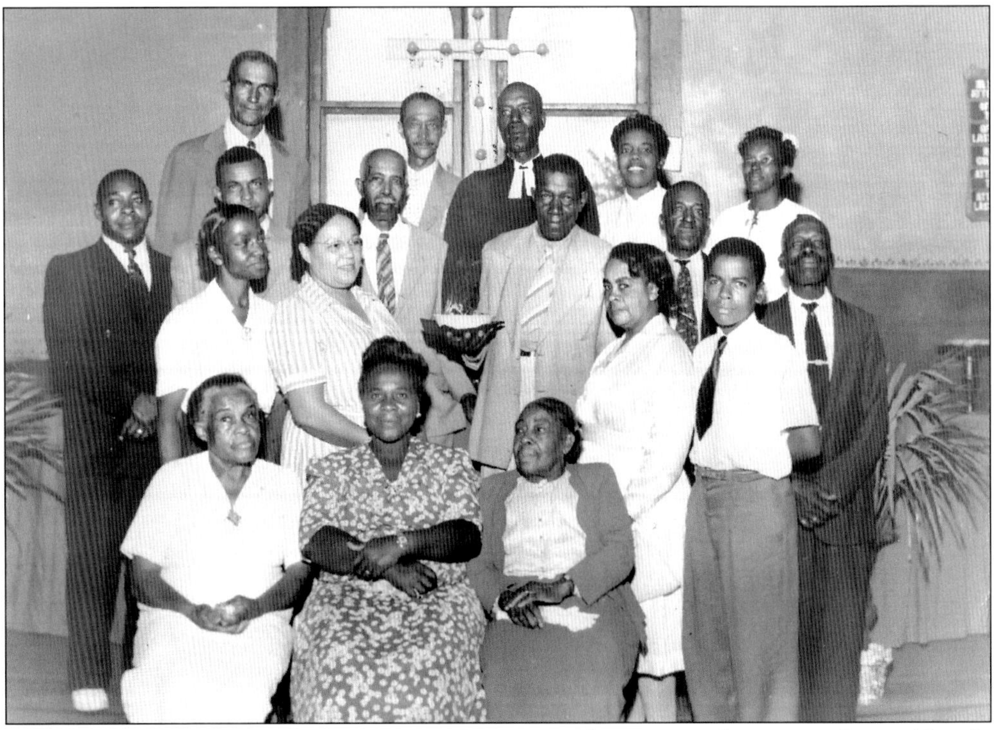

BARNES TEMPLE AME CHURCH MORTGAGE BURNING. The mortgage burning at Barnes Temple AME Church took place in the late 1940s. Pictured is the pastor of the church, Rev. Oscar H. Huggins, with members of the congregation. Holding the mortgage burning plate is Rueben Sanders. (Courtesy of Joyce Florence.)

RANDOLPH CAMPBELL. Reverend Campbell, first pastor of First Baptist Church, married Lucy Slaughter, whose brothers, Mat and Soney, helped found the church. (Courtesy of First Baptist Church of Elsmere.)

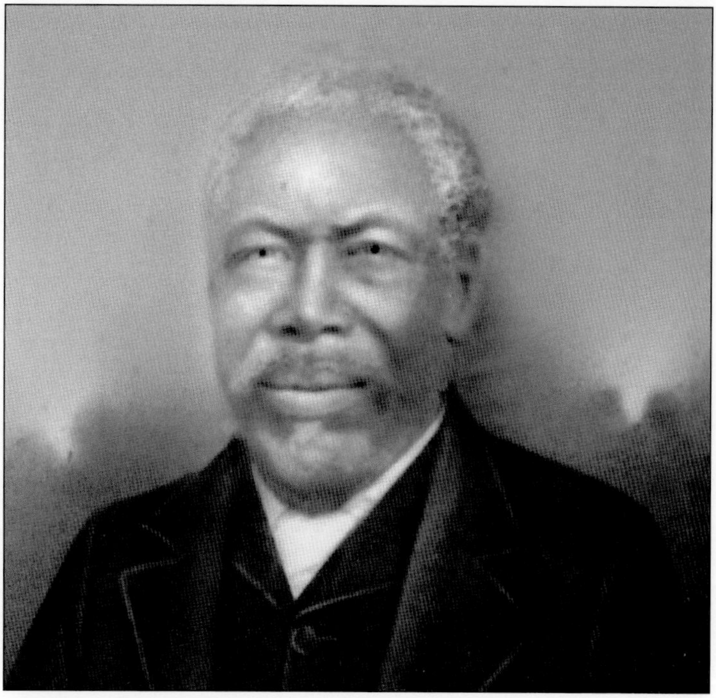

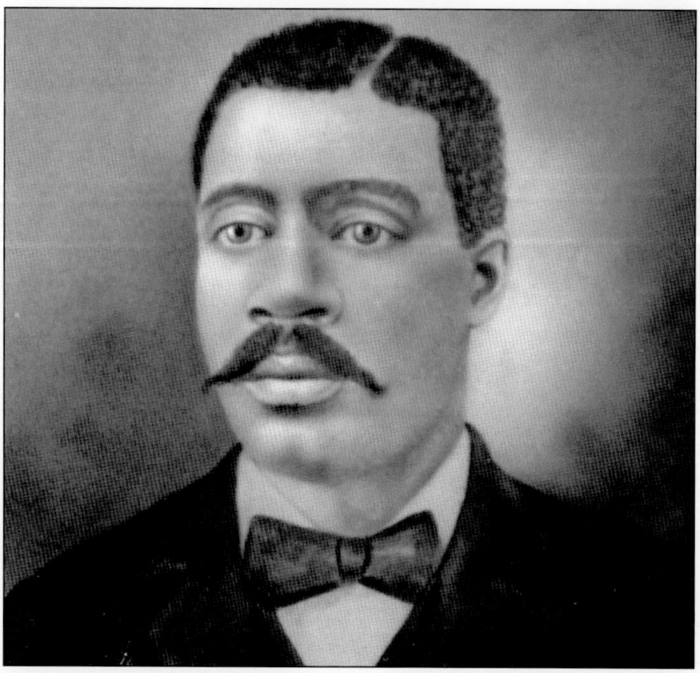

MADISON "MAT" SLAUGHTER. Pictured is Deacon Mat Slaughter, who, along with his brother Deacon Soney Slaughter, founded First Baptist Church of Elsmere in 1891. Before the church was organized, services were held in a dwelling on Spring Street that has now been converted to a home. (Courtesy of First Baptist Church of Elsmere.)

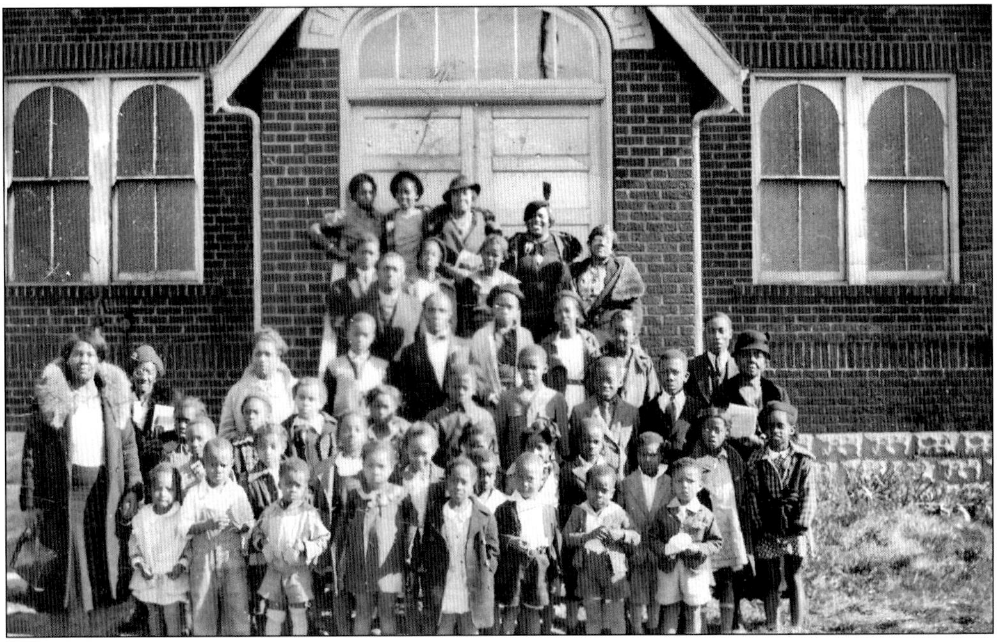

First Baptist Church. Above is the church congregation in the 1930s with Bunt Hopkins in the center. (Courtesy of Lillie Baker.)

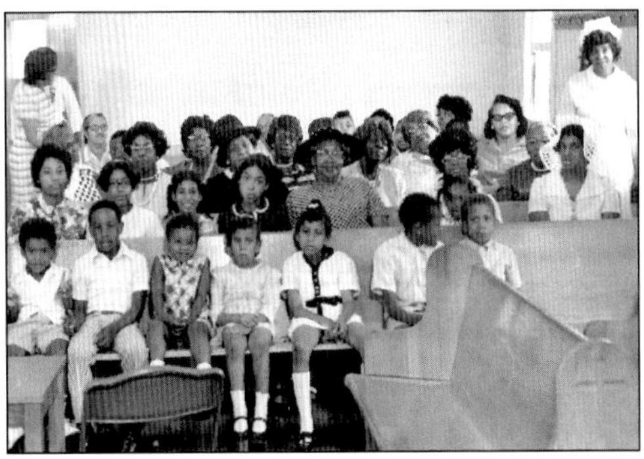

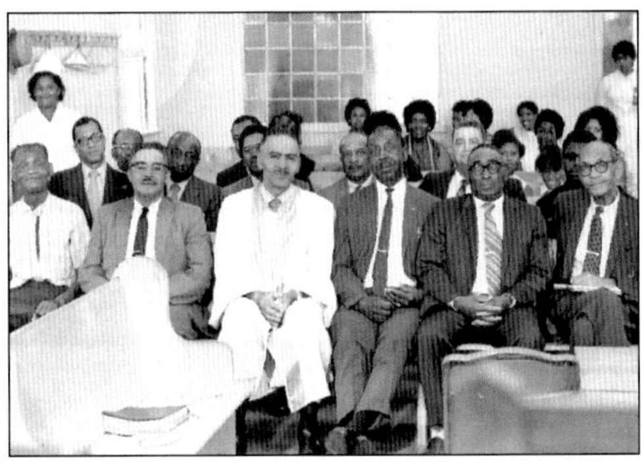

First Baptist's Anniversary Celebration in 1970. In the photograph on the left are, from left to right, (first row) Keith Chambers, Everett Samuels, Stacey Lewis, Maury Ludwick, Teresa Ludwick, Tony Ludwick, and Tracey Ludwick; (second row) Cornelia Lovelace, Bobby Jean-Finnell, Gwen Finnell, Karen Hines, Lillian Davis, Jennifer Spriggs Vance, Tammy Vance, and Selena Spriggs. Parishioners in following rows include Lutie Rice, Grace Alexander, Anna Mae Frazier, Margaret Terry, Willie Florence, Mrs. Louise Haygood, Katie Robinson, Mary Weaver, Ann Sleet, Gertrude Cavil, Marie Jones, Belle Baker, and Dolly Fowler. In the photograph on the right are, from left to right, (first row) John Henry Hamilton, Clarence Kenny, Rev. Falvin Haygood, Zack Williams, Archie Riddell, and Ace Davis. The parishioners in the rows behind include Howard Hines, Collie Luke, Charles Spriggs, Van Jones, Charles Alexander, Mary Chambers Ewing, Memphis M. A. Lovelace, Robert Samuels, Roslyn Luke, Tanya Porterfield, ? Hines, Margie Finnell, Geneva Williams, Vivian Ludwick, Angela Samuels, Ava Chambers, and Betty June Weaver. (Courtesy of Lillie Baker.)

FATHER CIANGETTI. In 1955, Fr. Paul Ciangetti was transferred from St. Henry Church in Elsmere and was appointed pastor of the newly established Mary Queen of Heaven parish by Bishop William Mulloy. Ground was broken in 1956 for a combined church and school building on Donaldson Highway. Prior to celebrating the first mass in 1957, services were held in the chapel of the Passionist Nuns on Donaldson Highway. Mary Queen of Heaven parish has continued to grow in facilities and in membership.

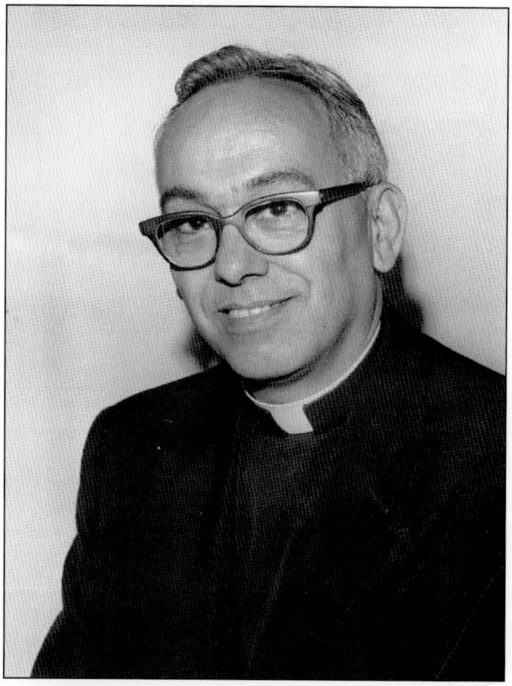

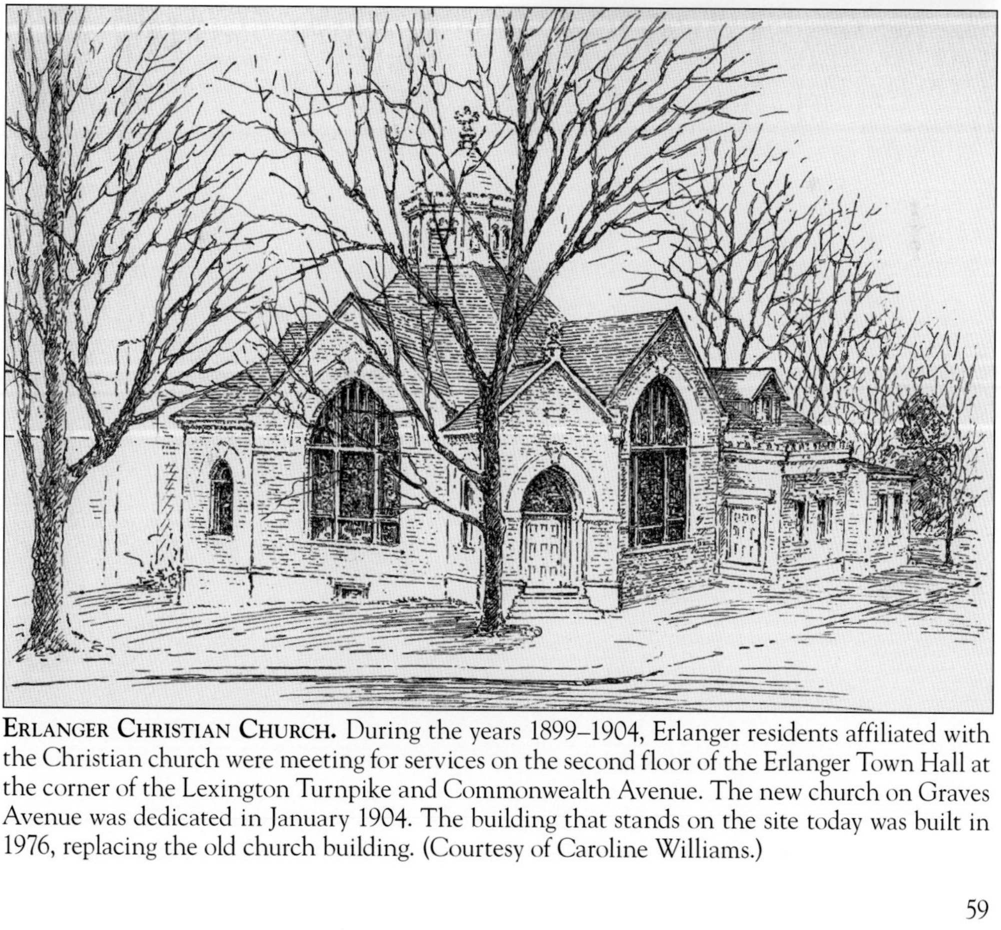

ERLANGER CHRISTIAN CHURCH. During the years 1899–1904, Erlanger residents affiliated with the Christian church were meeting for services on the second floor of the Erlanger Town Hall at the corner of the Lexington Turnpike and Commonwealth Avenue. The new church on Graves Avenue was dedicated in January 1904. The building that stands on the site today was built in 1976, replacing the old church building. (Courtesy of Caroline Williams.)

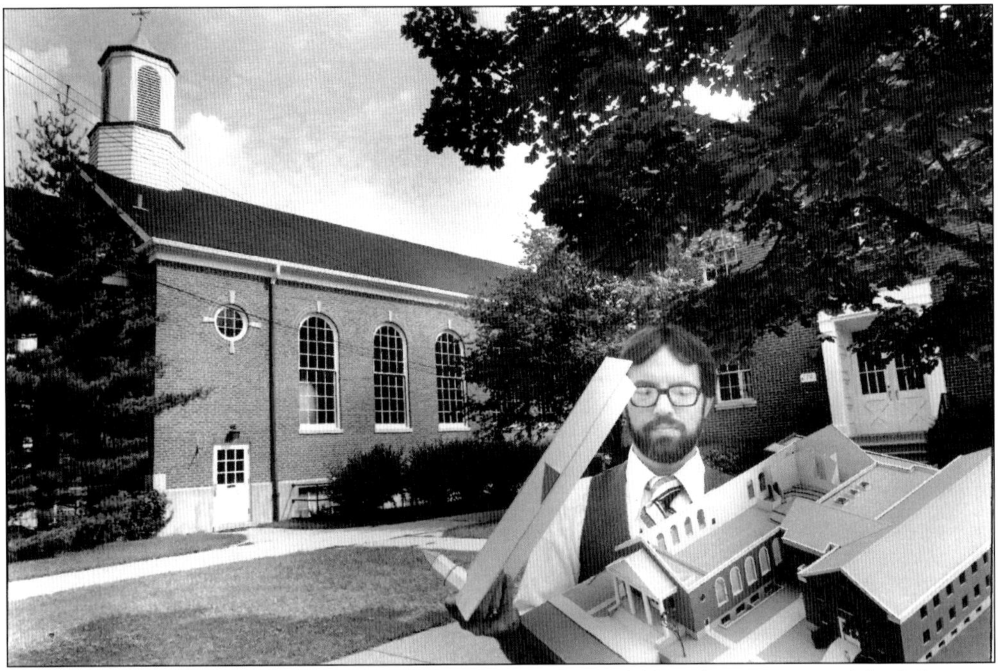

Erlanger Baptist Church. Dr. R. Dwayne Conner in 1980 is showing a model of the new church. Baptists have been represented in Erlanger since the earliest settlers. They worshiped in the Union Church in 1888, but in 1890, because of the generosity of the Erlanger Land Syndicate's gift of land, the Baptists built their first church on Commonwealth Avenue at a cost of $4,423.50. They had 13 charter members.

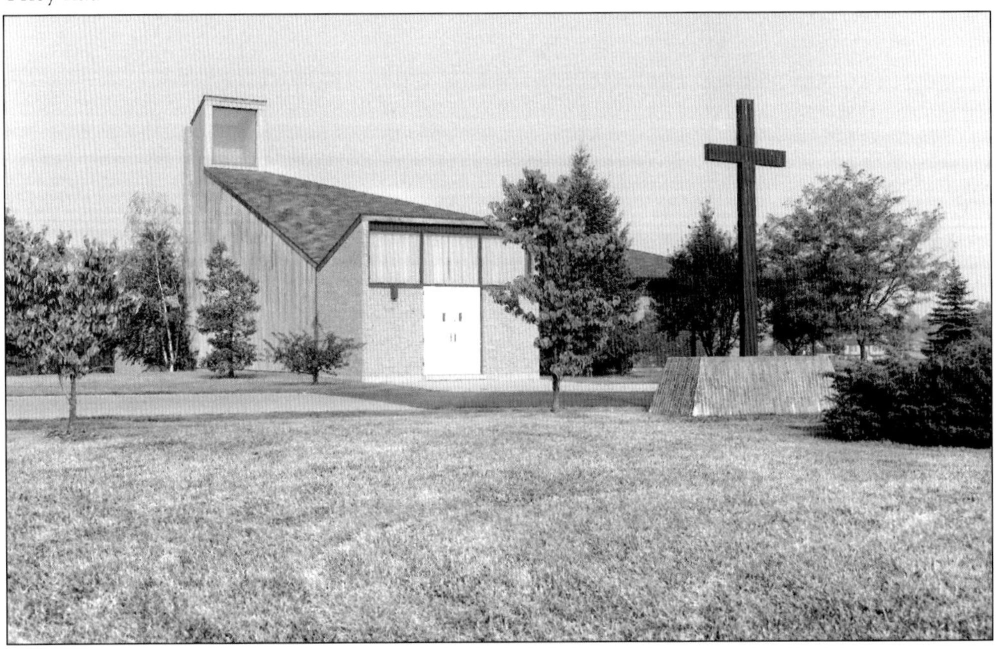

St. Barbara Catholic Church. The dedication of St. Barbara Church took place on July 21, 1969. The church was built by the Robert Emmet Hayes Architect Company. The first pastor was Rev. Albert Ruschman. St. Barbara's is located at 4042 Turkeyfoot Road.

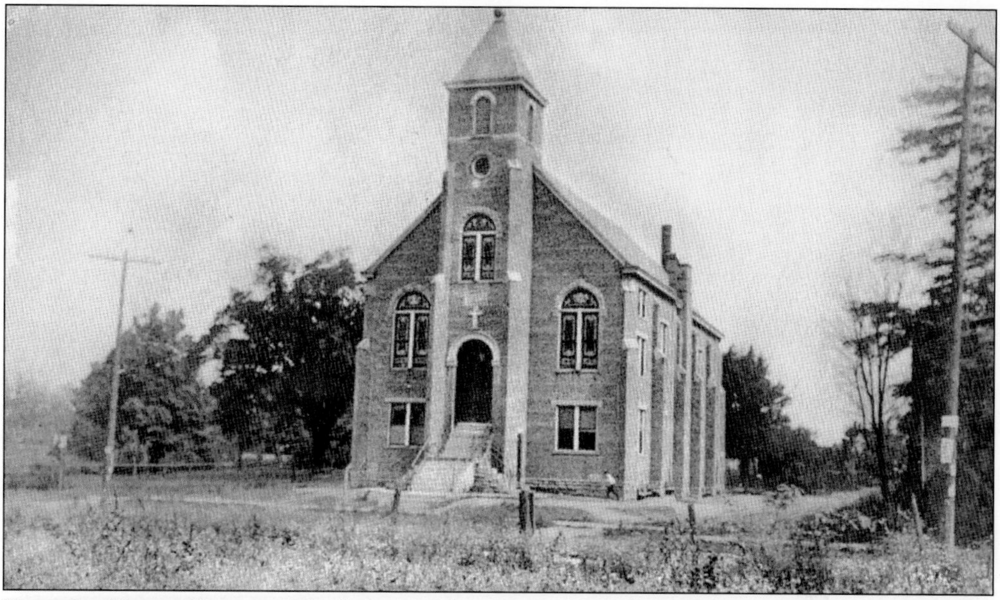

First St. Henry Church. The bishop of Covington, Camillus P. Maes, in 1890 commissioned the building of a new church at Garvey and Shaw Avenues. That church burned down in 1899, and a new church was built at Garvey and Dixie Highway. The name "St. Henry" was chosen because many of the members of the new congregation had moved from a parish of that name located in Cincinnati, near Crosley Field.

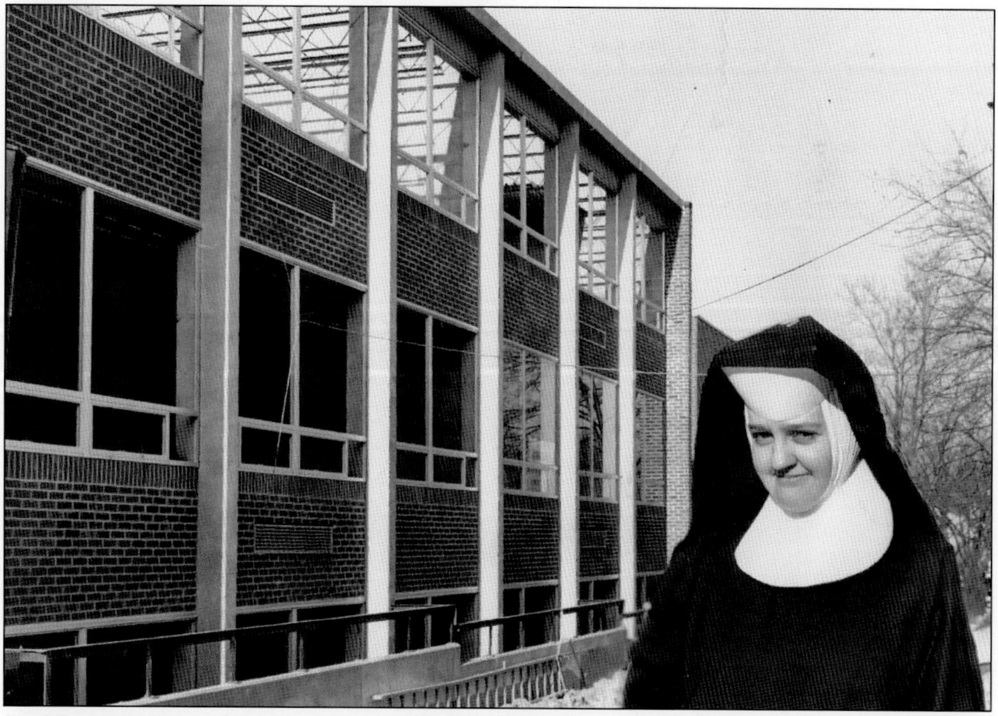

Sr. Herbert Scott. Sister was principal of St. Henry Elementary School during the 1950s. She is standing in front of St. Henry School. The middle school was built in 1963. Its enrollment of 1,105 children was the largest in the Covington diocese that year.

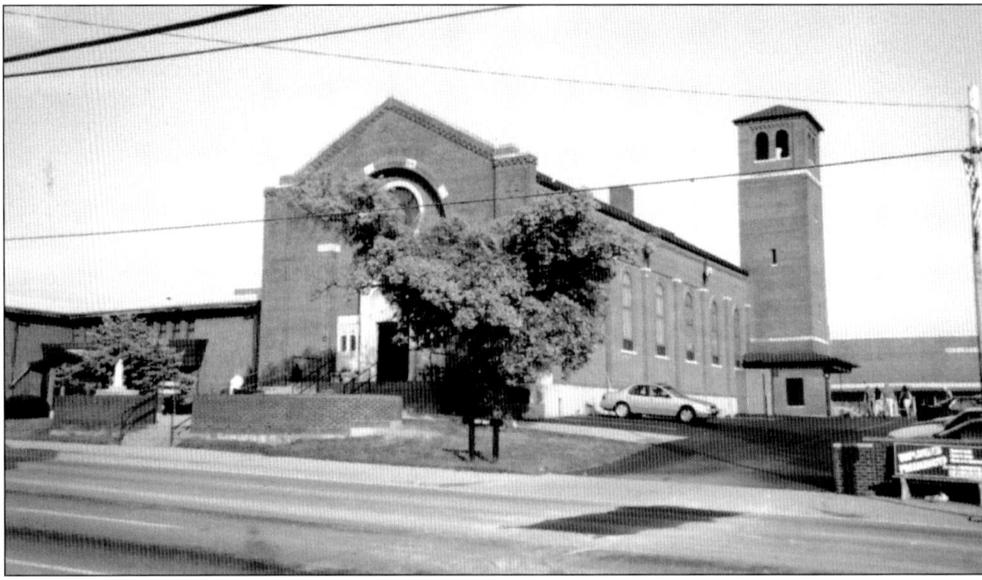

PRESENT-DAY ST. HENRY CHURCH. On Sunday, May 17, 1936, Bishop Howard dedicated the present attractive church constructed of brick in the Romanesque architectural design. There were 325 families registered at the parish at the time of the dedication. Rev. Edmund Corby was pastor of the parish.

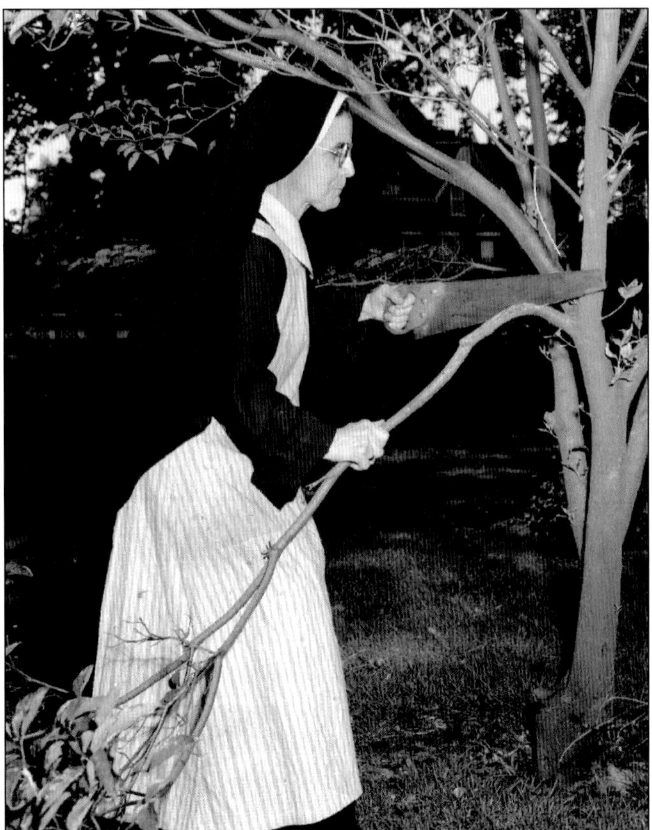

SR. ANSELM WEIBEL. The nuns at St. Henry church handled many chores. Sister Anselm of the Benedictine Order was in charge of the altar linens and was also the cook for the Sisters's house. It looks like she was also the groundskeeper.

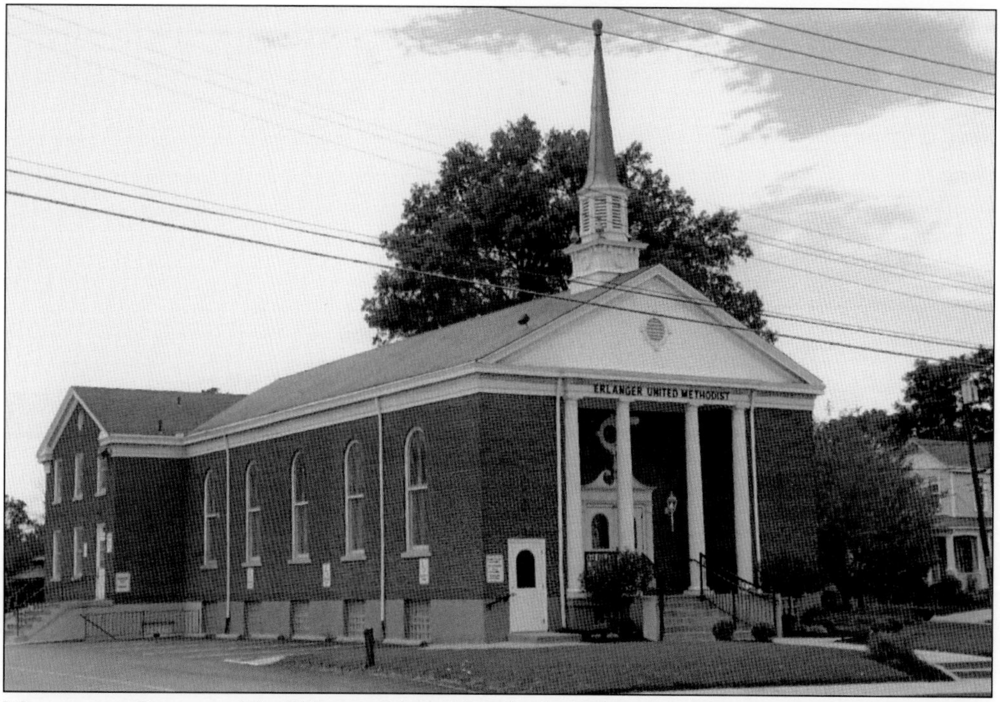

METHODIST CHURCH. The Erlanger United Methodist Church is on the land donated in 1889 by the Erlanger Syndicate at Commonwealth Avenue and Home Streets. All denominations worshipped in this church until about 1891, when the Erlanger United Methodist Church secured the title to the building. On January 4, 1948, the old building was demolished because of fire. In December 1955, a new church, with lots of improvements, was finally completed. The new church on this site is now serving the Methodist community.

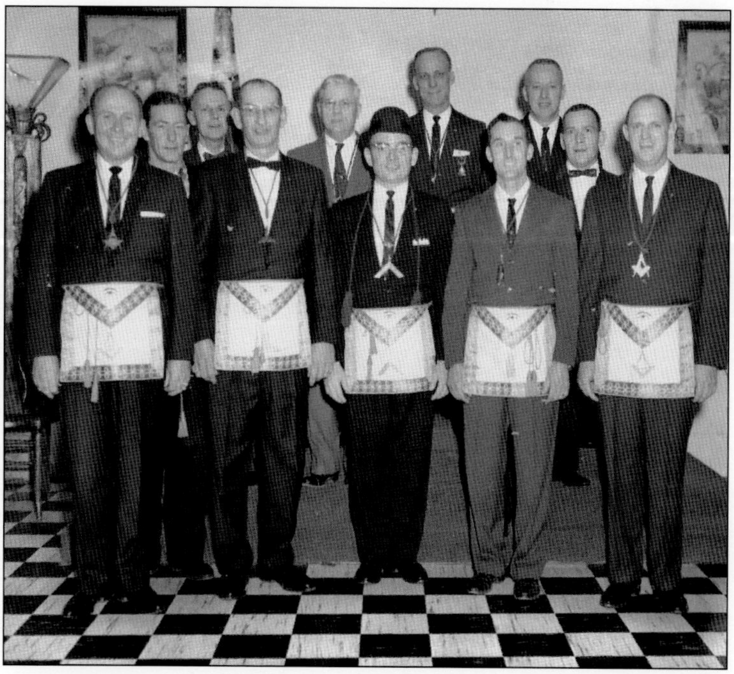

ERLANGER GOOD FAITH LODGE. This February 1964 photograph taken inside the Masonic Lodge on Graves Avenue shows, from left to right (first row) Howard E. Edwards, Joseph Jump, Roderick C. Grall, Alfred Martin, and Charles Points; (second row) Wallace E. Henneman, Harry B. Shyrigh, Arthur J. Lindeman, John A. Layne Jr., William B. Shotwell, and Robert Walters.

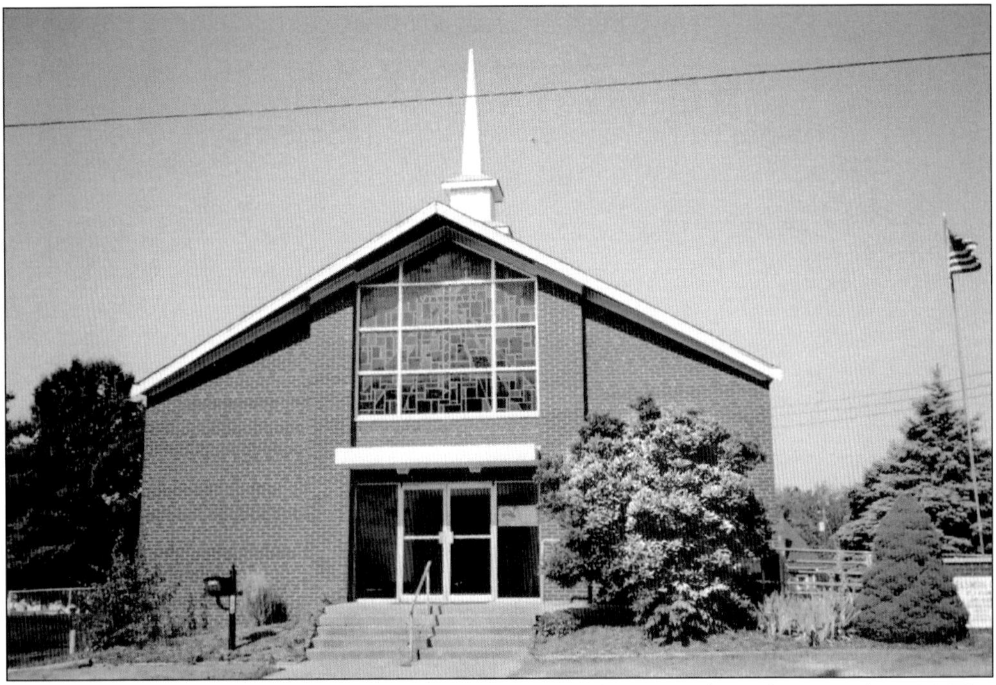

ELSMERE CHURCH OF CHRIST. The Elsmere Church of Christ was formed in March 1926. The initial congregation consisted of 104 men, women, and children. The first minister was Rev. Raymond Watson, who lived in Walton, Kentucky. The church property at 124 Carlisle Avenue was purchased from Elizabeth D. M. Hottendorf. The original building was damaged by fire in 1927 and rebuilt in 1928. The present structure was finished in 1965.

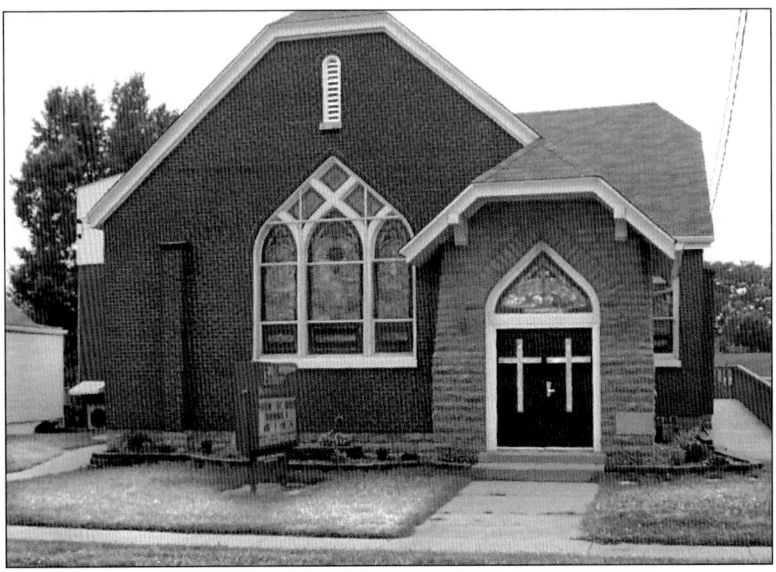

ELSMERE BAPTIST CHURCH, GARVEY AVENUE. In June 1914, the Erlanger Land Syndicate donated a lot to build the Elsmere Mission of the Erlanger Baptist Church. In 1922, Elsmere Baptist Church was officially organized at this location. (Photograph by Terry Collis.)

Three

Businesses

Restaurants, Shops, and Industry

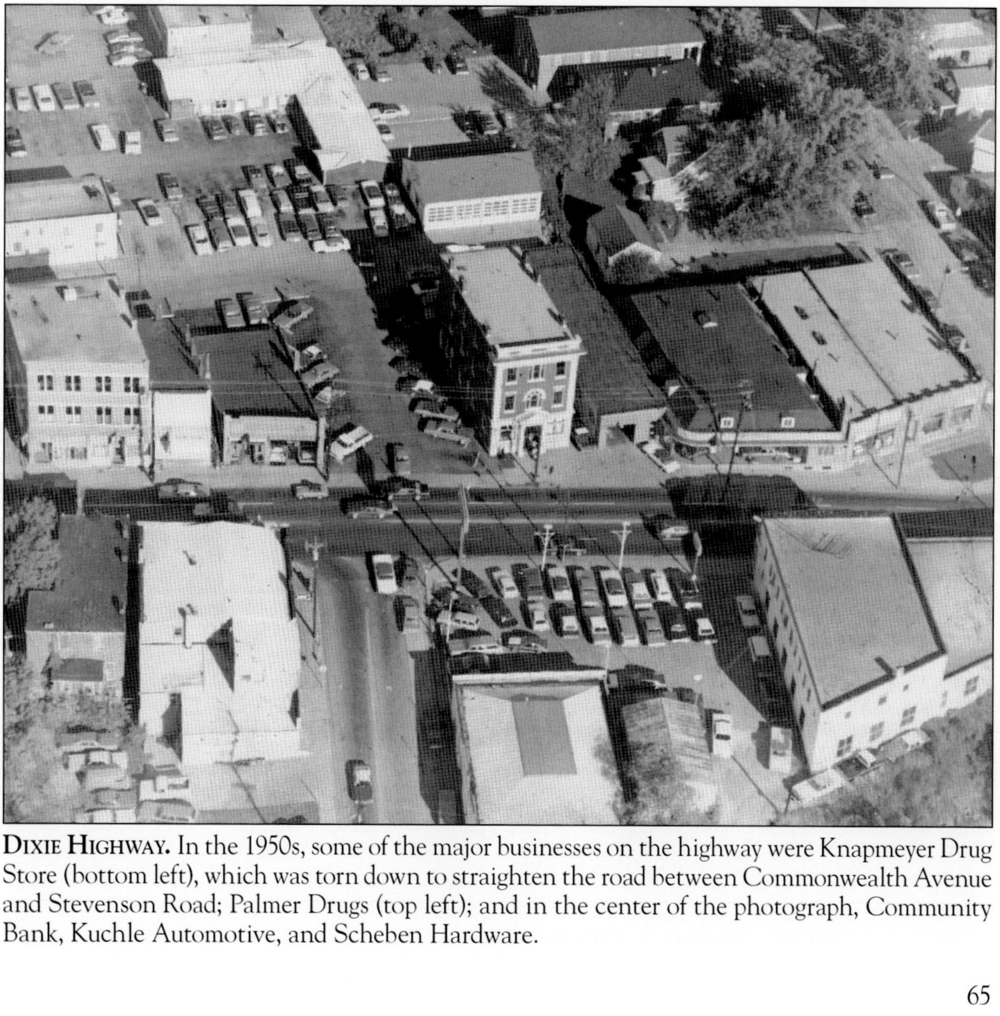

Dixie Highway. In the 1950s, some of the major businesses on the highway were Knapmeyer Drug Store (bottom left), which was torn down to straighten the road between Commonwealth Avenue and Stevenson Road; Palmer Drugs (top left); and in the center of the photograph, Community Bank, Kuchle Automotive, and Scheben Hardware.

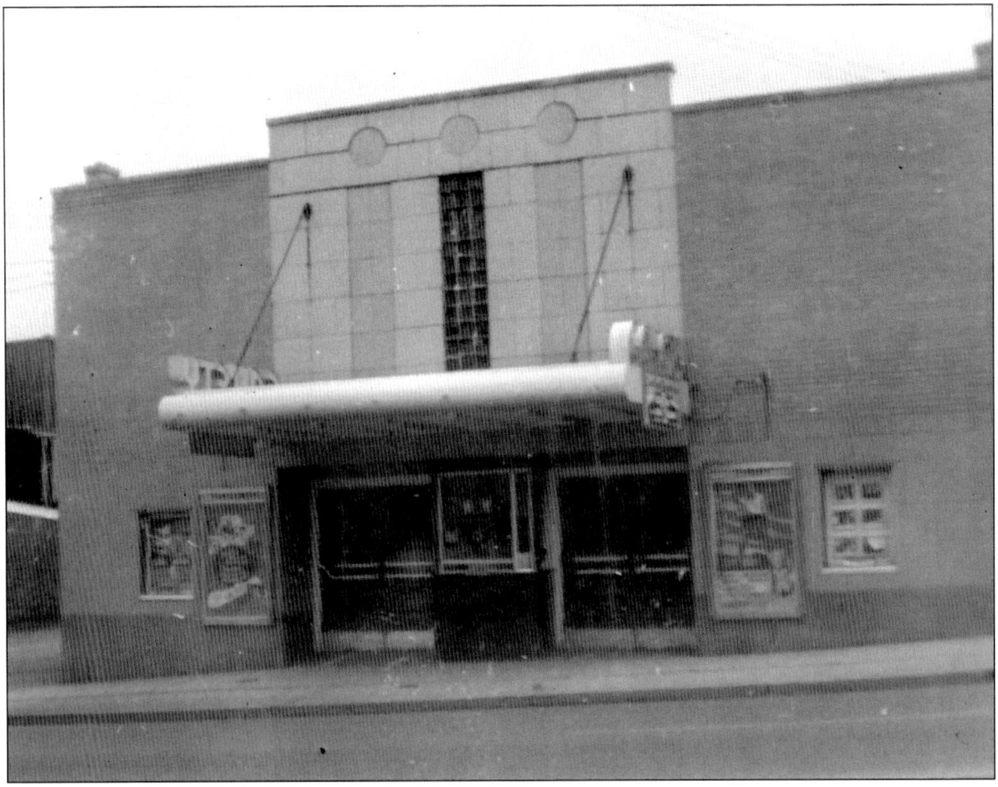

The Gayety Theater History. The first theater in the location next door to Dusing Brothers Ice House was built in 1914. It was torn down, and A. F. Herman built a new theater called the Gayety Theater in 1938. The first movie shown was *The Crowd Roars* with Robert Taylor. In 1960, the Gayety was sold and the name changed to Village Cinema. The Village Cinema operated until 1998, when Dusing Brothers Ice bought the property, tore it down, and built a new storage facility for their business. (Below photograph by Paul Dusing.)

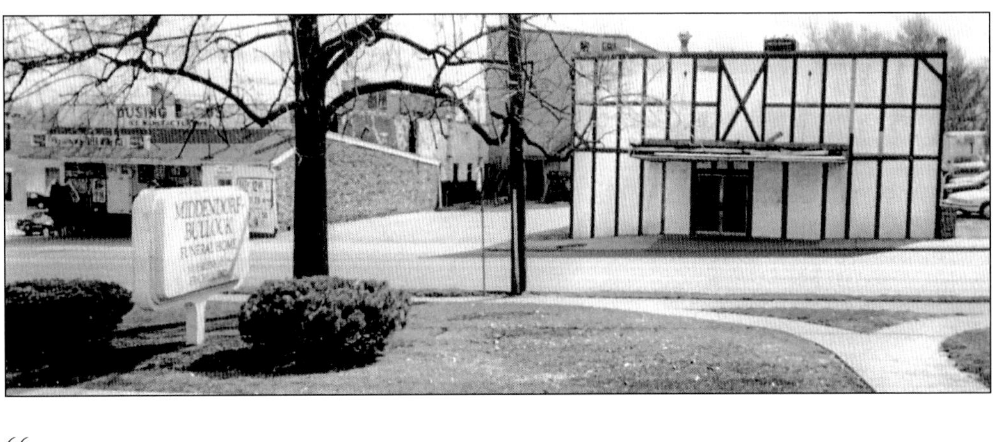

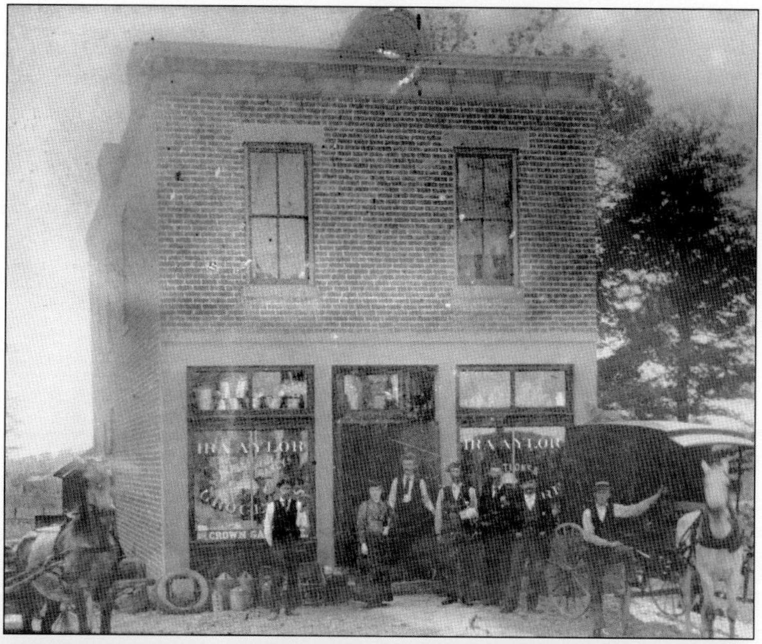

Ira Aylor Grocery Store. Ira Aylor and his wife, Arminta Glacken Aylor, operated the store located on Dixie Highway near Stevenson Road. By the 1900s, the city of Erlanger included 89 residences, 3 grocery stores, 2 livery stables, and a variety of other businesses. Aylor's grocery was typical of that time period.

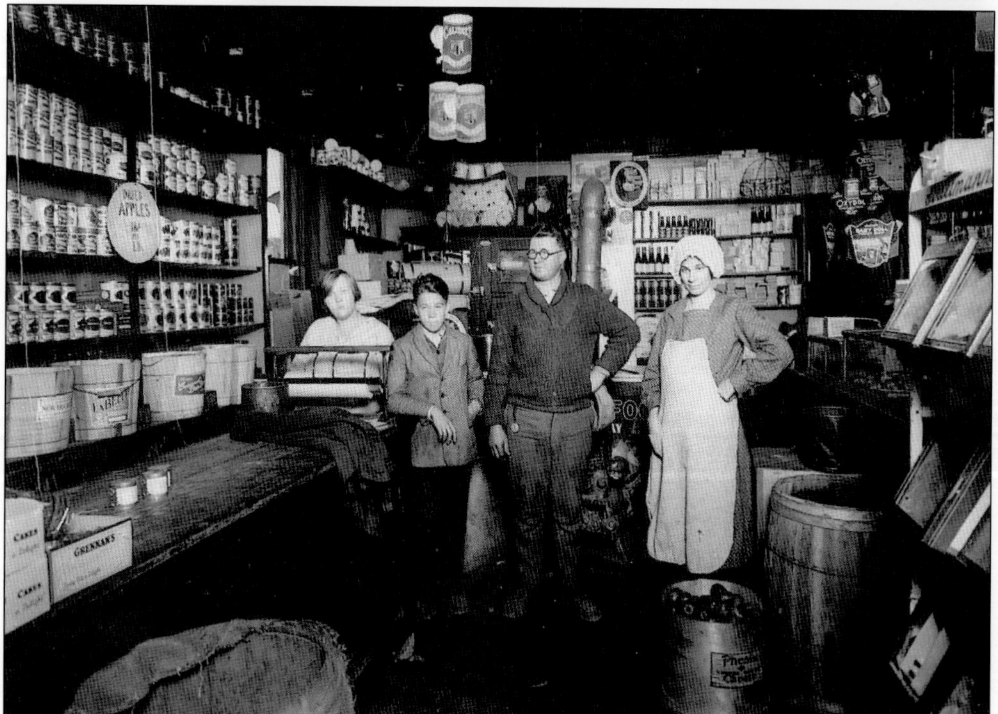

Hoard's Grocery Store. This photograph provides a rare look inside one of these early stores, showing fresh-baked products and a variety of canned goods. The store was located at Garvey Avenue and Cross Street. It was owned and operated by the Hoard family during the 1940s. It was one of many privately owned grocery stores on Garvey Avenue. Pictured from left to right are Beatrice Dunaway, Cecil Hoard, and his parents, Owen and Katherine Hoard. (Courtesy of Denney and Roberta Foster.)

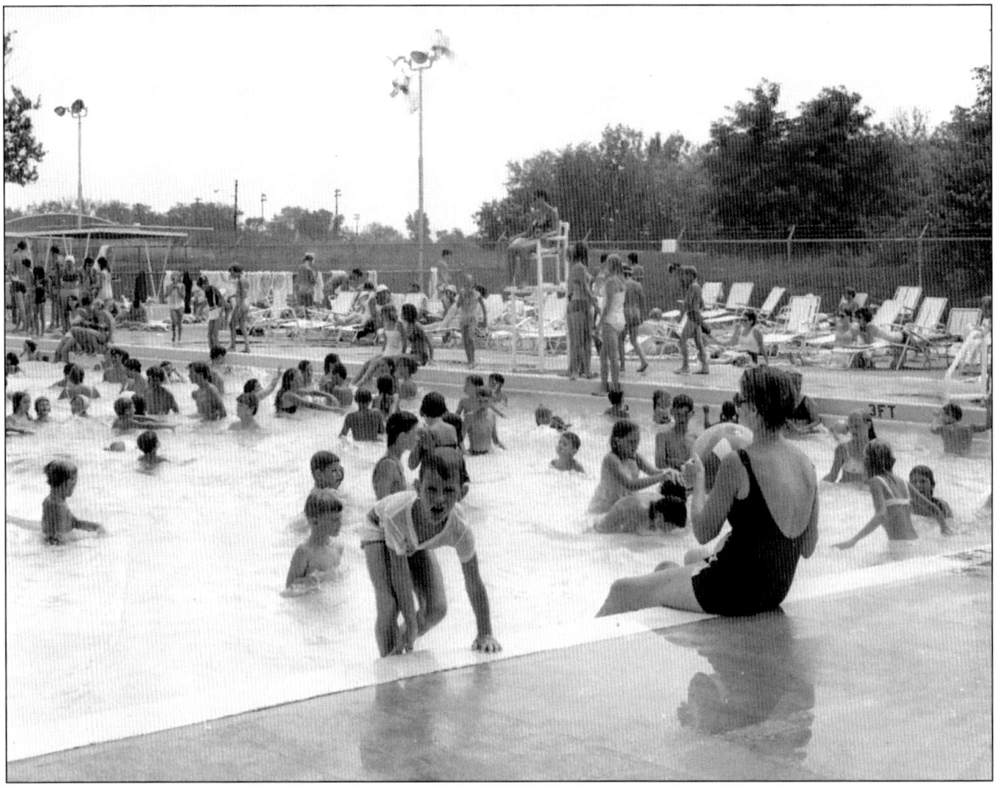

TRIPLE-E SWIM CLUB. The Triple-E Swim Club's history began with a ground-breaking ceremony in 1958. The pool was located at Commonwealth Avenue and Watson Road on land purchased from the Erlanger Lions Club. Triple-E opened on June 14, 1959. The name "Triple-E" was chosen to attract memberships from the Erlanger, Elsmere, and Edgewood neighborhoods. (Courtesy of the Kenton County Library.)

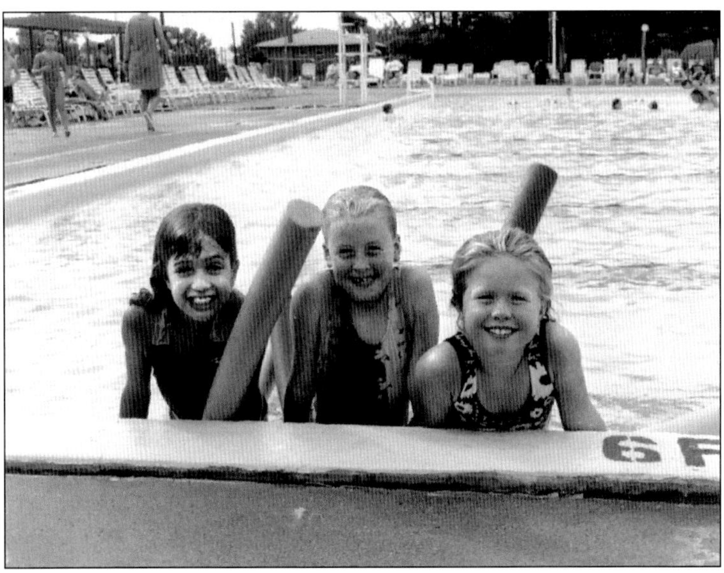

TRIPLE-E, 1990s. Three girls are pictured in the 1990s enjoying the pool. They are, from left to right, Karen Lageman, Melissa Braun, and Gabby Boiman. In 2005, the property was sold and the Erlanger City Center was built by the Drees and Hemmer Construction Companies. (Courtesy of the Kenton County Library.)

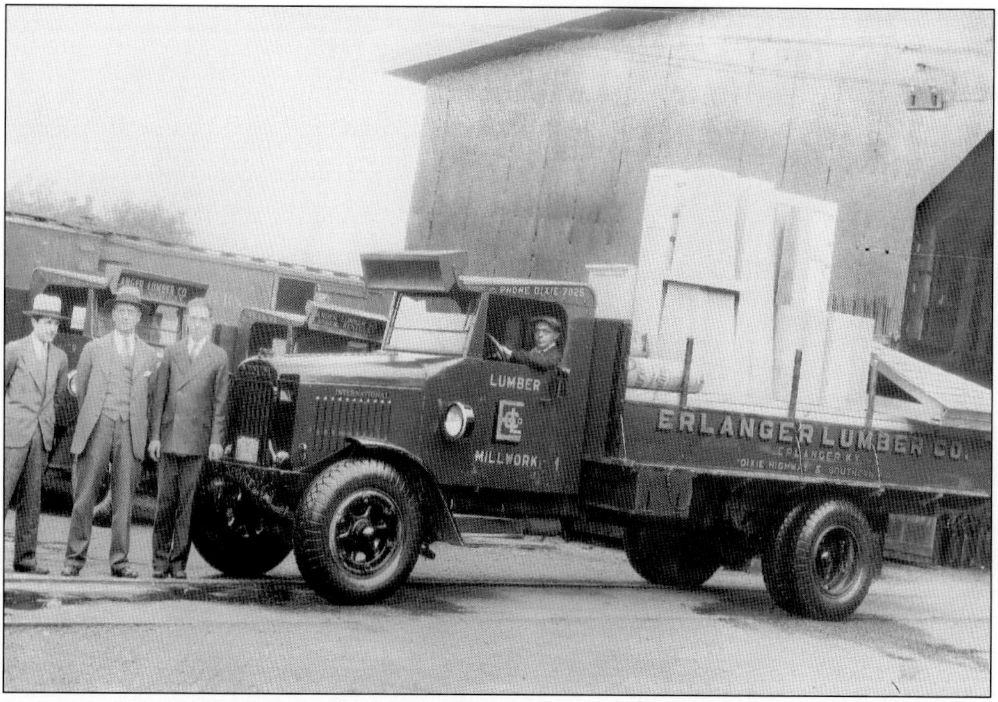

ERLANGER LUMBER COMPANY. Charles P. Hagemeyer was owner in the 1930s of Erlanger Lumber Company. The company was known for lumber, building materials, paints, and kitchen cabinets. In 1948, William Hagemeyer was president. He is one of the men standing in front of the truck. In 1953, William sold the company to Albert W. Goering.

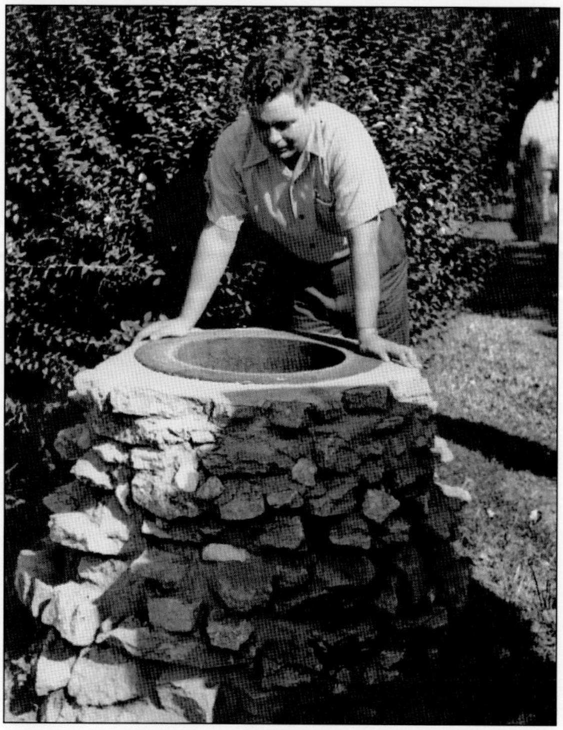

THE WELL AT DOC'S PLACE. This September 2, 1947, picture shows the opening to an old well on Dixie Highway. This well, along with a spring near Dry Creek and Kentaboo Avenue, was the only source of water for residents in that immediate area as late as 1932.

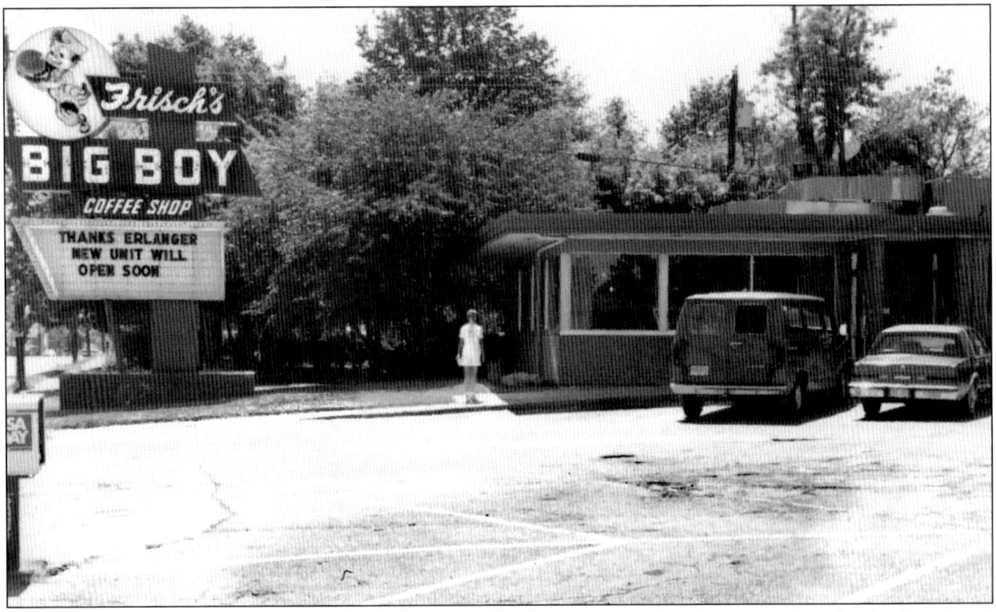

FRISCH'S BIG BOY. Frisch's opened in 1959 and became a major location for the high school crowd. Boone County and Erlanger-Elsmere teens used to congregate here or just "cruise" through. Curbside service was the main attraction, while the main menu item was a Big Boy double decker, french fries, coleslaw, and a Coke, all for about 85¢.

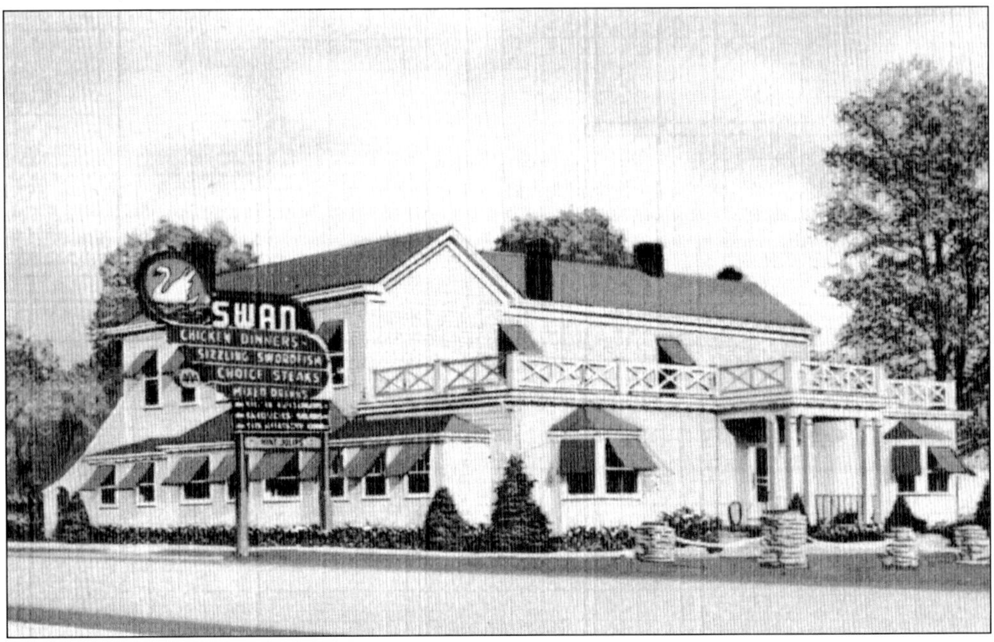

SWAN RESTAURANT. Built in the late 1880s as a stagecoach stop on the route from Cincinnati to Lexington, the Nine Mile House was remodeled and expanded to become the Swan Restaurant in 1947. The menu specialized in sizzling swordfish, frog legs, shrimp, and choice steaks. During this time, gambling tables were provided on the second floor and slot machines could be found throughout the restaurant. In 1956, this building was remodeled and a florist shop was established by the Schreiver family. (Courtesy of the Schreiver family.)

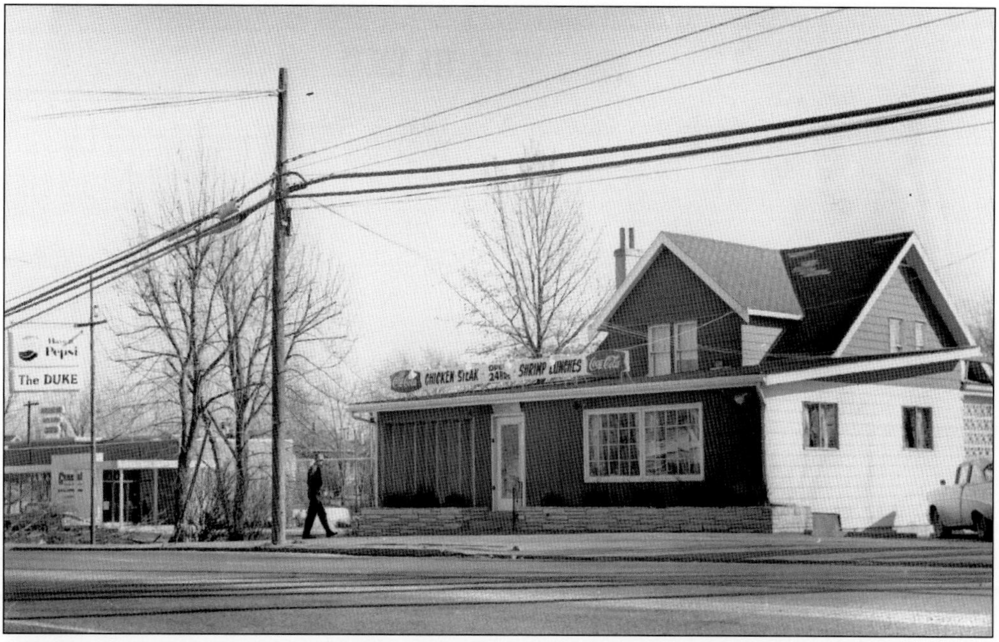

THE DUKE. Noted for its steak dinners, the Duke was located on 3709 Dixie Highway in the 1940s and 1950s. It moved up the road to 4503 Dixie Highway in the 1960s and 1970s. The bar in front of the restaurant was a popular hangout for ball teams. It was operated by Earl and Jack Howell. A fire destroyed the building in the 1980s and it was never rebuilt.

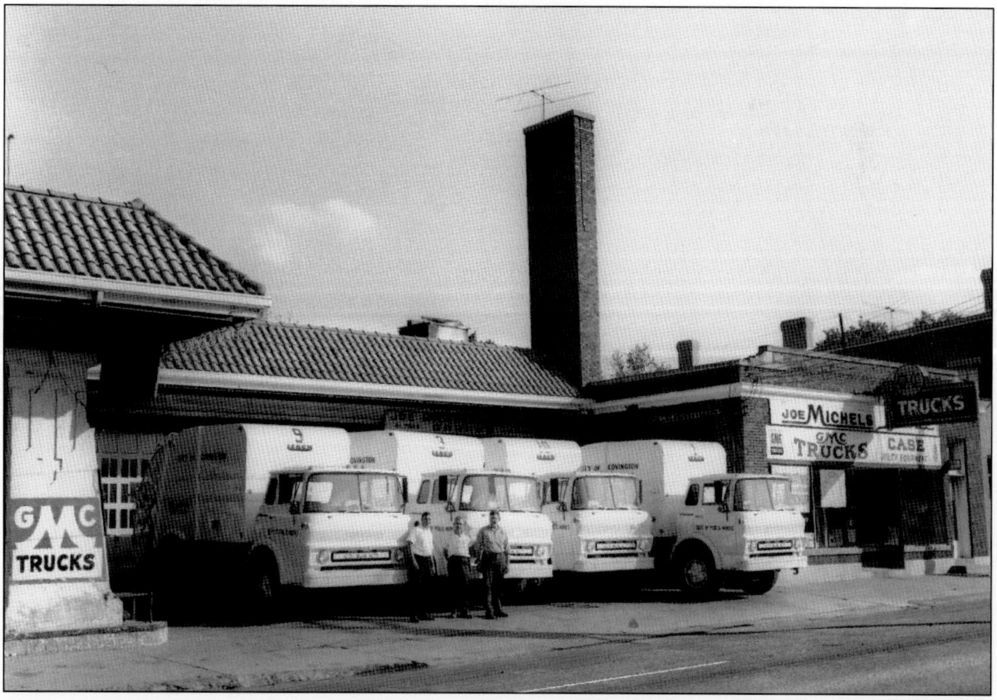

MICHELS SERVICE STATION. Joe Michels operated this GMC garage in the 1950s. This building is still located on the Dixie Highway across the street from Graves Avenue. The elm tree that divided Erlanger from Elsmere is located just to the left of the pillar with the logo "GMC Trucks."

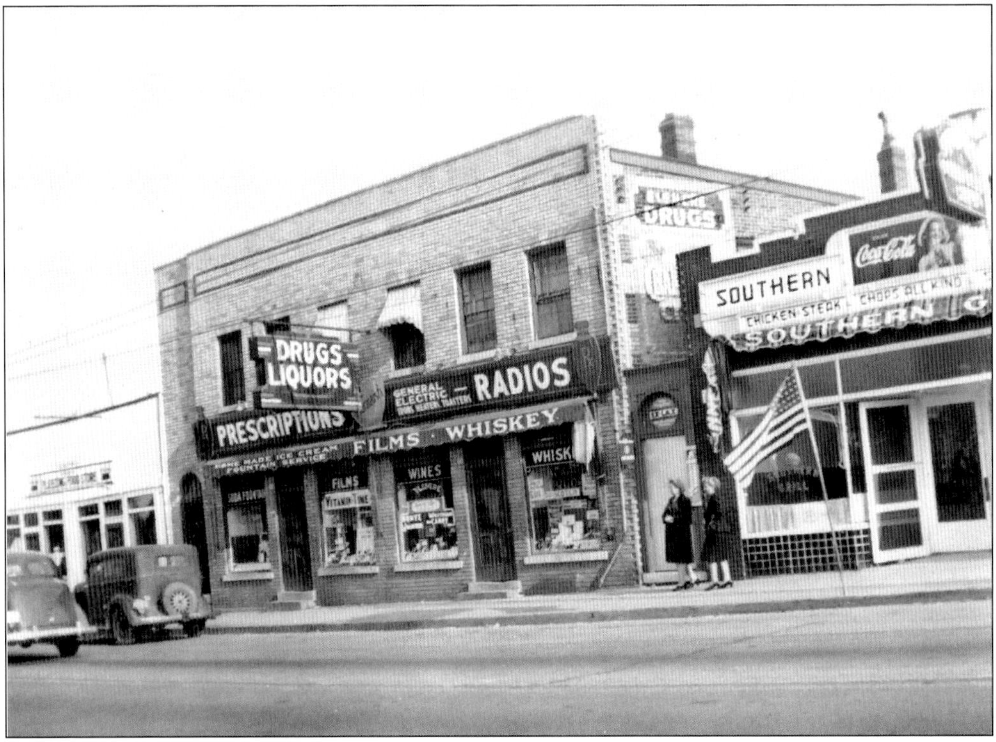

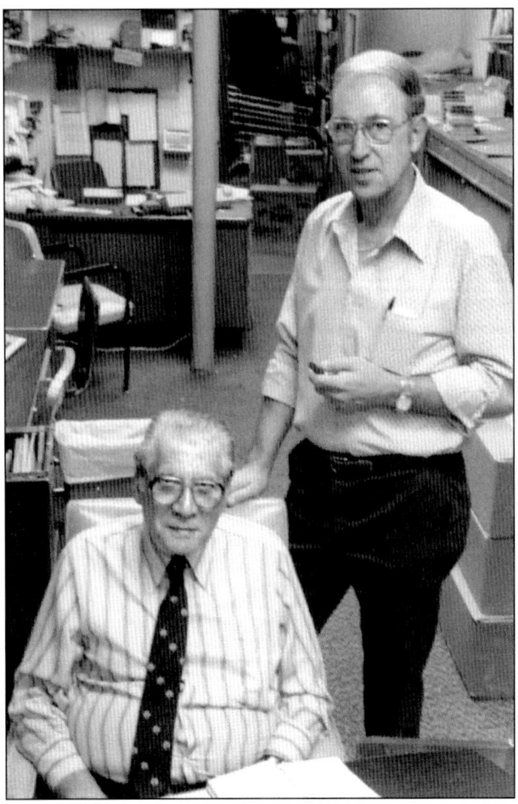

Elsmere Drugs. Known as Sid's, the drugstore was owned and operated by Sidney Horwitz. He was a very caring individual. A delivery service primarily for medicine was one of the amenities of his store. Many young men and women got their first job working for Sid. One of them was Don Koop. Don went to work for Sid as a delivery boy and worked his way up to assistant manager. Pictured at left are Sidney Horwitz (left) and Don Koop.

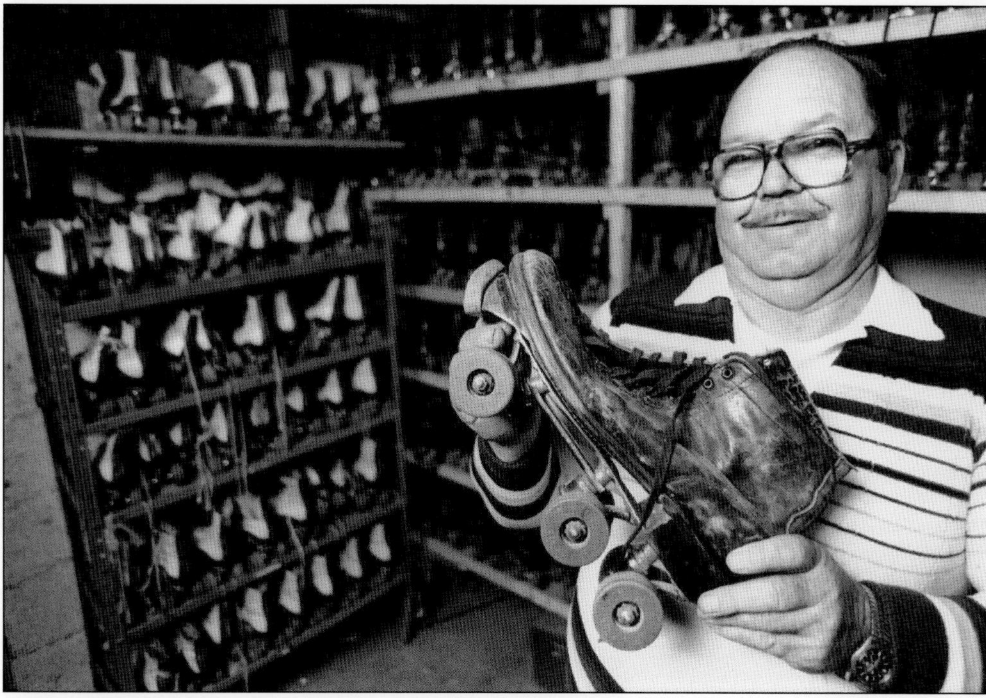

Jimmie's Rollerdrome. Jim Mullins returned from World War II and built his skating rink at 115 Main Street in Elsmere. It opened on New Year's Eve 1948. Jimmy is shown in this photograph with a special skate he designed to accommodate heavier skaters because they often broke the regular skates. Jimmie's wife, Marie, and his family continue to operate the rink at the same location.

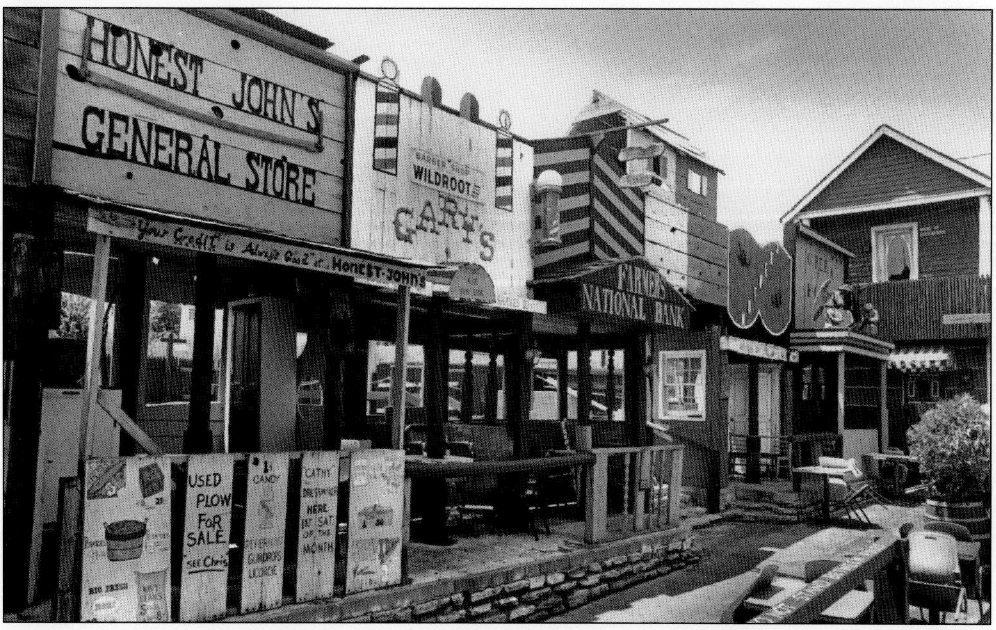

Round-up Club. The 1950s was a heyday for night spots in the Erlanger-Elsmere area. The first night spot in Erlanger was the Big Cowboy, which later became the Round-up club owned by Gene Kenney.

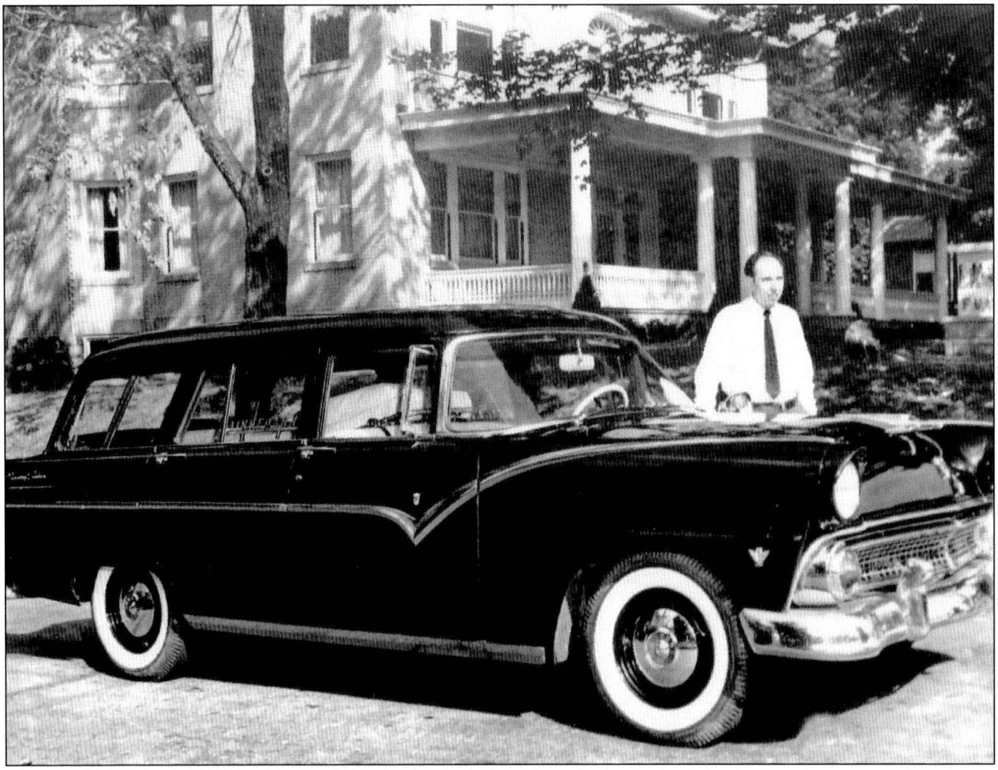

LINNEMANN FUNERAL HOME. The Linnemann Funeral Home is located on Commonwealth Avenue in Erlanger, Kentucky. Although there have been many additions and renovations, the building was the original home of the Buckner family, one of the first settlers in the Erlanger area. Above is a picture of Bud Linnemann, owner of Linnemann Funeral Home in its early years. Bud is shown with a 1955 Ford Country Squire, which he used as a limousine for his business. This vehicle was at times pressed into service as a backup ambulance for the Elsmere Life Squad. (Courtesy of Guy Linnemann.)

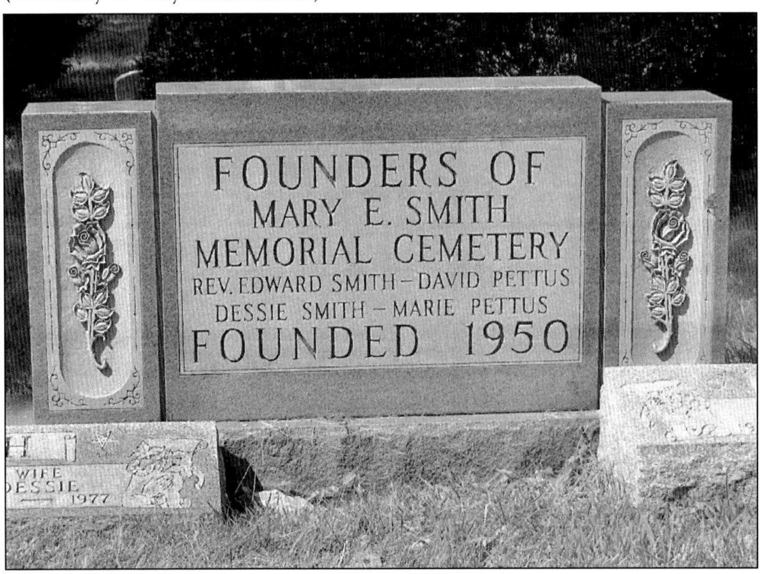

MARY E. SMITH CEMETERY. This cemetery was founded in 1950 by Rev. Edward Smith, Dessie Smith, David Pettus, and Maria Pettus as a memorial to Reverend Smith's mother, Mary E. Smith. (Photograph by Paul Dusing.)

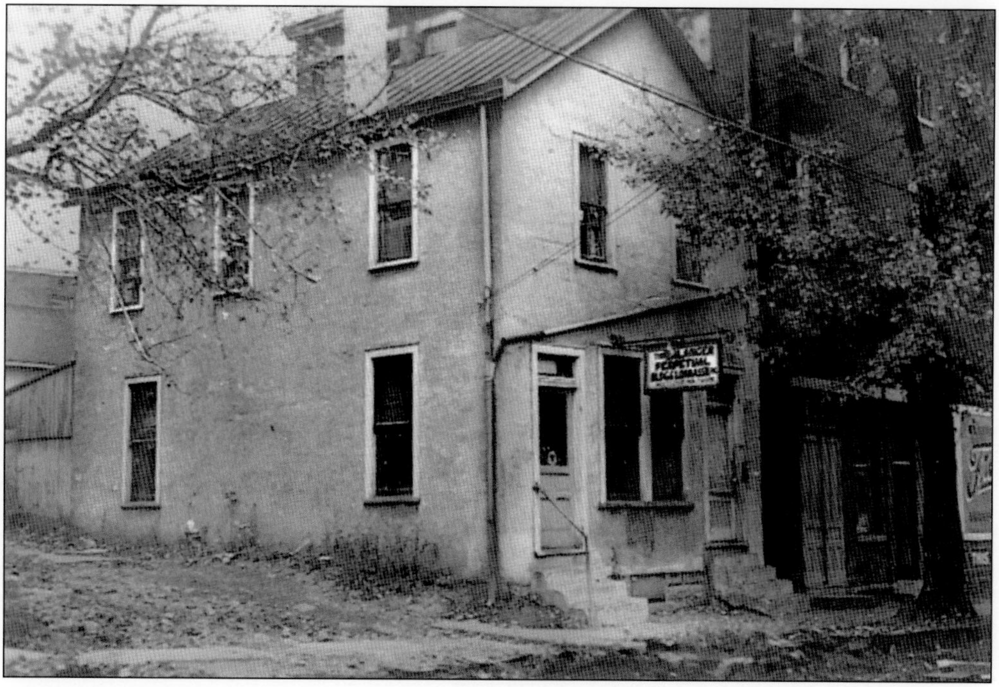

Erlanger Building and Loan. In the early 1900s, this home located on Commonwealth Avenue housed the Erlanger Perpetual Building and Loan Association, which survived the 1929 Depression. In the 1940s, the photograph below shows the new building on Commonwealth Avenue, which stands today.

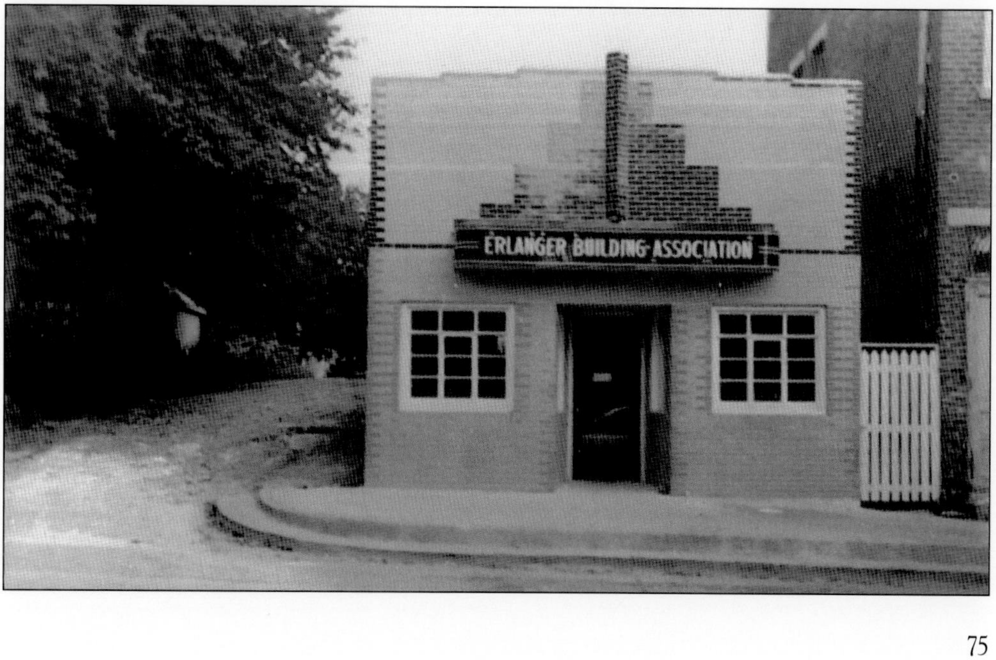

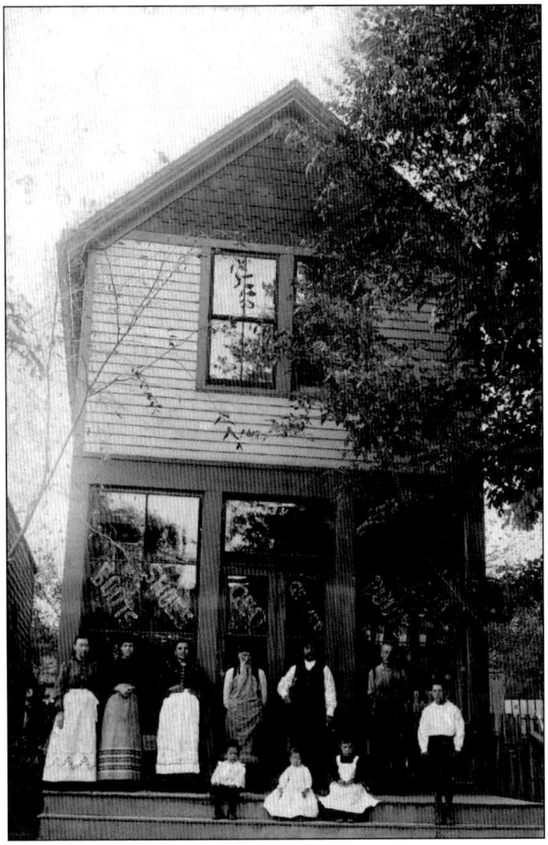

GEBHARD'S SHOE STORE. About 1894, Gebhard's Shoe Store was located on the Lexington Pike (Dixie Highway) in Erlanger, Kentucky. In the photograph, standing in front of the store are, from left to right, Mrs. Alex Ficke DeMarsey, Hattie Mack, Mary Gebhard, Grandpa Fred Ficke, George Gebhard, and an unidentified shoemaker. The Children shown are identified from left to right as Gus, Hanna, Maggie, and Mark.

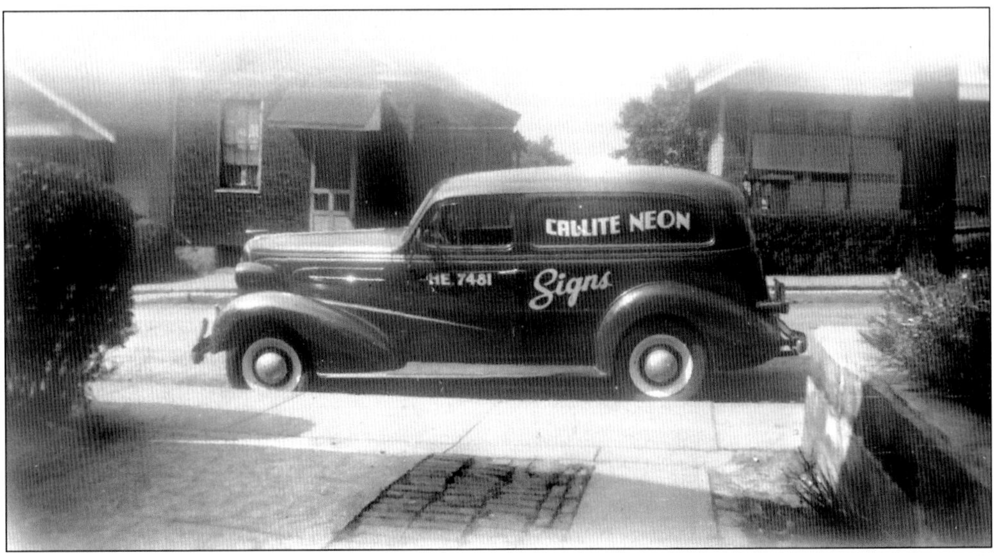

CALVIN TRITSCH. January 27, 1933, the skillful designer of neon lighting made a huge sign, which was claimed to be the largest skeleton neon sign in this part of the country. He was working for Dixie Sign Company at the time. Calvin was married to Esther Whitefoot. At one time, he had his own business, Cal-Lite Neon Signs, in the city of Erlanger at 3804 Dixie Highway. Calvin passed away January 3, 1994. (Courtesy of Mark Tritsch.)

Joe Stetter. Pictured is Joe Stetter's helicopter landing on the roof of the Family Motor Inn, which Stetter owned and operated in Erlanger. Ironically, he died in a helicopter crash in 1981.

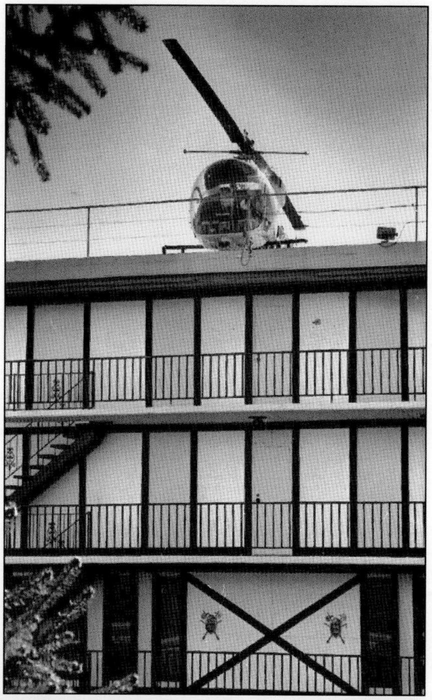

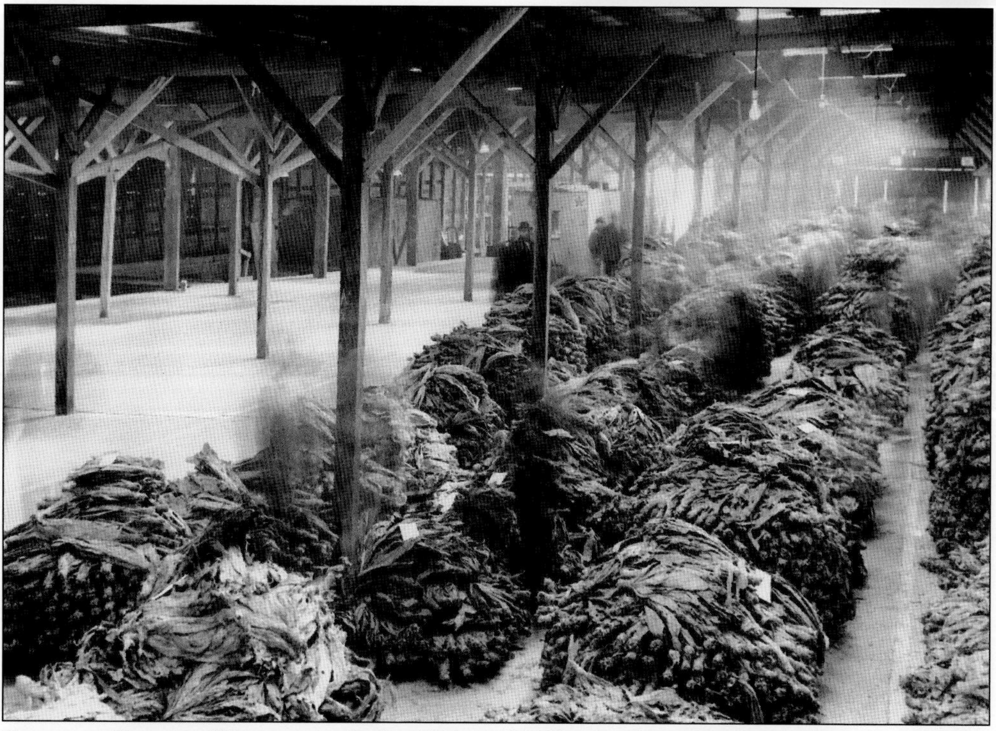

Erlanger Tobacco Warehouse. In the 1940s and 1950s, there were two huge tobacco warehouses in the area now known as the Kroger shopping center located off the Dixie Highway. Starting about mid-August, farmers brought their tobacco here to be auctioned. This area was very busy, especially in the mornings around Christmas.

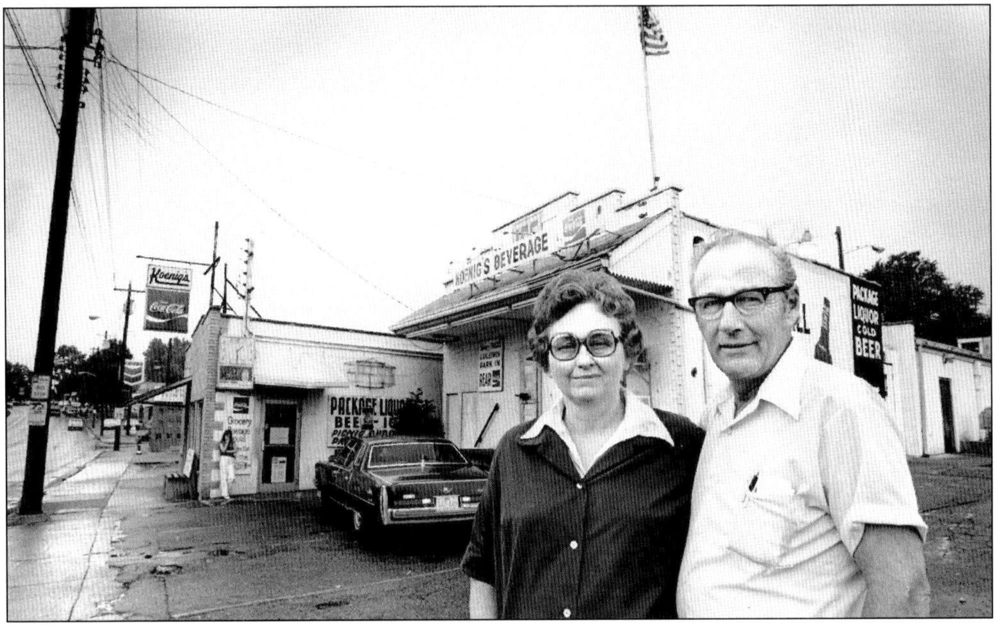

KOENIG'S GROCERY. From the 1940s to the 1970s, Koenig's Grocery was located next to the Bentler Building on the Dixie Highway. Specializing in meats, it was a popular shopping venue for folks in the Erlanger-Elsmere area. In the later years, the store was operated by the Tom Koenig family. The store was razed in the 1970s due to the widening of the Dixie Highway, and a new store was constructed at 3516 Dixie Highway. Pictured are Tom and his wife, Betty.

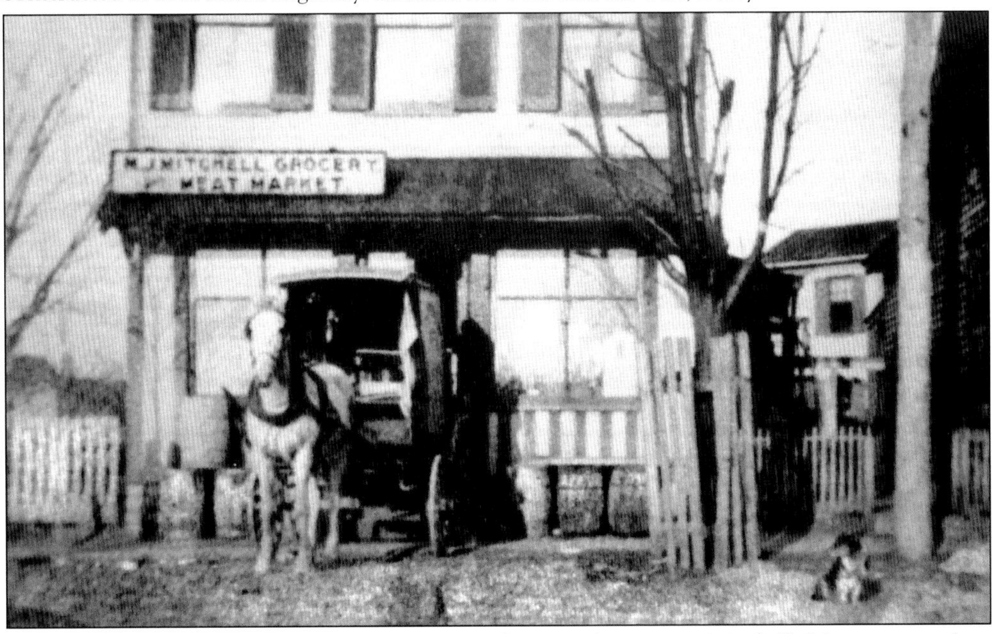

MITCHELL'S MEAT MARKET. This store was opened in 1891 by Morgan Mitchell. Morgan went door to door selling meats from a wagon. After establishing a customer base, Mitchell added groceries to his list of products and continued his meat wagon. His home delivery business continued until the mid-1940s. The building still stands on Crescent Avenue in Erlanger. The original telephone number was 36, the second telephone in Erlanger.

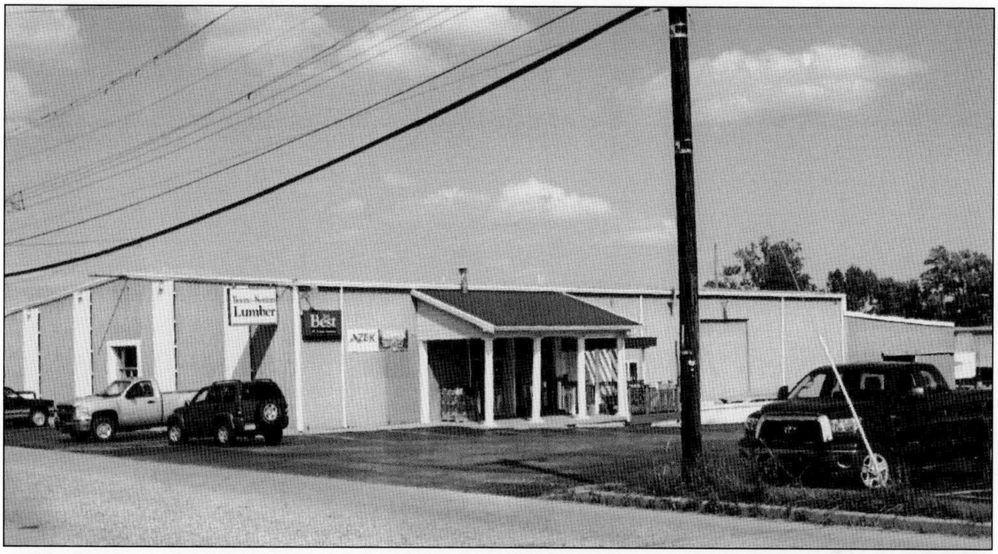

Boone Kenton Lumber Company of Erlanger. The business is the oldest business in Erlanger and is still in operation at the Crescent Avenue location. In 1914, Blaine Fulton owned and operated the business. It was then purchased by R. C. McNay, later by Gene Kelly, and at the present time is owned by Herbert Works. Every owner of the lumberyard has been an active citizen of Erlanger, and many family homes in the community have been serviced by this lumberyard.

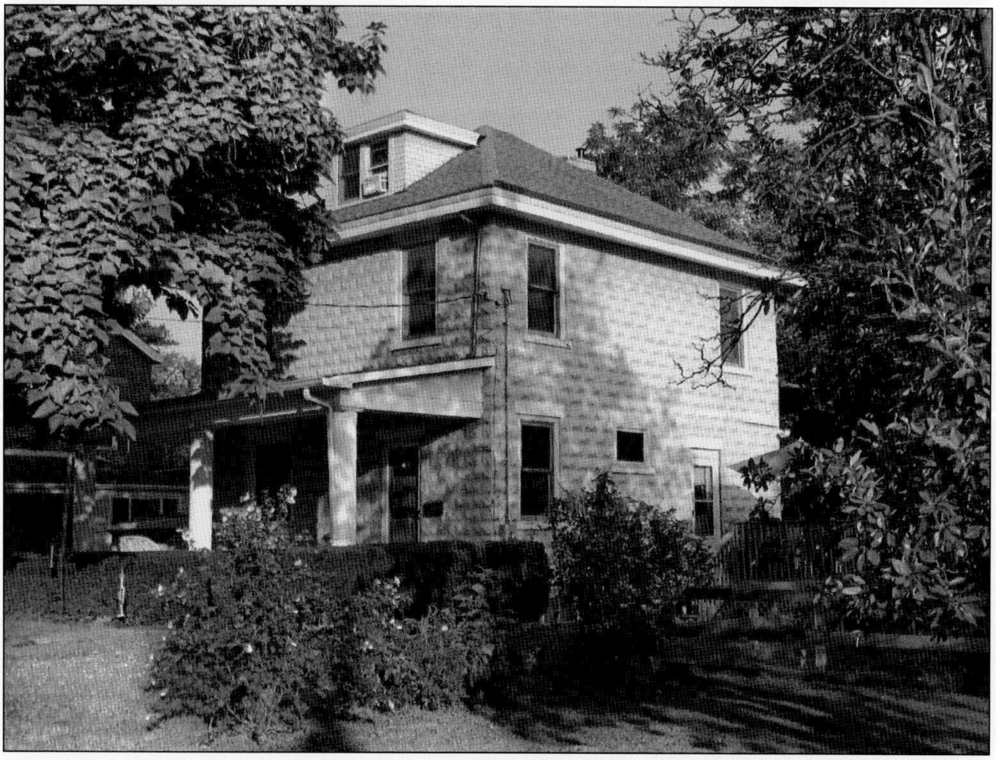

John Merk Home. Located at 3224 Riggs Avenue in Erlanger, this is an example of a concrete-block home. John was a supplier of concrete blocks. He made the mold and made each block by hand. This home gives an example of the ornate architecture. (Photograph by Paul Dusing.)

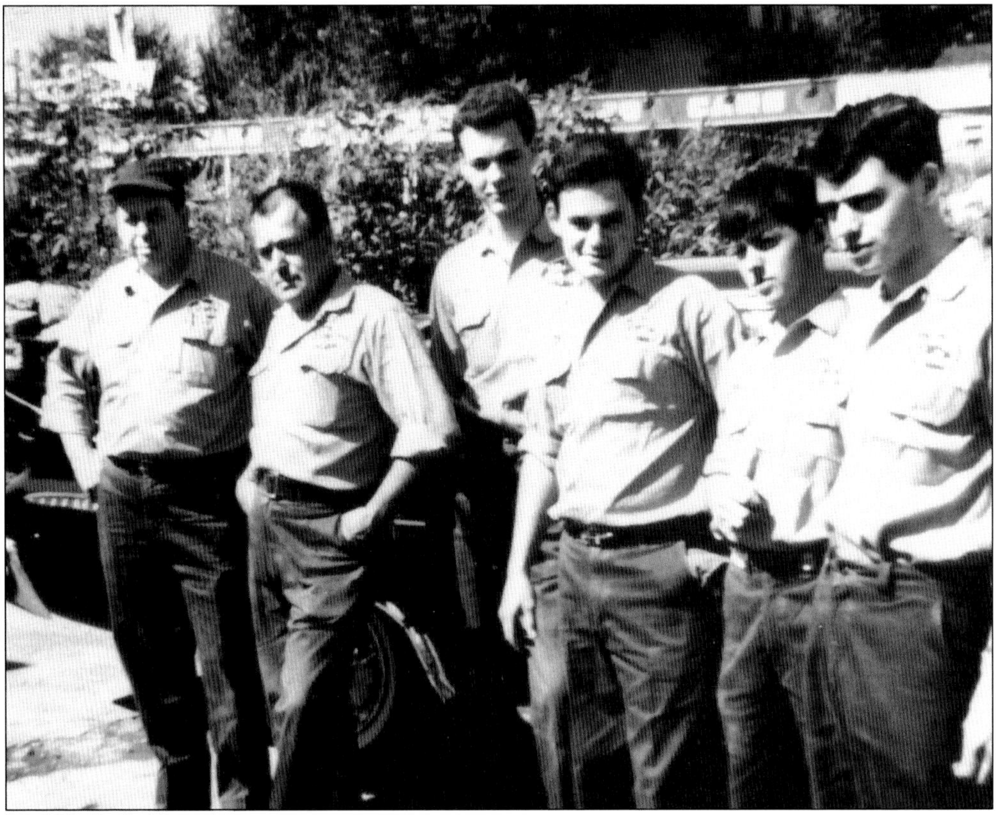

Hartke Auto Body Repair. Hartke's has been a long-standing enterprise in Erlanger. Located on Dixie Highway near Kentaboo Street, Hartke's was founded by Lee Hartke in 1945. Those in the picture are, from left to right, Mel Reincke, Lee Hartke Sr., Dave Cummins, Lee Hartke Jr., and Jim and Paul Hartke. (Courtesy of the Hartke family.)

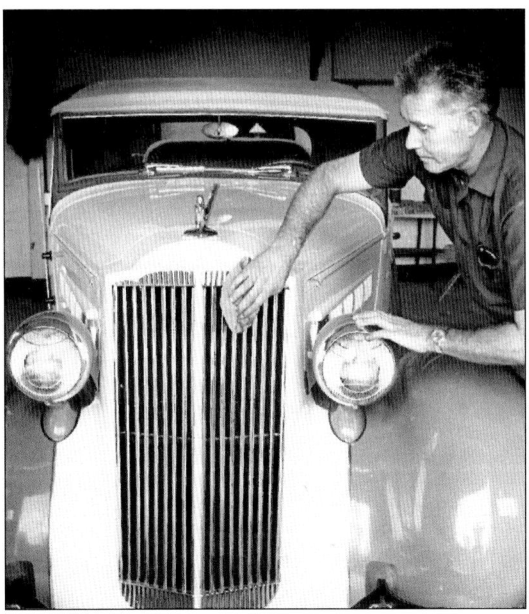

Joe Vagedes. Pictured is Joe Vagedes, brother of Fred and Ray. From 1969 through 1989, Fred and Ray Vagedes ran a vintage and antique car restoration business on Lytle Avenue in Elsmere. Cars were shipped into this Elsmere location from around the country.

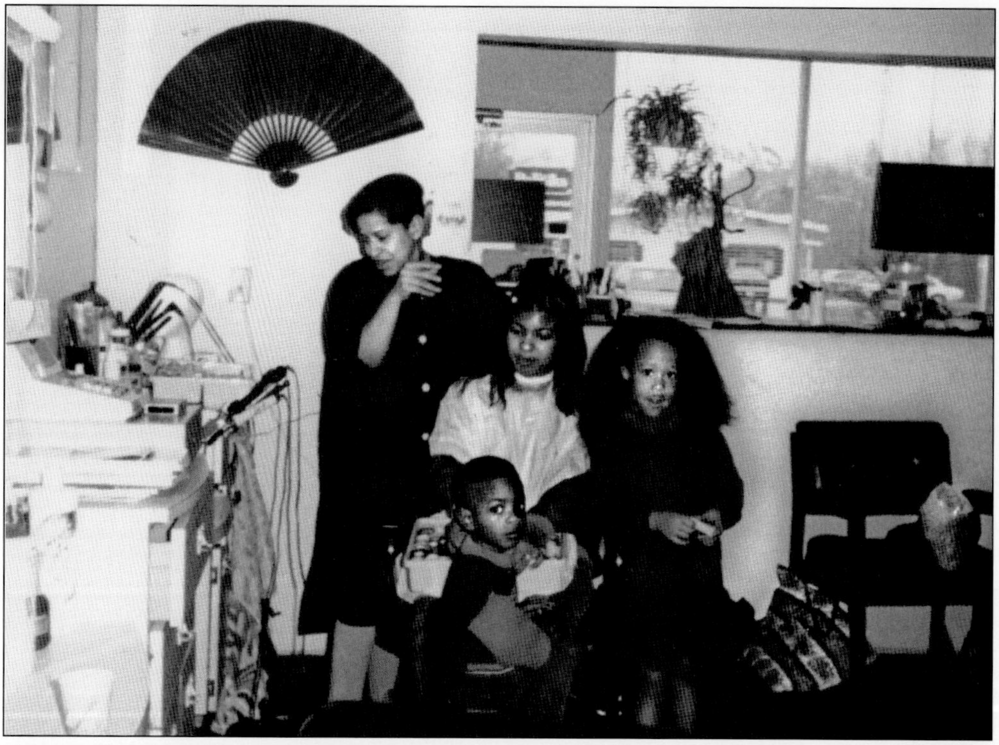

EBONY CREATIONS BEAUTY SALON. Owned by Mary E. Warner Lewis, Ebony Creations was established in 1992 and was the first African American–owned salon outside of the home. First located at the corner of Dixie Highway and Lytle Avenue, it was inspired by the home salon on Capital Avenue owned by Vicki Riddell in the early 1960s. It was later moved to 3309 Dixie Highway. Pictured is Mary working on her daughter, Stacey Lewis Carter, while Ashley Botts (right) and Aubrey Carter look on. (Courtesy of Mary Lewis.)

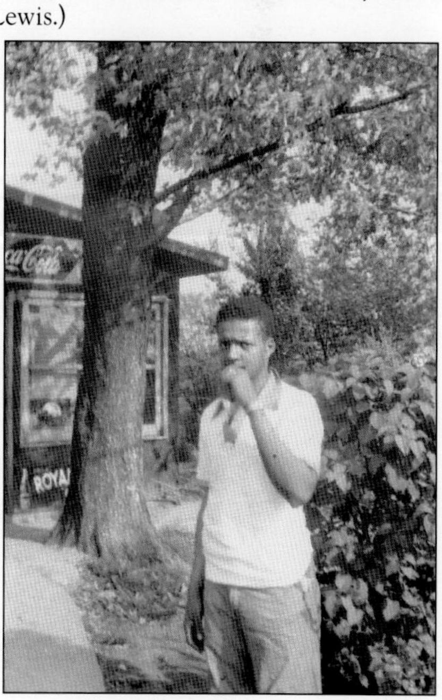

JUKE JOINT IN ELSMERE. Prior to the civil rights movement, many places were off-limits to African Americans. In response, the community established their own businesses that would provide a social outlet as well as needed goods. The Juke Joint belonged to John and Mamie Weaver and sat at the corner of Garvey Avenue and Plateau Street. Pictured is John "Buster" Weaver. (Courtesy of Nancy and Rosella Weaver.)

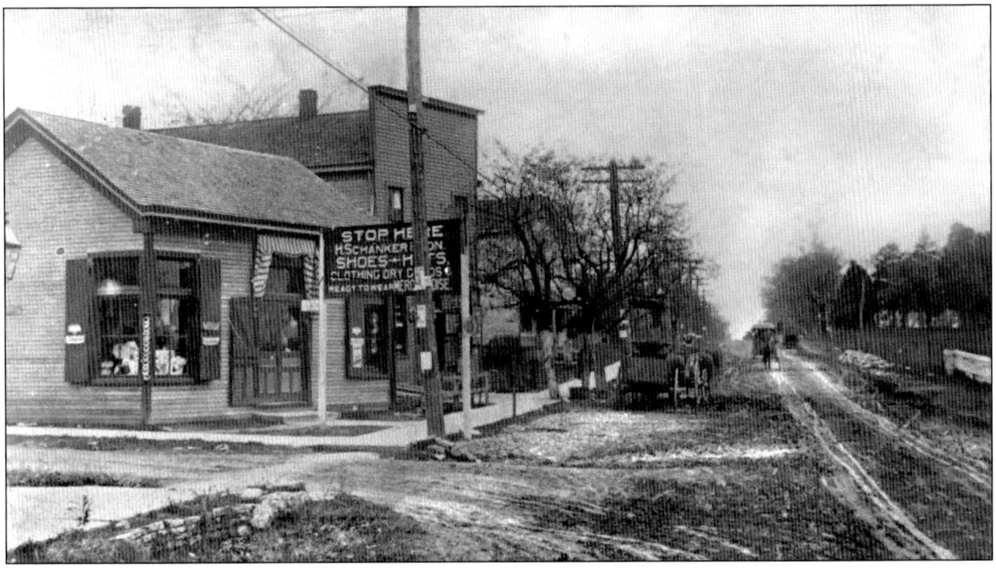

SCHANKERS DRY GOODS, 1890S. One of the early dry goods stores in the area was located at the corner of the Dixie Highway and Garvey Avenue. Schankers offered ready-to-wear merchandise. A brick structure eventually replaced the wooden structure in the 1940s.

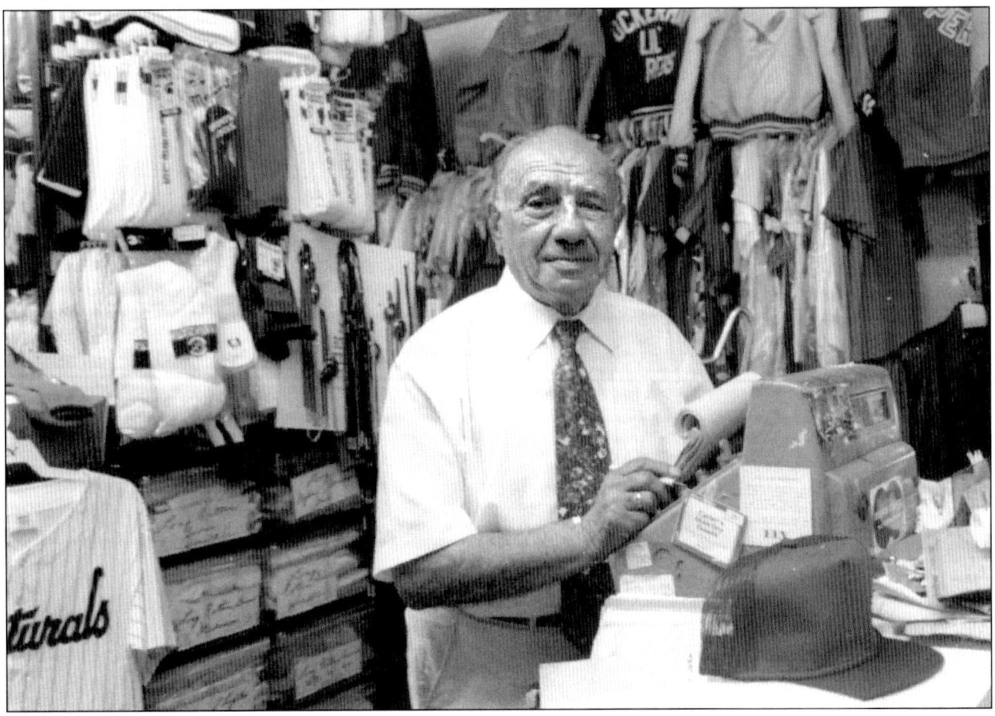

DIXIE DRY GOODS. After losing most of his family members at the Auschwitz concentration camp, Henry Carter immigrated to the United States, where his older brother had settled at the outbreak of the war in Europe. In 1946, Henry started Dixie Dry Goods in Erlanger, Kentucky. The store was originally located on the east corner of Dixie Highway and Garvey Avenue but was later moved to the west side of the highway, where it eventually occupied three buildings. Henry operated the store for 50 years.

Putt-Putt Golf. In the cool summer evenings, the Putt-Putt golf course offered a relaxing, although sometimes frustrating, experience. Saturday mornings were tournament times for all the youngsters in the area. Everyone wanted to win a trophy. It is located at 3143 Dixie Highway behind the present-day post office complex.

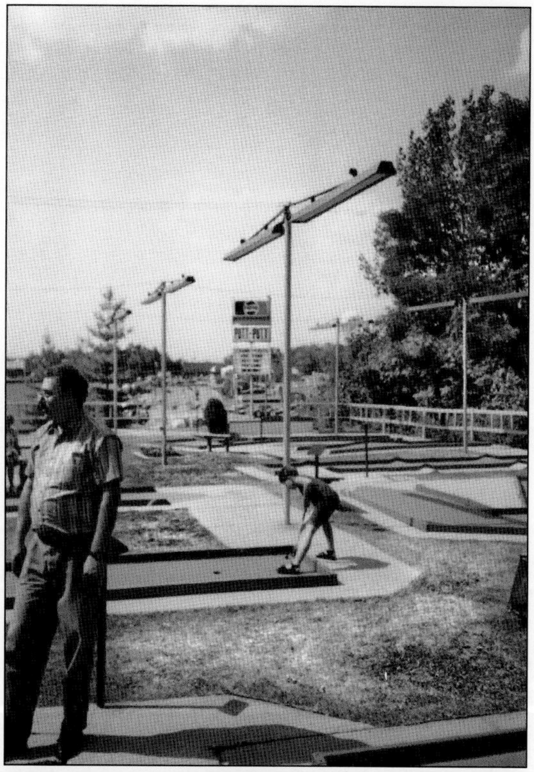

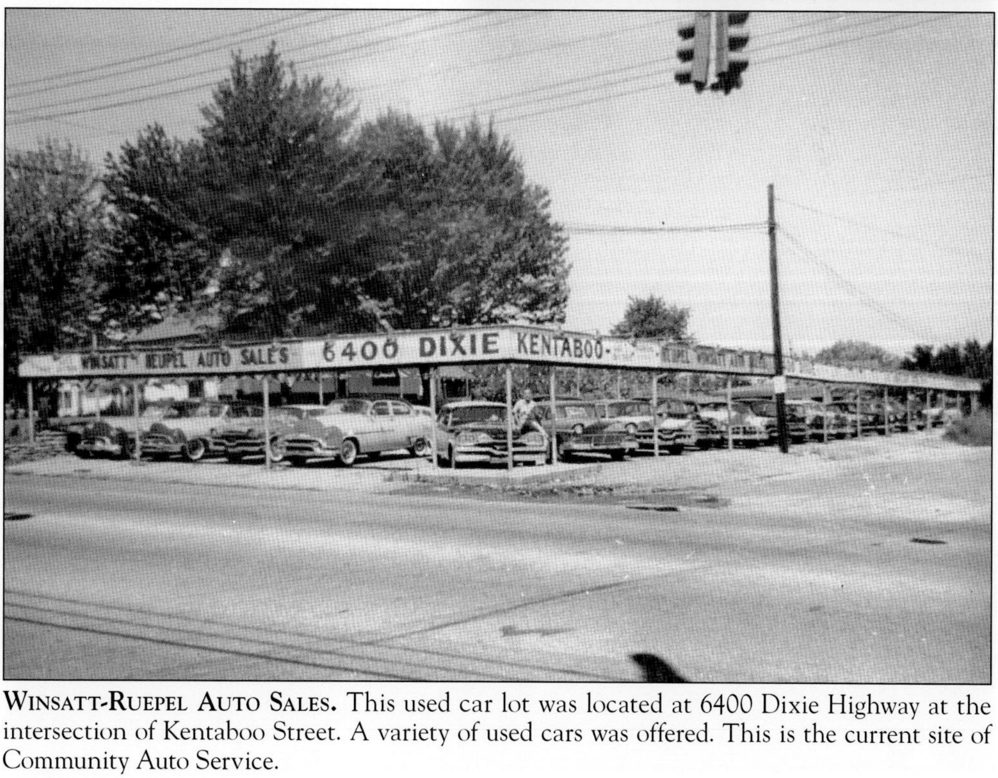

Winsatt-Ruepel Auto Sales. This used car lot was located at 6400 Dixie Highway at the intersection of Kentaboo Street. A variety of used cars was offered. This is the current site of Community Auto Service.

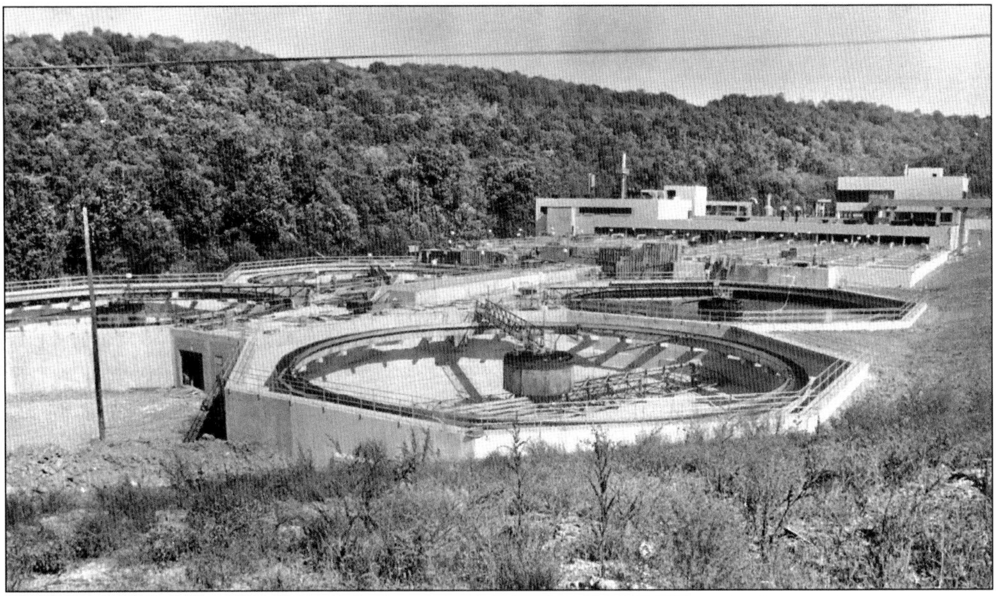

DRY CREEK SEWER PLANT. Sanitation District No. 1 installed this large facility in the northeastern part of Erlanger just a few hundred yards from the Ohio River. Originally treating waste from Northern Kentucky cities with chlorine gas, it now uses a less dangerous industrial bleach solution as the preferred oxidizing agent.

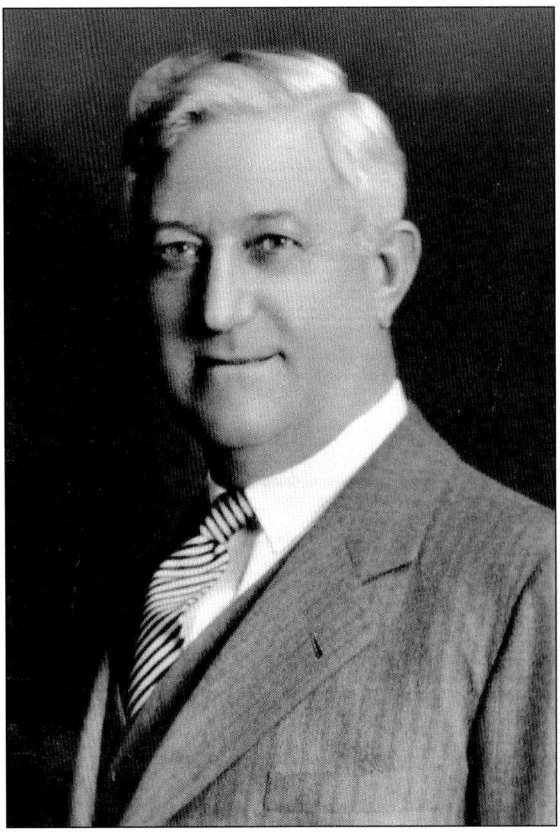

GEORGE STETTER. George Stetter bought the old Caleb Manly Mansion property in the 1930s. He was from the Vonderhaar and Stetter Funeral Home in Newport. Stetter served as president of the Forest Lawn Board of Directors until his death in 1950. His daughter Thelma Stetter Owen's husband, James L. Owen Sr., then managed the property. More than 11,000 burials have taken place at Forest Lawn Cemetery.

Four

People and Events
Families, Citizens, Scenes, and Sports

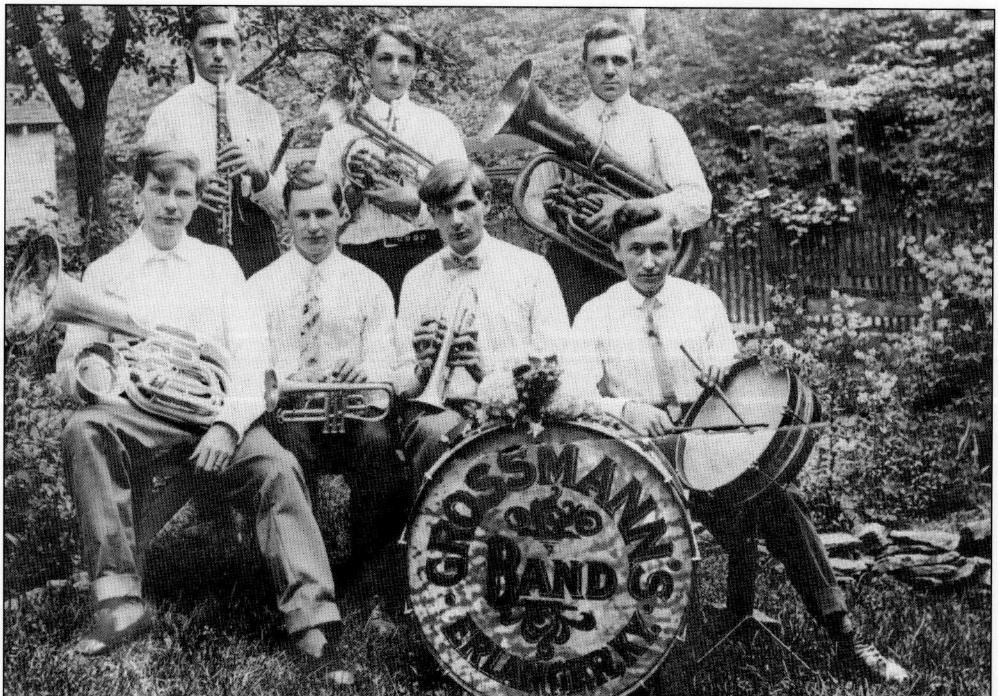

Grossmann's Band. In the late 1890s, as the Erlanger community continued to grow economically, social organizations also developed dances, plays, and Chautauqua lectures. They were usually presented in the town hall's second-floor stage area. Grossman's Band usually furnished the music for the events.

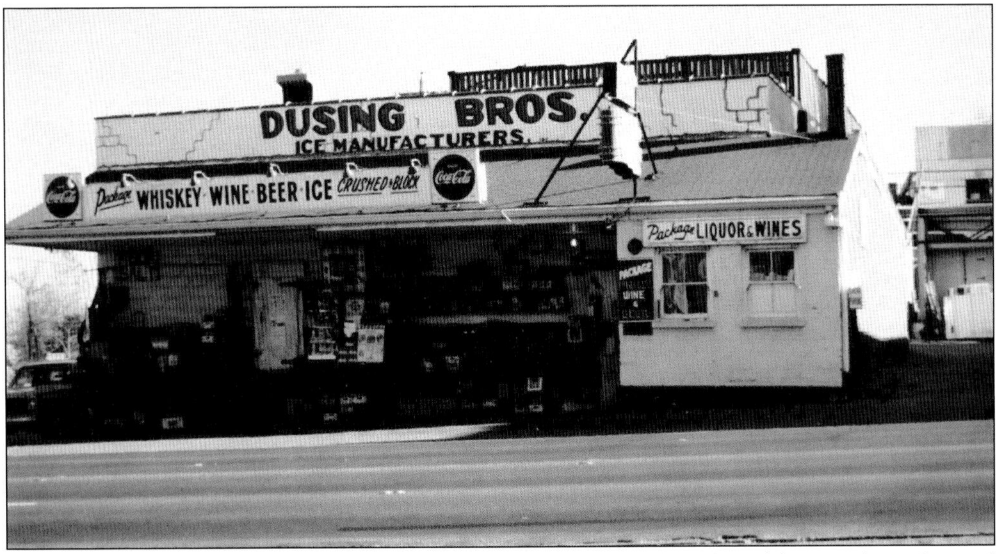

Dusing Brothers Ice Manufacturers. In 1928, Dusing Brothers (Franklin, on the right, and Ben) opened in Elsmere, Kentucky, the only independent ice manufacturing plant in Northern Kentucky. They sold ice from the front dock or delivered it by wagon or truck. Before refrigerators, ice was carried into homes and businesses by the driver, using a heavy leather cape on his back to keep from getting wet. When the Gayety Movie Theater opened next door, the ice house provided cool air via two large pipes and a fan at each location. Over these 81 years, four generations of Dusings have served and cared for citizens on both sides of the Dixie Highway. (Both courtesy of Dusing Brothers Ice.)

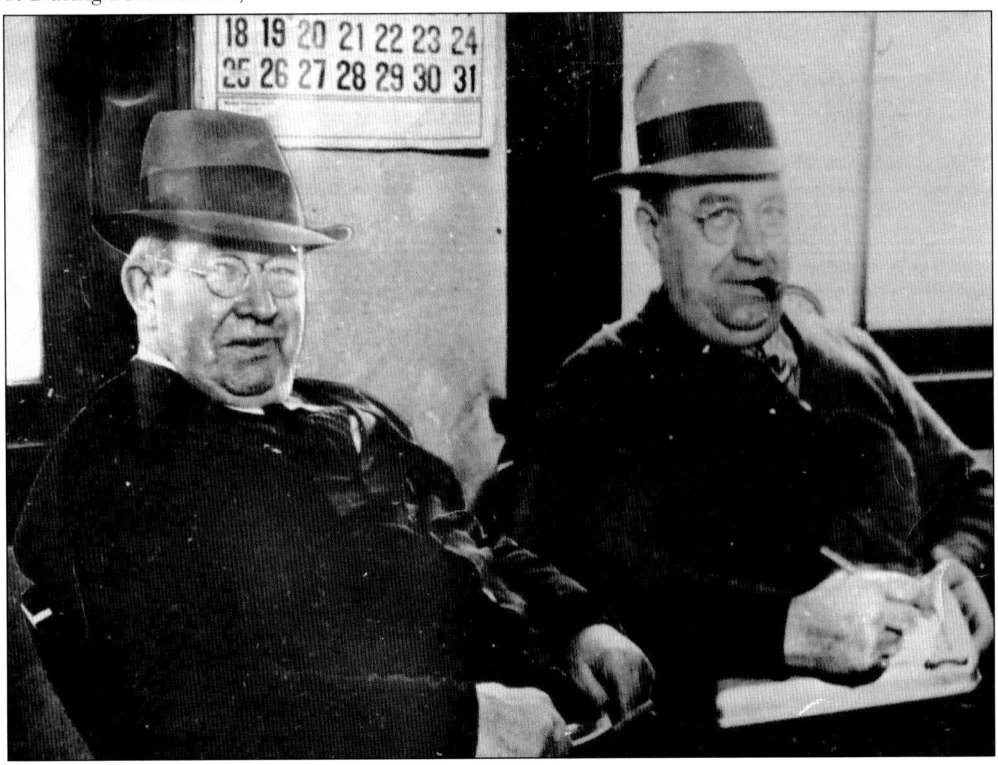

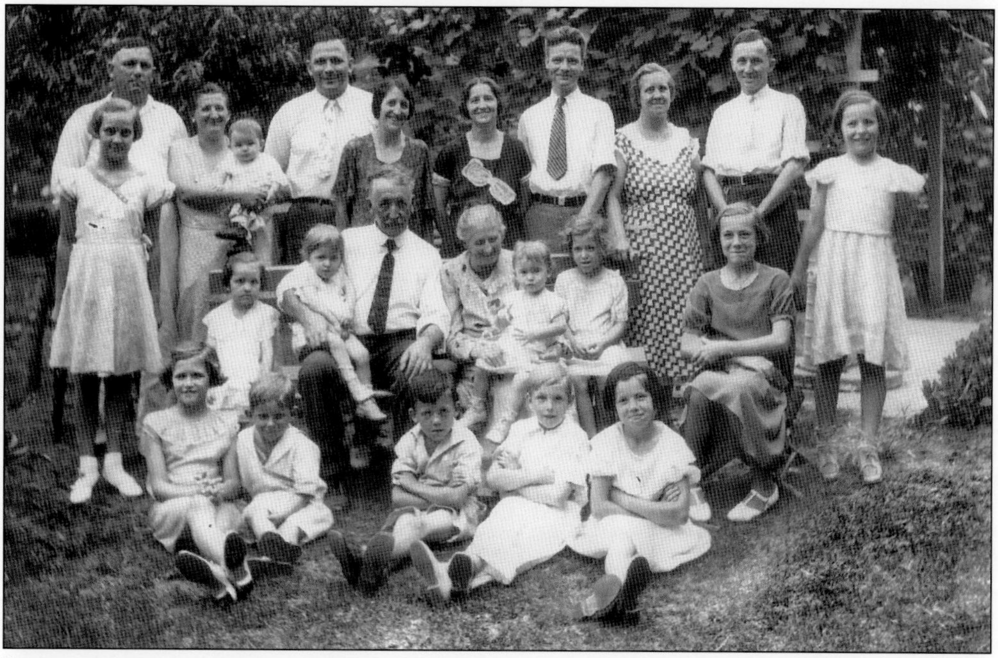

John and Johanna Waginger Family. John and Johanna, seated in the center of the photograph, pose with a child on each of their knees celebrating a special occasion in 1934. Their four children are standing in the back row. From left to right are George and Mary Waginger Hartman, Dick and Katherine Waginger Koenig, Ted and Matilda Waginger Feldman, and Catherine and John Waginger Jr. (Courtesy of Rita Behler.)

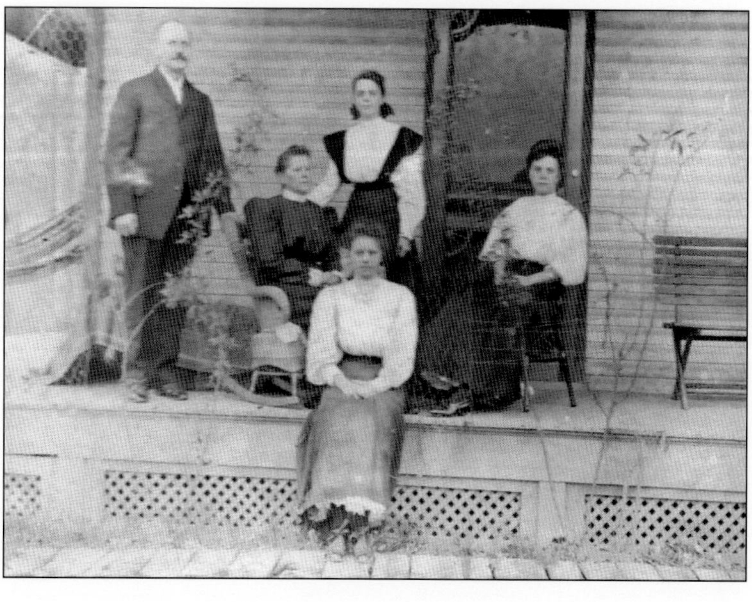

Hoehn Family Home. The home was located on Hulbert Avenue in 1910. The owners were Frank Hoehn and his wife, Freda, born in Baden, Germany. Frank and Freda had three daughters, Florence, Elizabeth, and Frances, all pictured on the porch. (Courtesy of Ruth Wolking.)

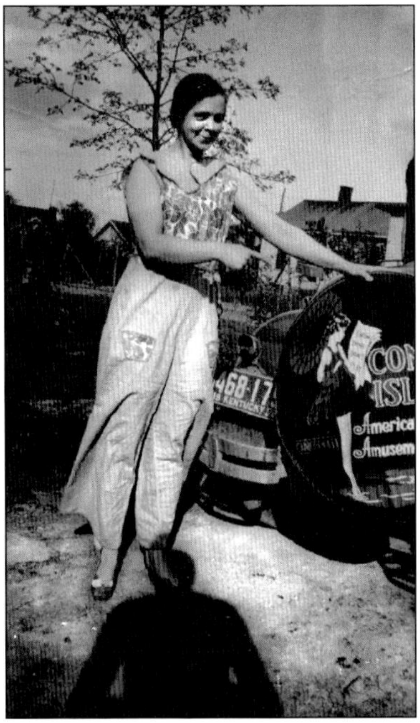

Martha Hall Victor. Martha Hall came to Erlanger and taught for many years in the Erlanger-Elsmere school system. She married lawyer Russell Victor.

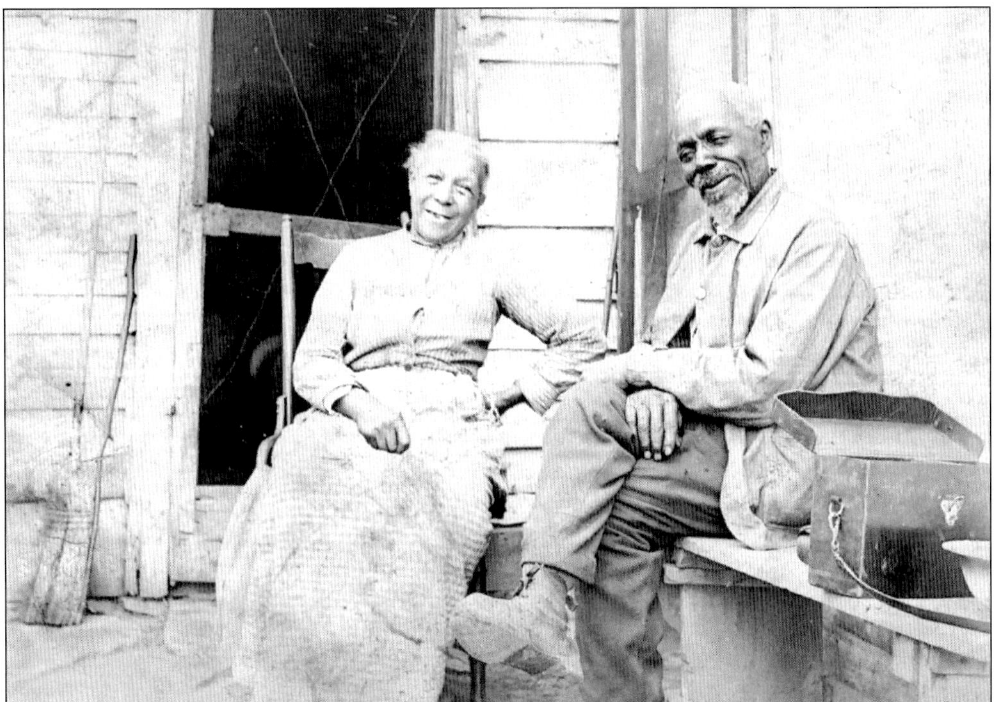

Judy and Henry Brooks. The Brookses lived on the Dennis Conway, and later Mose Black, property on Erlanger Road from the late 1800s until the 1920s. Henry was one of a number of African American stone workers in the area. He would bring stones from Dry Creek that would later be used for buildings in the Erlanger and Elsmere area. (Courtesy of Fred and Betty Hartman Black.)

Morgan Mitchell. Mitchell served in World War I, and the family donated his uniform to the Erlanger Historical Society, where it is on display. The Mitchell family started a grocery and meat business with a horse and buggy as a traveling meat market. In 1891, they opened a store on Crescent Avenue. They had the second telephone in the community. He received orders by telephone and had a delivery service. This business was operated by them for 60 years at the Crescent Avenue location.

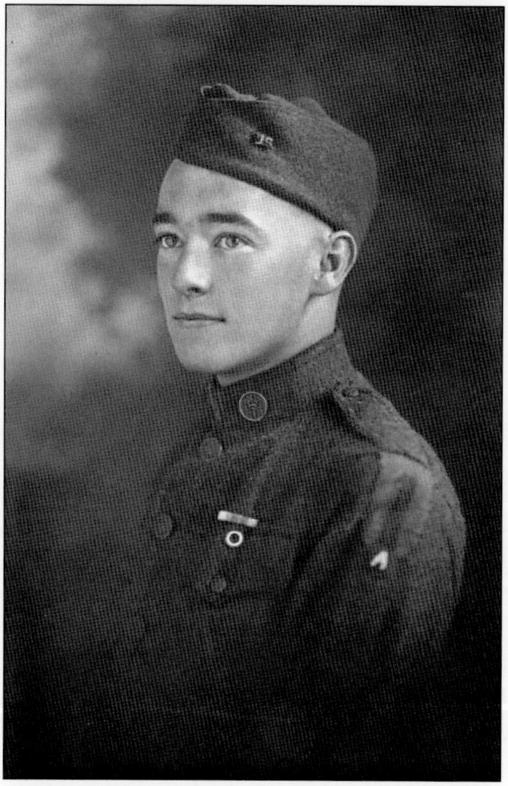

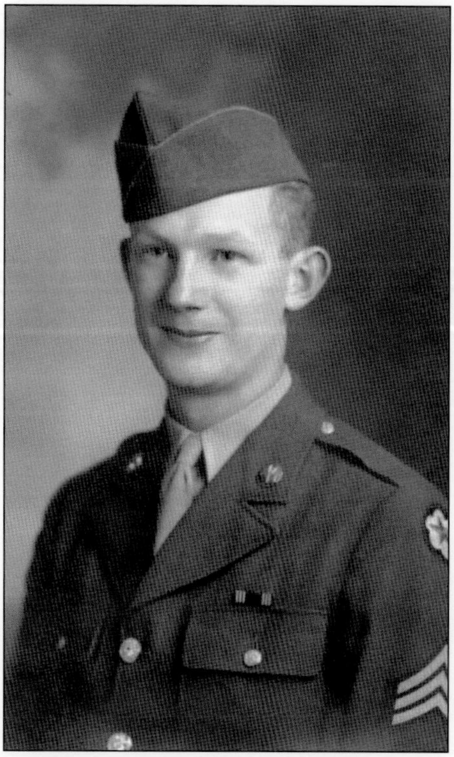

Russell McClure. Russell served in World War II on a code team in General McArthur's headquarters in Manila and handled the messages between the president and the general. He was also stationed in Camp Crowder, Missouri. One night, he went to a USO dance and met his wife, Mary. They moved to Erlanger in January 1946. Russell served on city council for 12 years, and Mary served as president of the Erlanger Historical Society for eight years. (Courtesy of Mary McClure.)

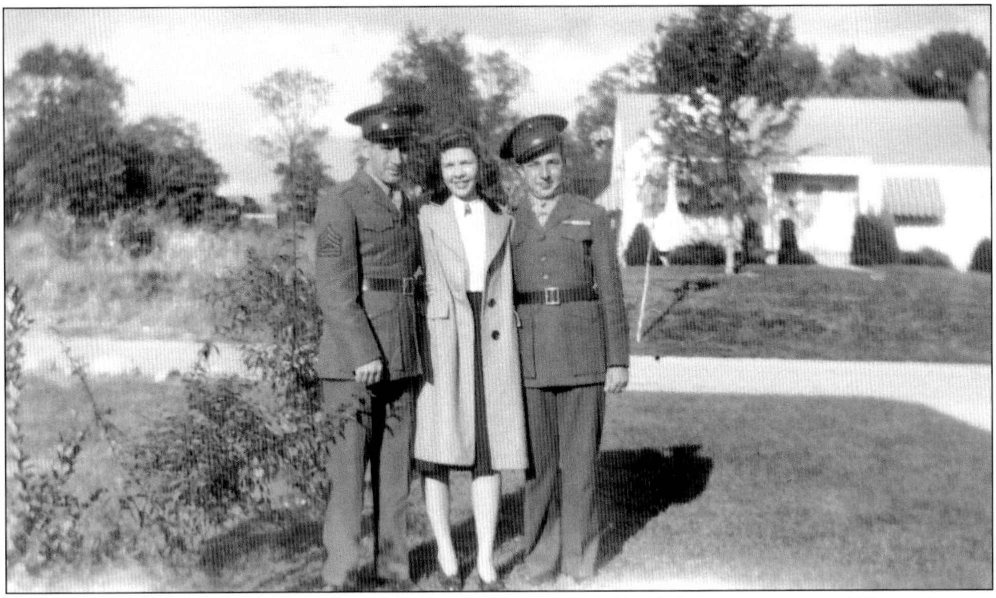

HOME FROM THE WAR. In October 1945, Frank Hopkins (left), Dolores Jansen, and Harry Jansen Jr. are standing at the end of McAlpin Avenue in Erlanger, Kentucky. At the time, the address was 55 McAlpin Avenue. The field across the street became Cowie Avenue. In 1945, McAlpin Avenue ran into the yard of Lloyd High School. (Courtesy of Jansen family.)

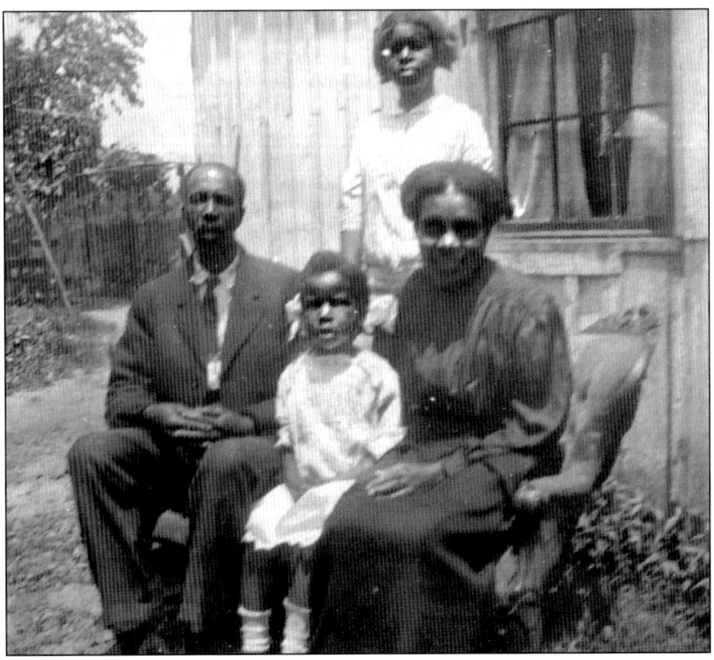

CARNEAL FAMILY. William and Mary Carneal pose with their daughters, Cora (standing) and Wilma. Both girls received bachelor's degrees from Wilberforce University in the 1930s and later taught in Elsmere at either the Dunbar or Wilkins Heights school. William's father, Orlando Goodrich Carneal, served with the 117th Regiment, U.S. Colored Infantry, during the Civil War. He received an honorable discharge in August 1867. (Courtesy of Eleanor King.)

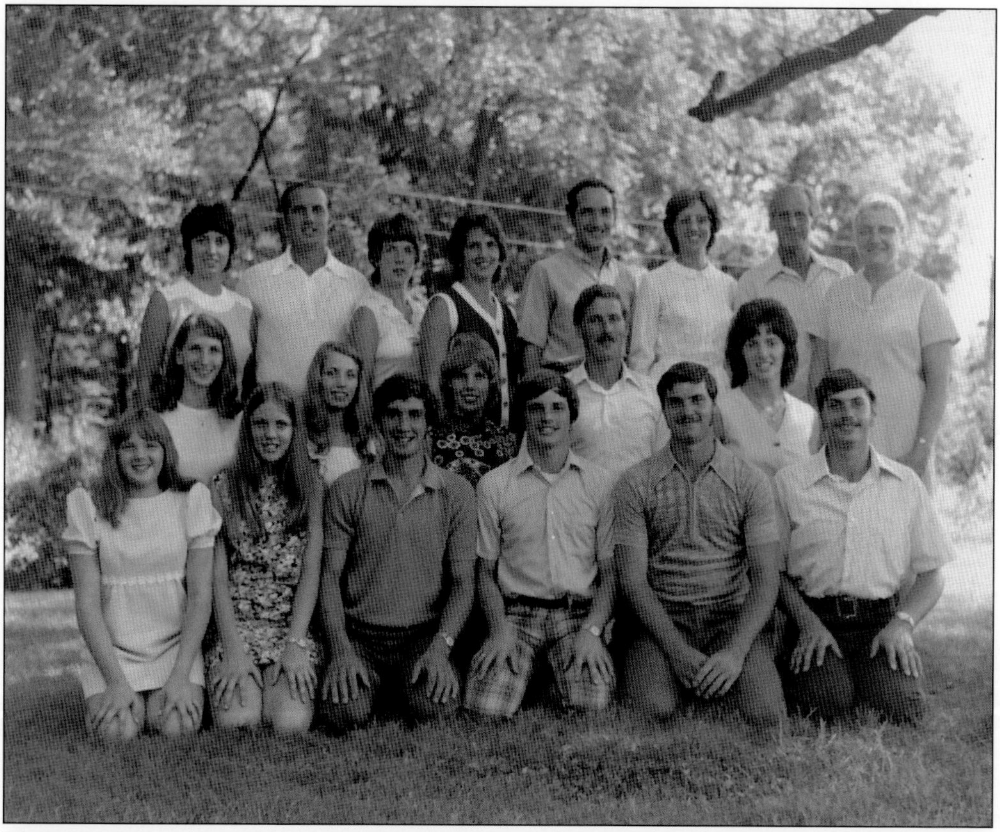

Tewes Family. John and Mary, owners of the Tewes Poultry Farm in Erlanger, are shown with their 17 children. Pictured are, from left to right, (first row) Cathy, Teresa, Joe, Mike, Dan, and Ed; (second row) Ann, Patsy, Trudy, Tom, and Peggy; (third row) Laura, Bob, Joyce, Rita, John, Sister Mary (OSB), and parents John and Mary Tewes.

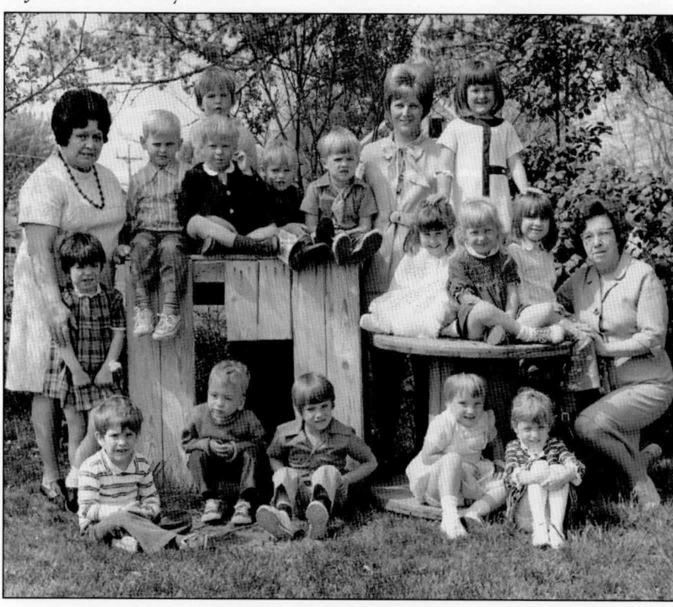

Martha Arnett Montessori School. This school was located on Hulbert Avenue in Erlanger. Pictured in 1976 are, from left to right, (first row) Jay Liddington, Andy Howard, Doug Rapp, Amy Arnett, and Karyn Fogie; (second row) Mrs. Frances McCarty, Sharon Stegman, Paul Neltner, John Crossen, Jimmy Heilmann, Scot McChain, Bruce Ravenscraft, Mrs. Blanche Rawe, Elizabeth ?, three unidentified girls (seated), and Mrs. Martha Arnett on the far right.

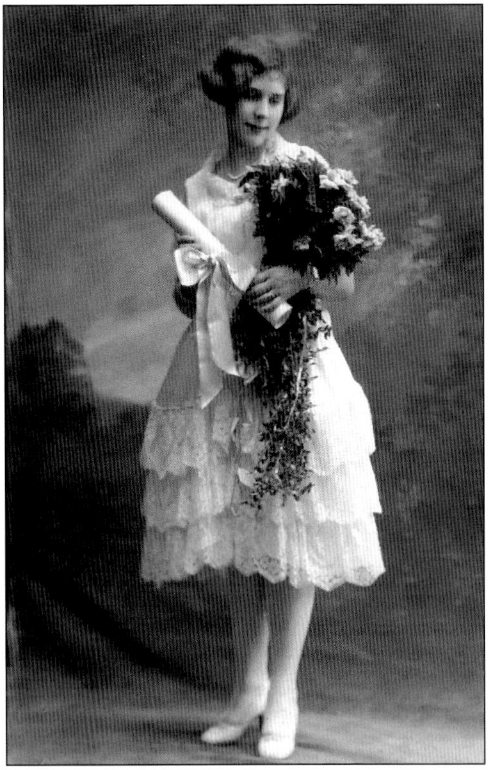

RUTH WOLKING. This is Ruth's high school graduation photograph from Villa Madonna Academy around 1943. The daughter of Peter A. and Frances E. Wolking and the granddaughter of Frank and Elizabeth Hoehn, Ruth was born in 1925. Ruth lived on Hulbert Avenue. (Courtesy of Ruth Wolking.)

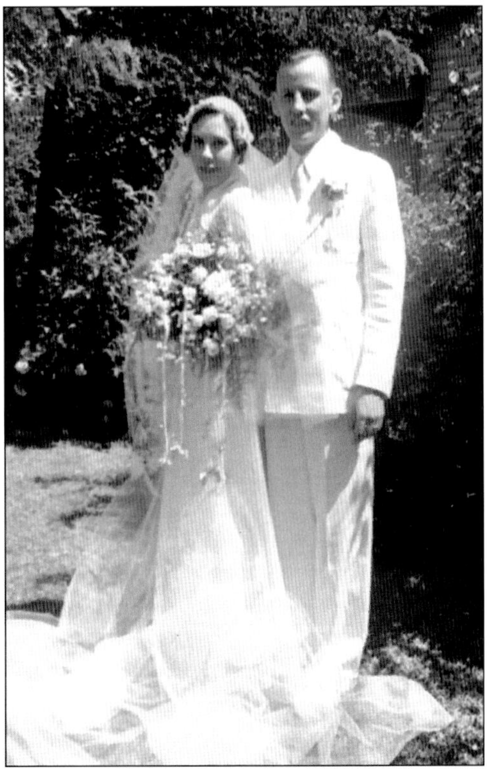

DOROTHEA WOLKING AND RALPH KEMPHAUS. The couple was married on July 4, 1937, at St. Henry's Church. Ralph was the son of Joseph and Elizabeth Kemphaus of Covington, and Dorothea Wolking was the daughter of Peter A. and Frances E. Wolking of Erlanger. Ralph coached basketball at several area high schools, one of which was St. Henry's High School. (Courtesy of Ruth Wolking.)

VIVIAN ALDERSON LUDWICK. Vivian was the daughter of Maury and Elmore "Mose" Alderson. She was a teacher at the Elsmere Head Start Center, which was in the Wilkins Heights School Building. (Courtesy of Stacey Carter.)

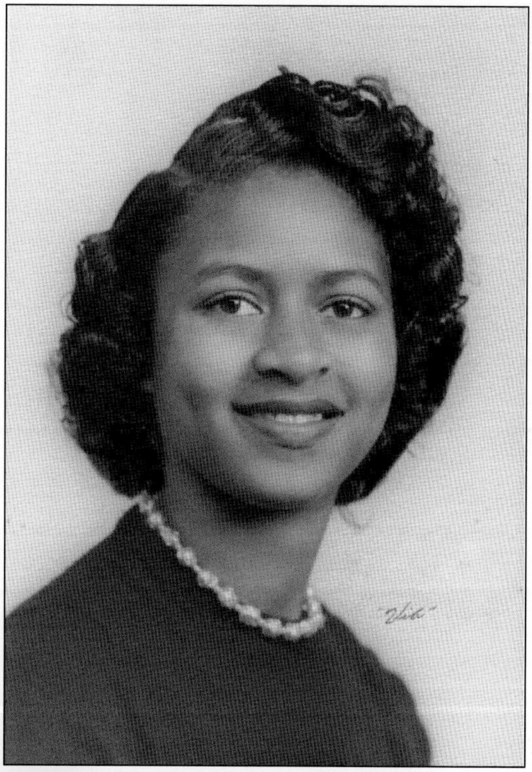

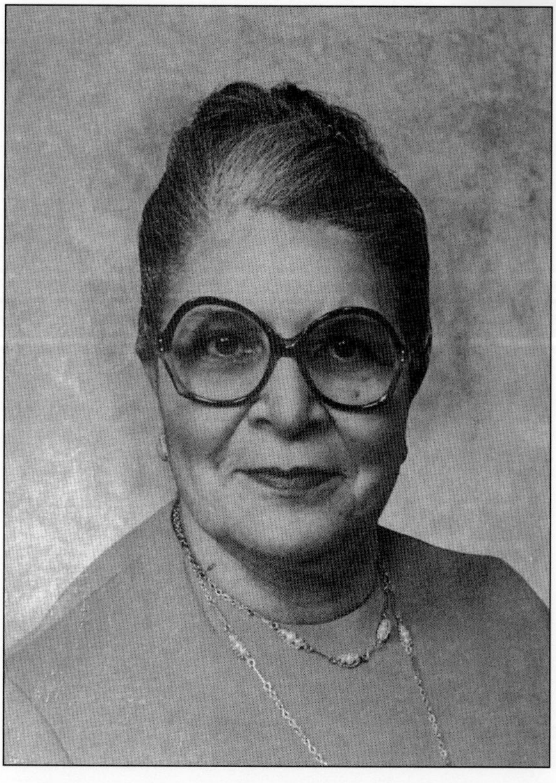

ROSELLA FRENCH PORTERFIELD. Rosella was born in 1918, the granddaughter of slaves. She grew up on a farm in Daviess County and went on to graduate from Kentucky State University in 1940. Soon after, she began her teaching career in Elsmere at Barnes Temple AME Church on Spring Street and later at Wilkins Heights School. In 1955, less than a year after the U.S. Supreme Court abolished segregated schools, Rosella persuaded Edgar Arnett, the superintendent of Erlanger Elsmere Schools, to integrate the schools. These events were documented in the September 17, 1956, issue of *Life* magazine.

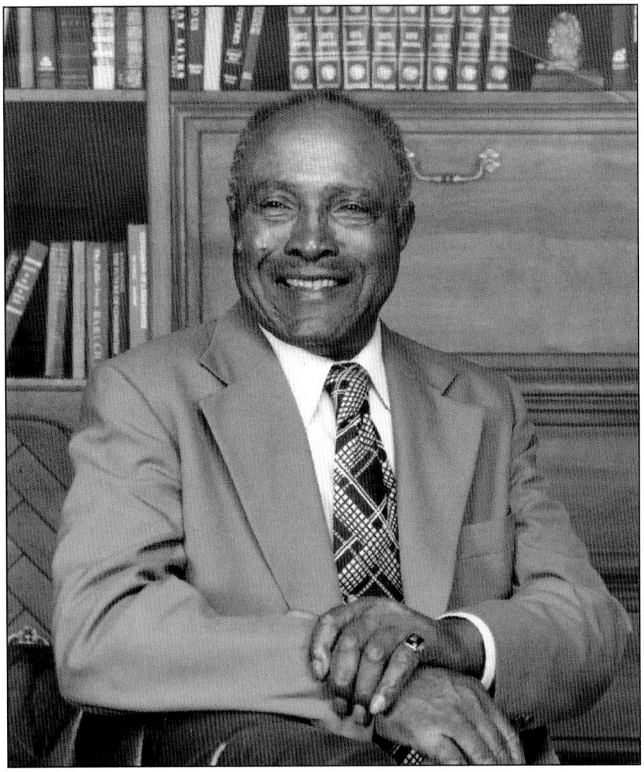

John T. Hopkins Sr. John is the grandson of Madison Slaughter, who helped establish the schools for the African American population in Elsmere and was one of the founders of Elsmere's First Baptist Church. John T. Hopkins served two terms on the Elsmere City Council. (Courtesy of Elmore and Harlene Hopkins and Gloria Jean Coleman.)

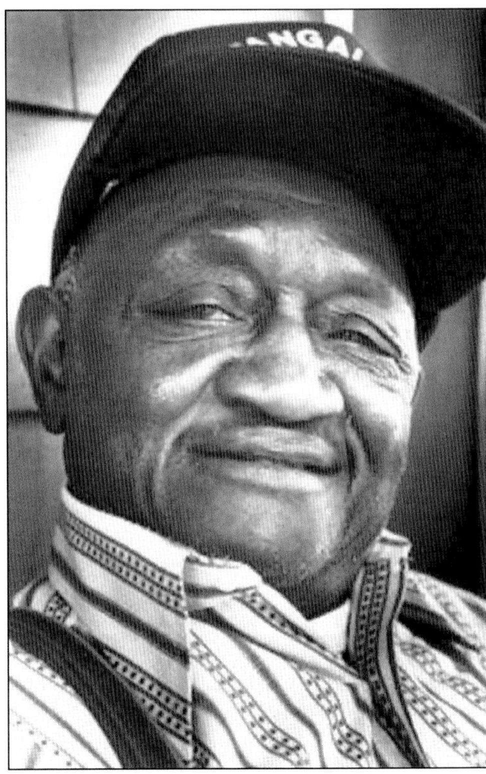

Oscar Johnson. Oscar "Popeye" Johnson was a son of Sherman and Emma Baker Johnson. Raised in Elsmere, he later lived in Covington and is featured prominently in a mural of "Local Heroes" at the Covington Branch of the Kenton County Library. (Courtesy of Brenda Thompson.)

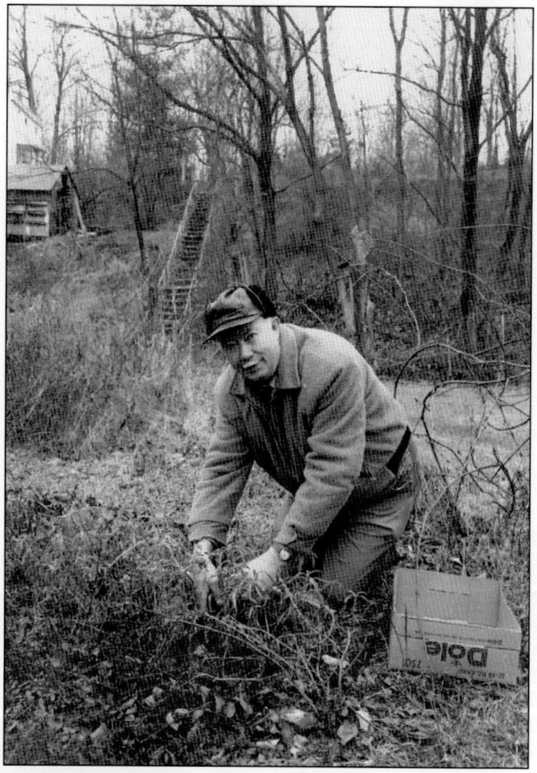

George Bolte. George was mayor of Elsmere in the 1950s and a scoutmaster for 10 years. He owned a farm on Garvey Avenue, where he raised vegetables, herbs, and rabbits. George passed away in 1986.

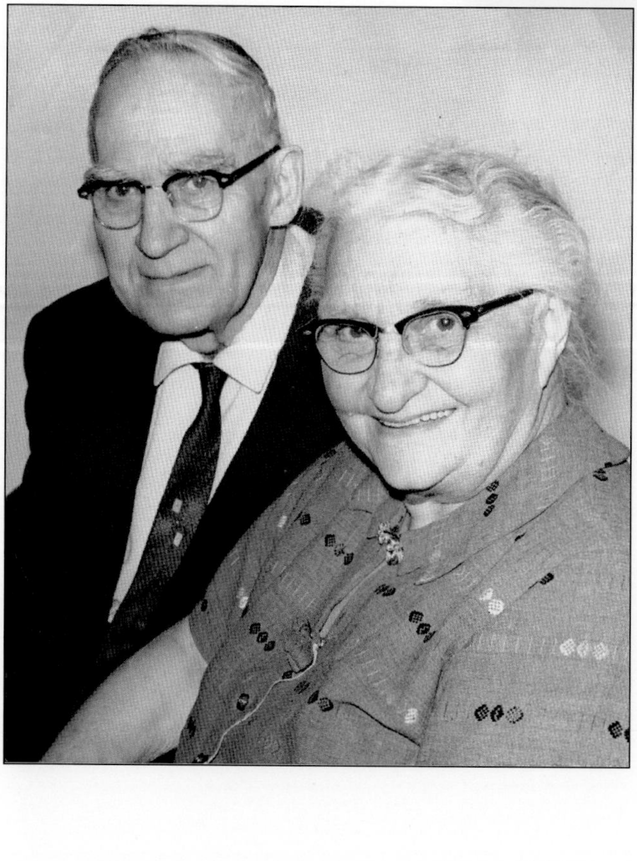

Mr. and Mrs. Mayo Taylor. Mayo Taylor was employed by the city of Erlanger in 1954 as the first city coordinator. He was the husband of Mary Alice Stevenson, great-granddaughter of William Thornton Timberlake. The Taylors were the fourth generation of Timberlakes to live in the Stevenson Road home. Mayo and Mary Alice Taylor received many awards from the community of Erlanger for their civic contributions.

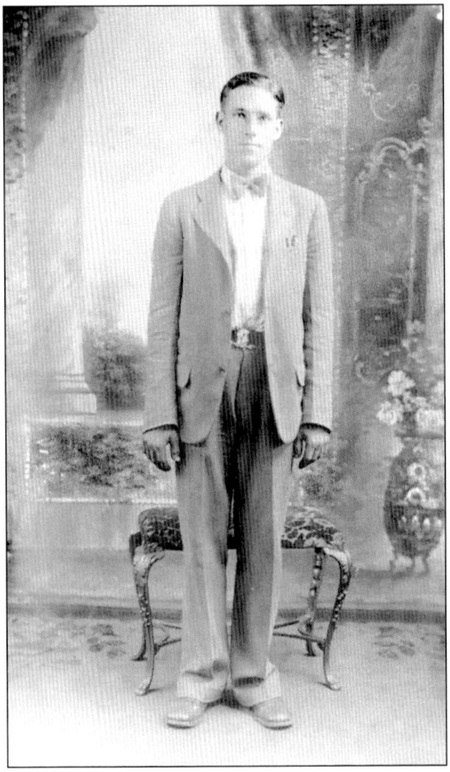

Tearl Burton. The photograph on the left shows Tearl in his younger years. Tearl came to Kenton County in 1931. In 1945, he purchased a little two-room house on Henry Street. He built additional rooms onto it and raised six children there. In 1975, he retired from his job with the City of Elsmere and lived to be 98 years old. He is pictured below with his daughter Fay and son Billy. (Both courtesy of Fay Burton Whaley.)

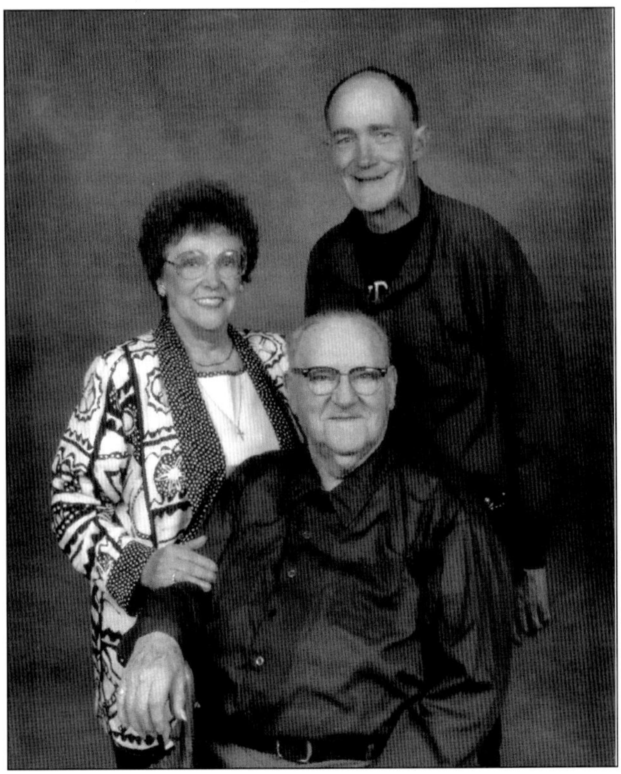

Mary Kathryn Bell. Resident of Erlanger for 60 years, Mary Kay was one of the first 150 graduated licensed practical nurses of the state of Kentucky in 1951. Mary worked for 28 years at the tuberculosis hospital, which was located on Farrell Drive in Fort Wright, Kentucky. Mary Kay is a charter member of the Erlanger Historical Society. (Courtesy of Mary Kay Bell.)

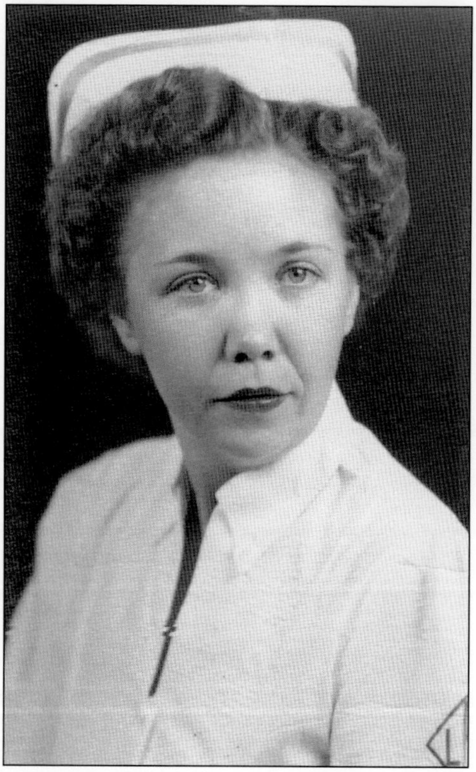

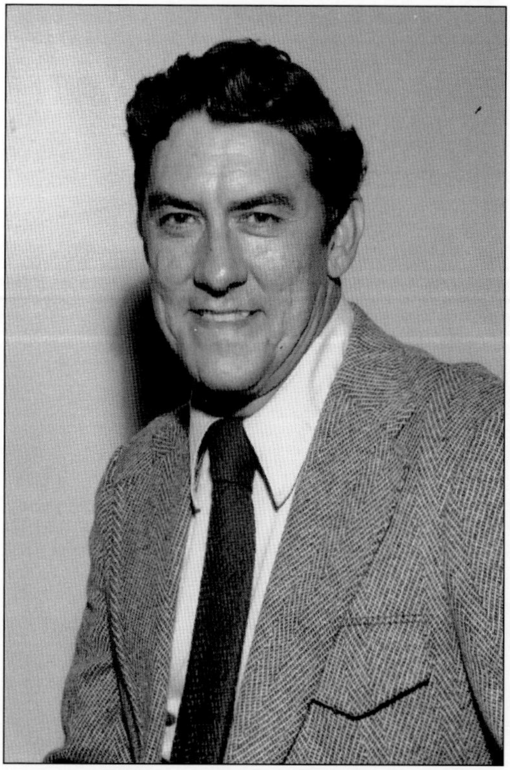

Fred Dietz Jr. Fred served on the Erlanger Elsmere School Board starting in 1971. He retired December 9, 2006, after 35 years of service. The Lloyd Memorial High School Auditorium was named Dietz Auditorium after Fred on September 16, 1995. Fred served in World War II from 1939 to 1945 and was manager of Doc Rust Heating and Air Conditioning. He raised his family in Erlanger and served as an usher at St. Henry's Catholic Church for several years.

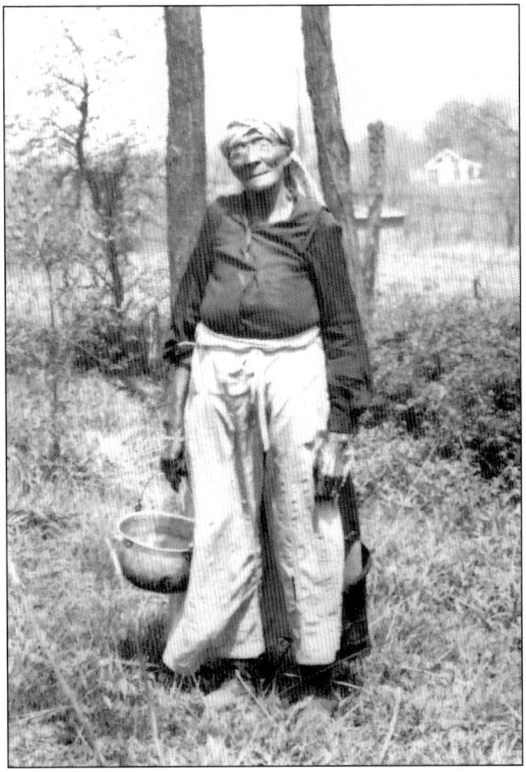

Fannie and Thomas Green. The Greens, both ex-slaves, were instrumental in starting schools for the African American population in Elsmere in the 1880s, including the Dunbar School on Spring Street. Their daughter, Nellie, was a teacher and married William Lewis, who owned a farm on Watson Road in Erlanger. The Greens purchased their farm from the Bedinger family in the 1890s. (Both courtesy of Bill and Linda Lewis.)

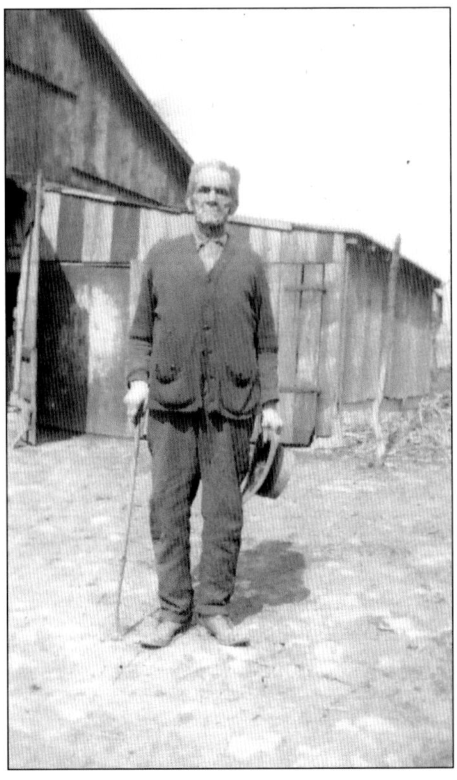

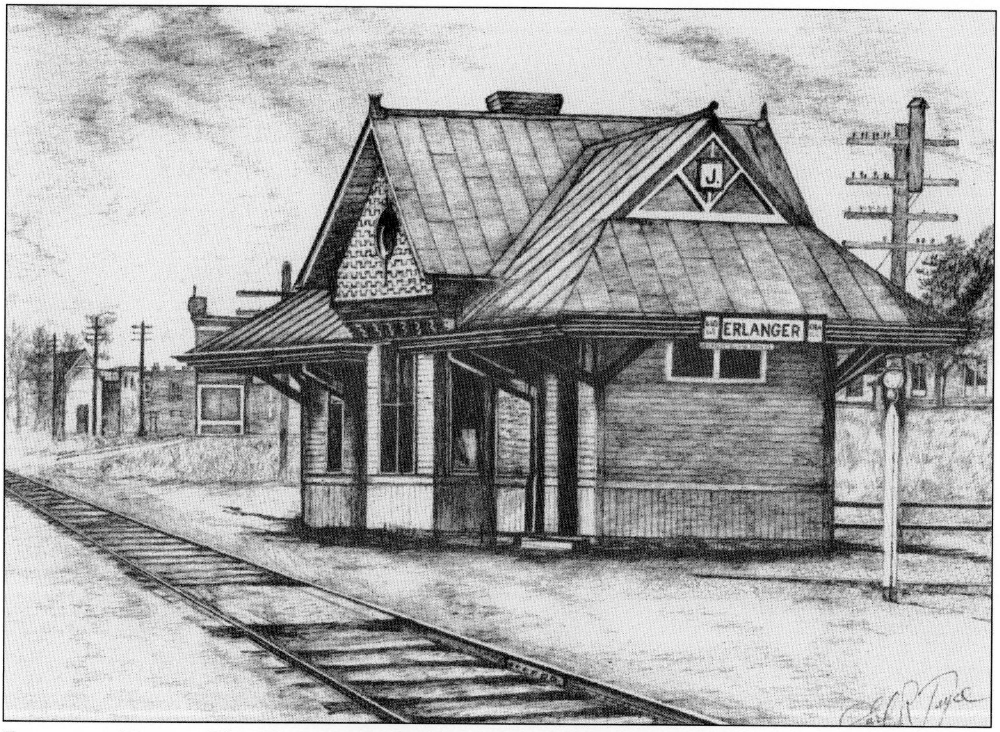

Erlanger Depot. The Community Bank commissioned Earl R. Tayce to do a series of four drawings of old buildings in Erlanger as a promotional advertisement. The Erlanger Depot was one in the series. When Community Bank went out of business, they gave permission to the Erlanger Historical Society to use the prints.

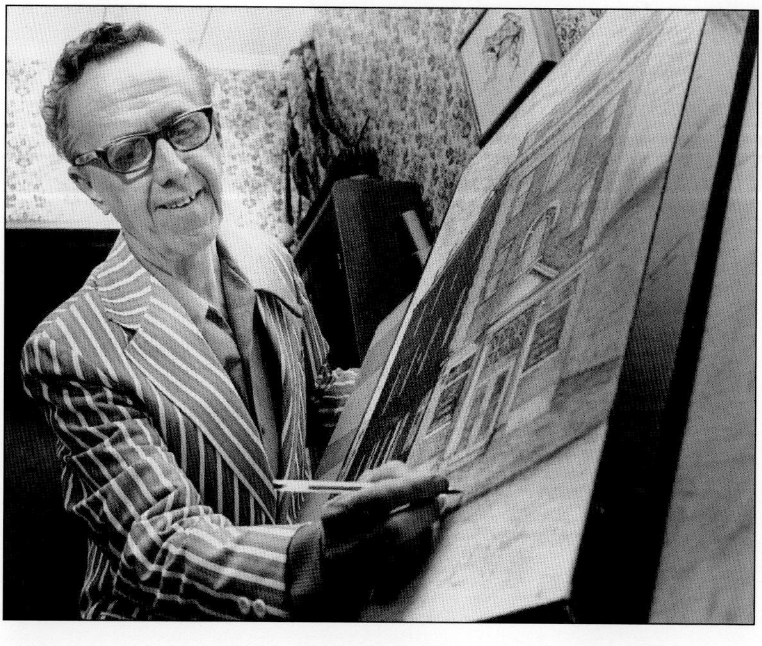

Earl R. Tayce. The artist lived at 205 Locust Street in Erlanger. Tayce was quoted as saying it was normal to spend 100 hours and use 25 pencils on his pen-and-ink drawings. He was born in 1914 in Elsmere. His subjects of preference were historic buildings.

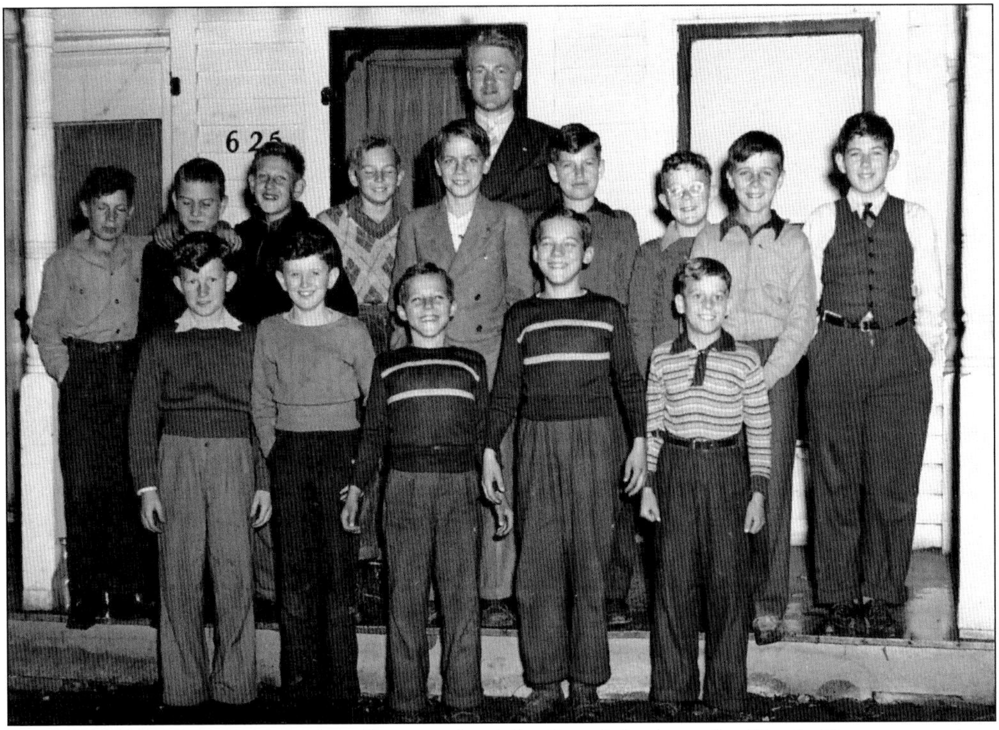

ELSMERE BAPTIST CHURCH. This photograph of the Royal Ambassador Youth Group was taken at the Perkins home on Spring Street in Elsmere in 1942.

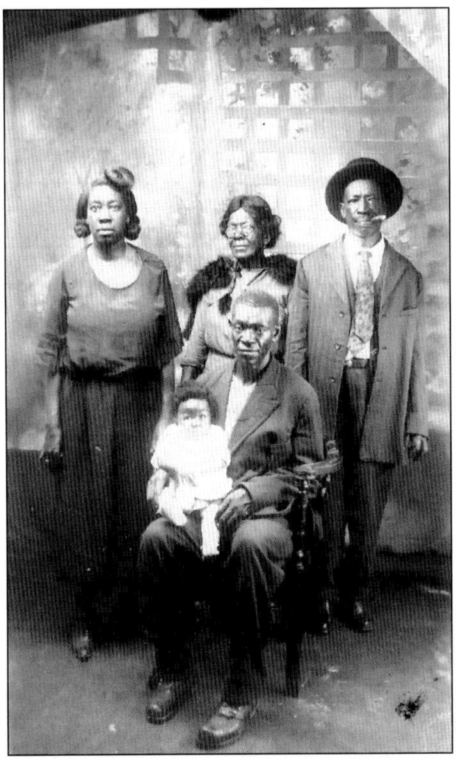

TOLLIVER FAMILY. Here in the early 1900s, Etheline Johnson Tolliver is standing on the left. Seated in front, holding his son Harrison Clifford Tolliver, is Etheline's husband, Robert Tolliver. Standing in back are Robert's brother, Harrison Tolliver, and his wife Stella. Robert and Harrison are the sons of Solomon Tolliver. Etheline's parents were James and Malinda French Johnson. Both families lived in the Elsmere area since the 1800s. (Courtesy of Emma Tolliver and Vicki Blanchett.)

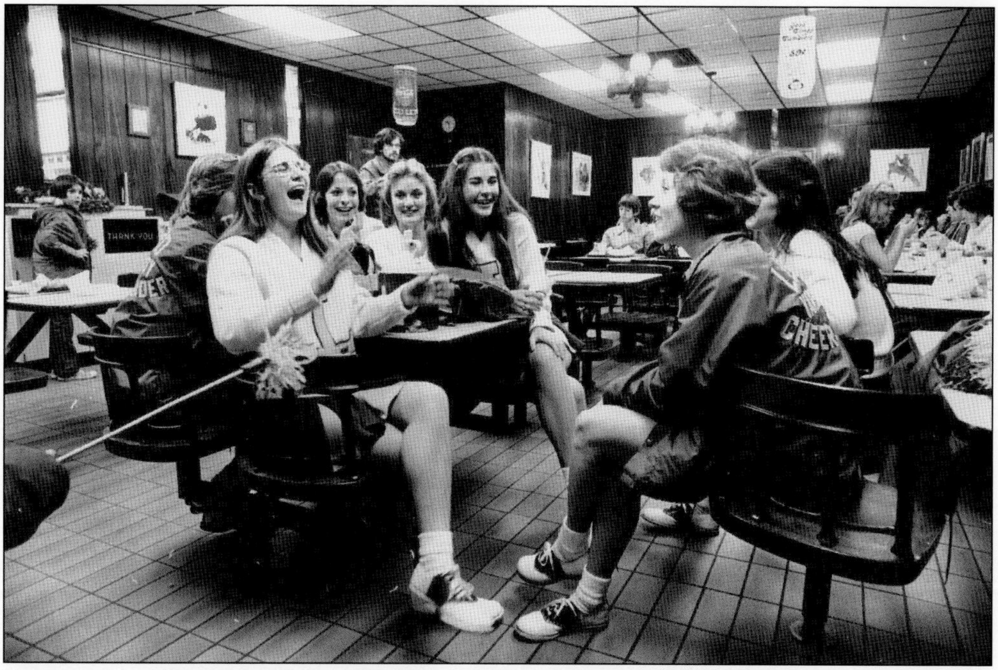

FUN AFTER THE FOOTBALL GAME. The Burger Queen on Commonwealth Avenue was a great place to meet after a game in the 1960s and 1970s. Since it was right across the street from Triple-E Swim Club, it was always busy at lunchtime during the summer.

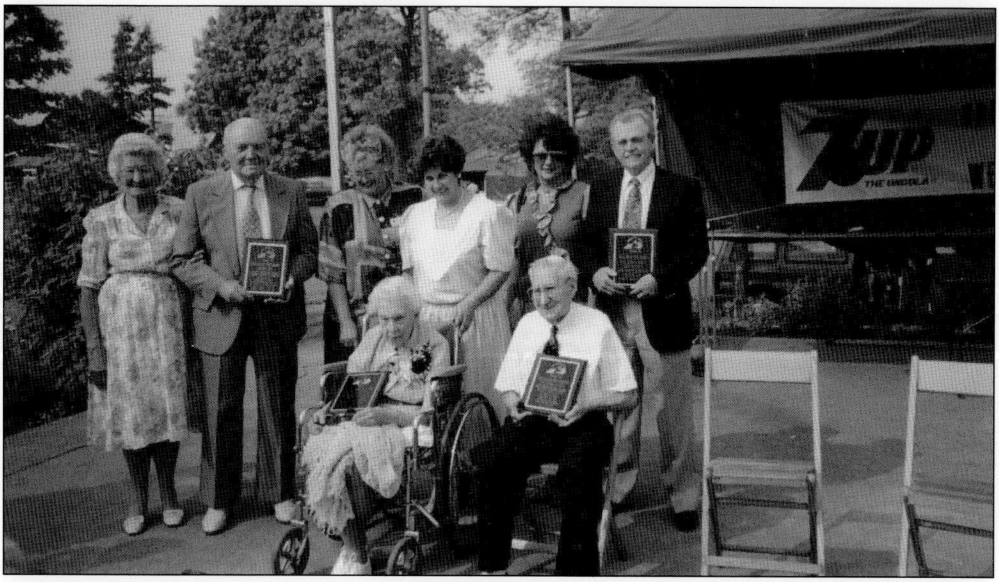

GOLDEN OLDIES AWARD. In May 1993, the Erlanger Historical Society presented awards to specific Erlanger residents. An award was presented to, from left to right, (first row) Esther L. Gschwind, born January 6, 1895, honored as the oldest teacher, and Henry Schneider, born in 1894, honored as the oldest living veteran; (second row) Anna and Everett Kidwell, married in 1928, for being the longest married couple (65 years), and (far right) Nancy and Herbert Works, owners of Boone-Kenton Lumber Company, incorporated in 1919, for the oldest business. Behind Esther Gschwind are two unidentified female caregivers.

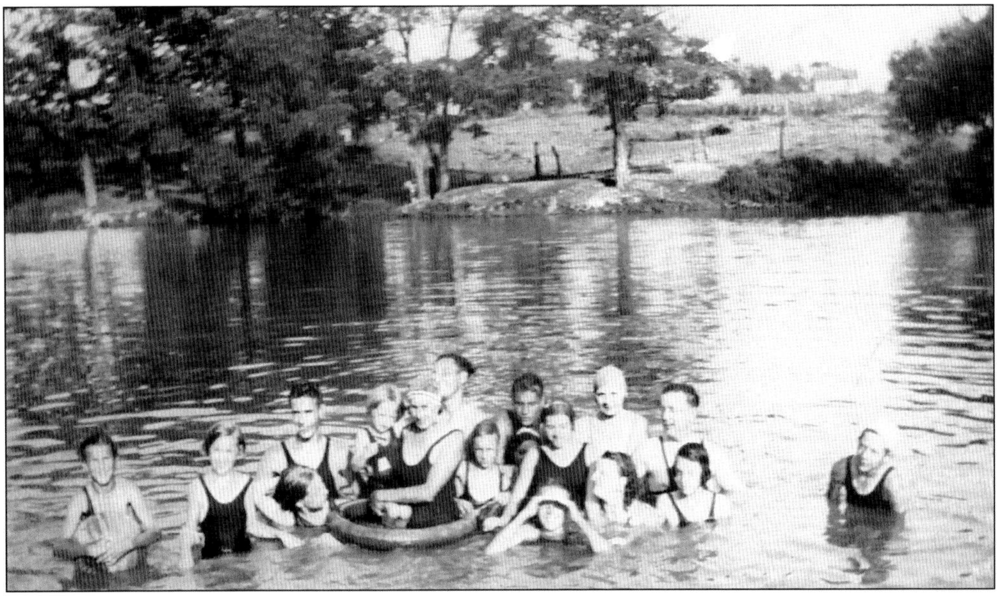

SILVERLAKE. Large amounts of water were needed to power the steam engine. To provide this reliable supply of water, the railroad builders decided to construct a large reservoir. This reservoir became known as Silverlake, and the citizens enjoyed the lake for swimming and fishing. This 1933 photograph of swimmers includes Virgil Dunaway, Floyd Mohr, Doris Mohr, Roger Gill, Alice Gill, Peggy Lou Gass, Harley Ketring, Bernard Finck, Mildred Finck, Delores Boyce, and Eleanor Boyce . The others are unidentified. Below, the young boy fishing is Larry Lindemann. In 1969, the City of Erlanger purchased the land from the railroad, drained the lake, and made the baseball and soccer fields. In 1976, one hundred years after the lake had been built, Silverlake Park was dedicated.

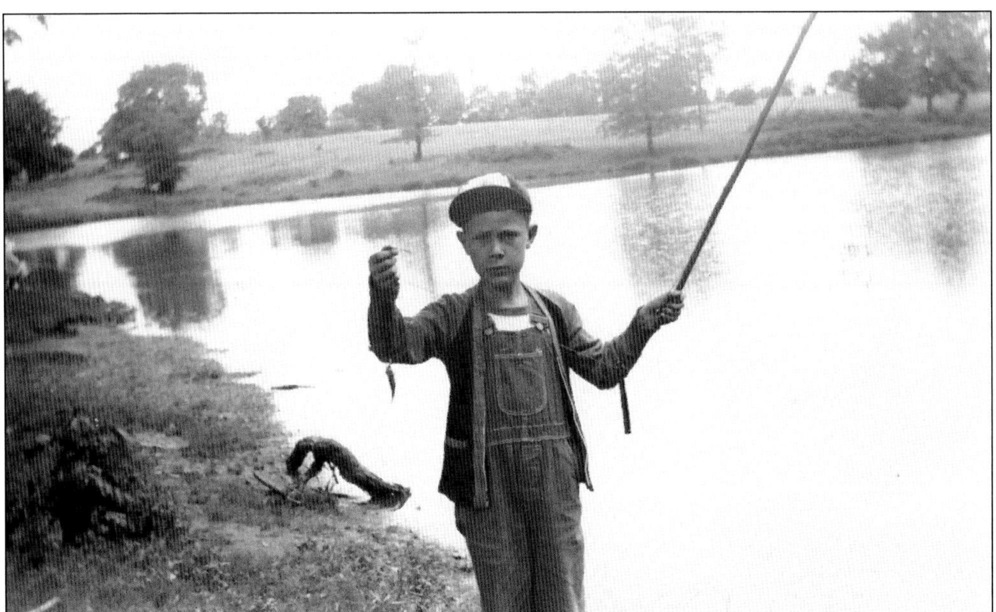

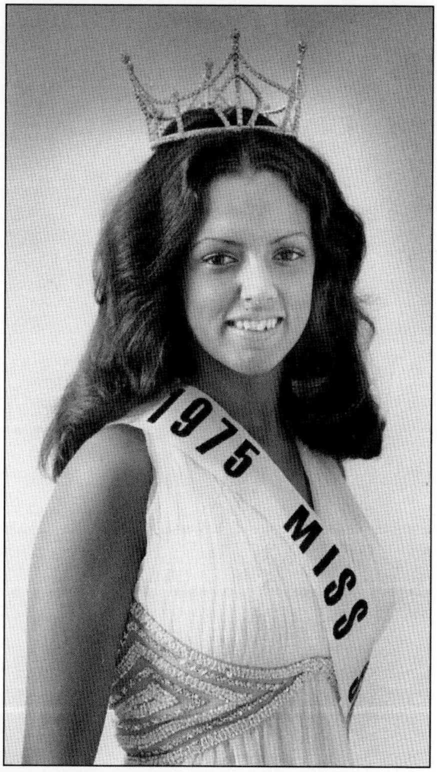

MISS SPIRIT OF 1976. Cheryl Fernandez was elected at the July 1975 pageant as the bicentennial princess. Cheryl lived on Alice Street in Erlanger and attended St. Henry High School.

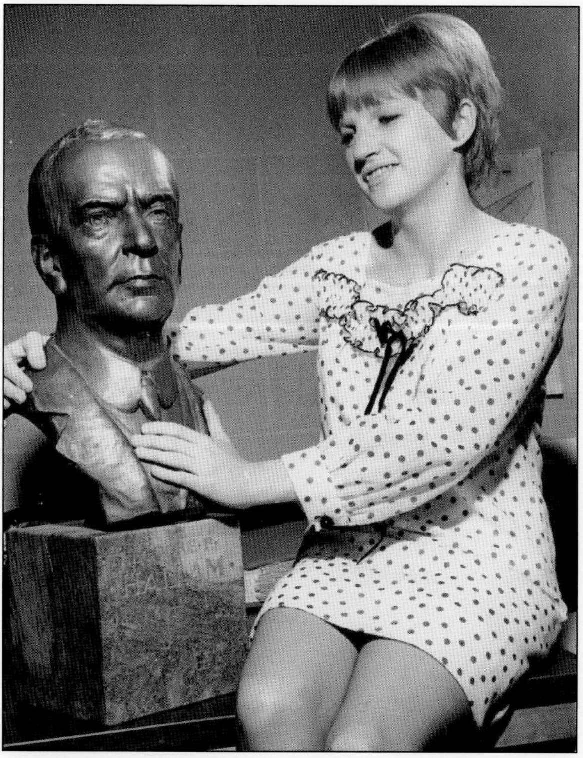

THEODORE HALLAM, 19TH-CENTURY LEGISLATOR. Hallam was married to Betty Timberlake. Kentucky-born author Irvin S. Cobb called Hallam "the orator in a state of orators and almost the quickest thinking man on his feet." In 1970, the City of Covington gave the bust of Hallam as a gift to the City of Erlanger. Peggy Bauer (in this photograph) is proudly accepting the gift. In 1992, the City of Erlanger gave the bust to the Erlanger Historical Museum for display.

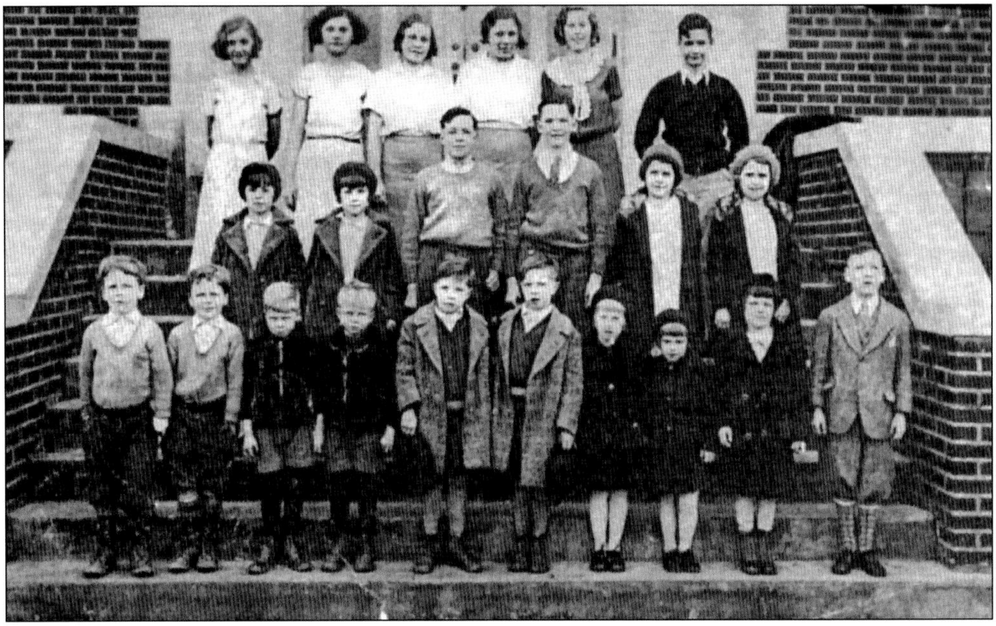

A RARE PHENOMENON. There were 11 sets of twins in the Erlanger-Elsmere School System in the 1930s. The two tall boys in the center of the picture are identified as Ralph (left) and Bruce Fulton. They served in World War II. Ralph was killed in action in Africa, and the Veterans of Foreign War Post No. 6423 Elsmere was dedicated in his honor.

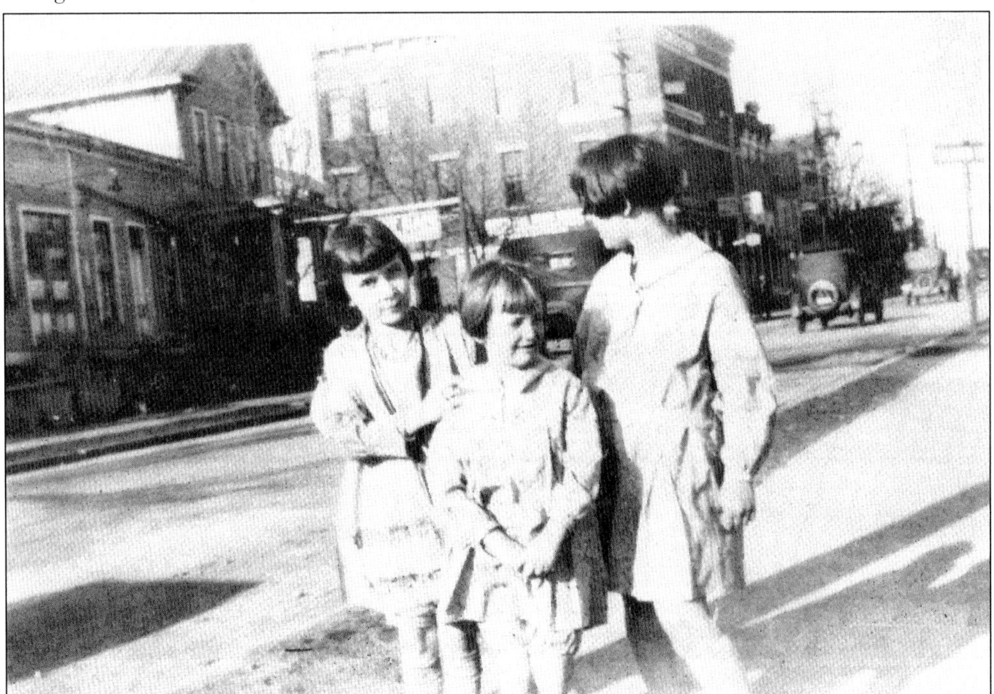

POSING ON THE DIXIE. These three little girls, from left to right, are Katherine Keeney, Betty Gurney, and Lydia Rose Keeney in the 1920s. Notice the Kohorst Hotel and the Bentler Building in the background. (Courtesy of Donald Thomas.)

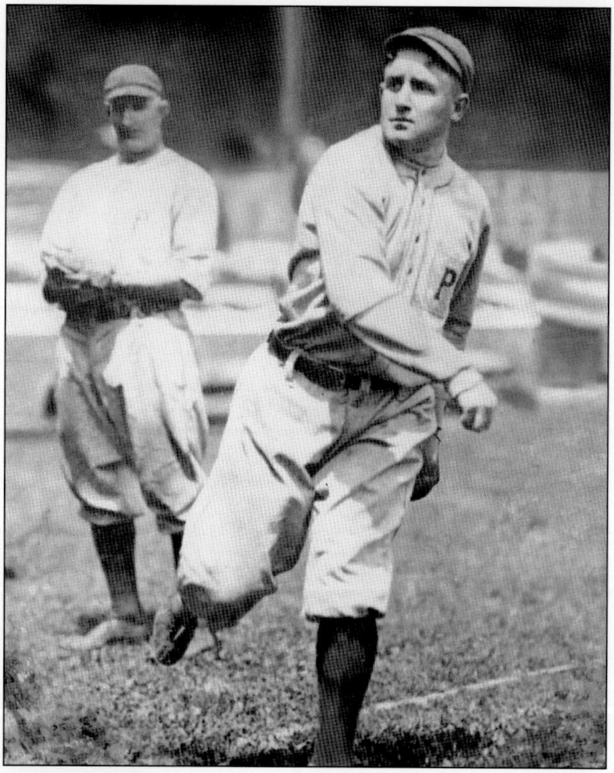

JAMES HARRY VIOX SR. Jimmy started his major league baseball career in 1912 at the age of 21. As second baseman for the Pittsburgh Pirates, Viox hit .317 in 1913, his first full major league season—good for third place in the National League and besting teammate Honus Wagner (seen on the left in this photograph). Jimmy's batting average that year set a long-standing record for rookie second basemen, only equaled by Dustin Pedroia in 2007. Viox and his wife, Nell, came to live in Erlanger, Kentucky, in 1927. (Courtesy of James Viox Jr.)

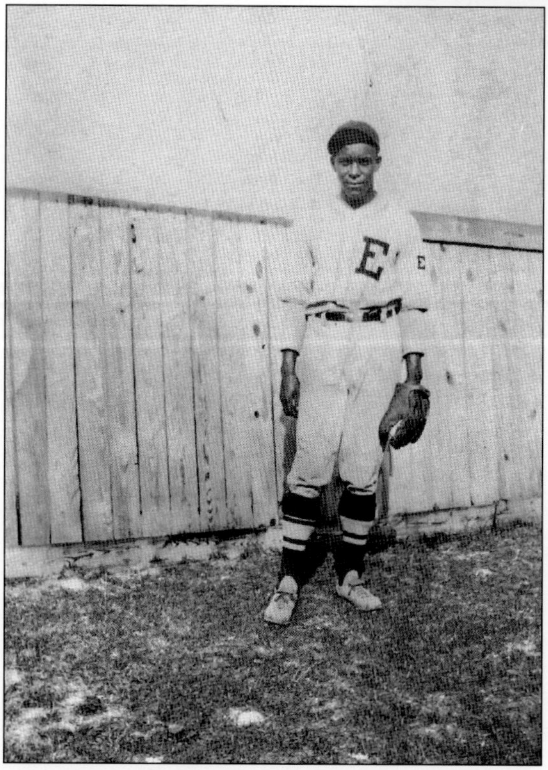

THOMAS LEWIS. Son of William and Nellie Green Lewis, Thomas played baseball in the Negro Baseball League for the Lexington Hustlers, where he pitched against Satchel Paige. He later taught at the Dunbar School on Spring Street in Elsmere in the 1930s. (Courtesy of Bill and Linda Lewis.)

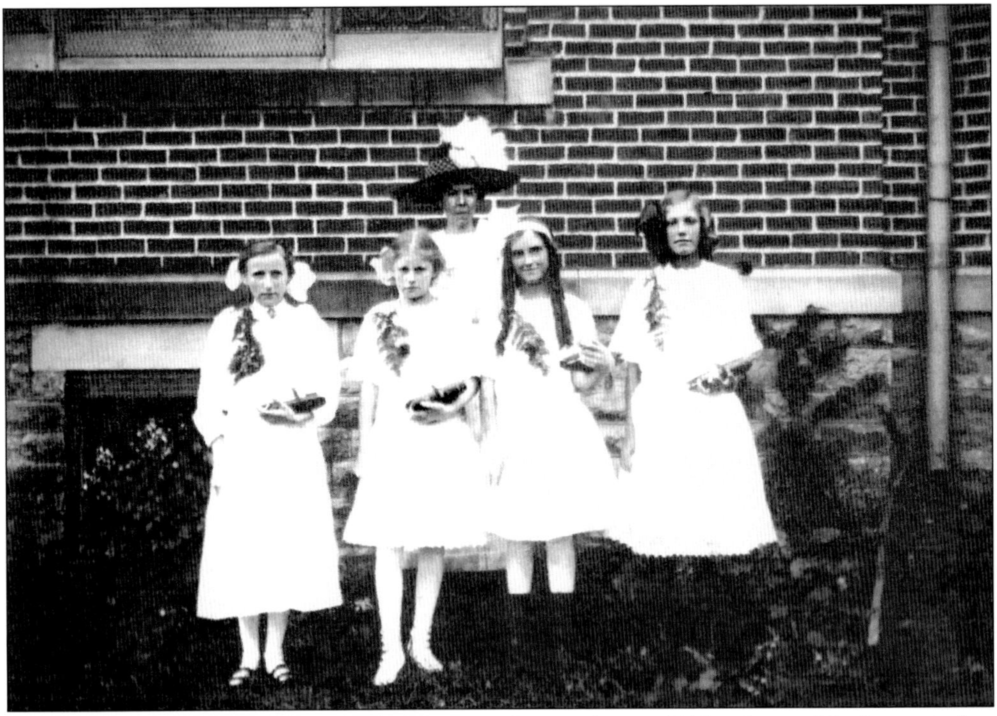

Graduation from Bible School. This photograph was taken in 1912 in front of the large window at the Erlanger Christian Church; the girls are standing in front of the cornerstone. The only name known in the photograph is the young lady on the far right. She is Georgia G. Hummell Cahill. The Hummells lived on Hulbert Avenue. (Courtesy of Georgia "Birdie" Michels.)

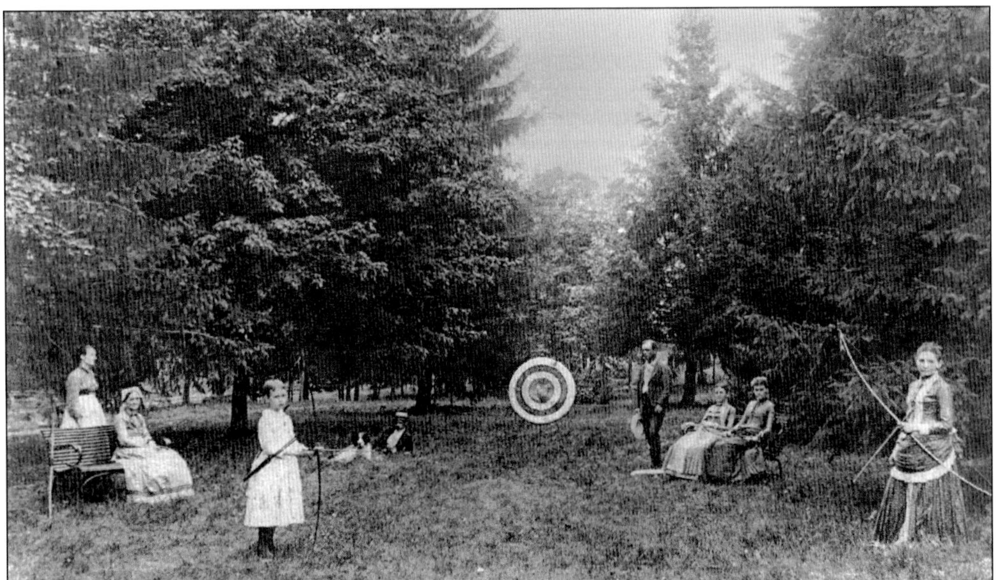

Archery Fun. The Stevenson family is pictured in 1888 on the grounds of the Stevenson Road Timberlake home. From left to right are a maid, Alice Timberlake Stevenson, Alice Hallam, T. J. Stevenson, Theodore Hallam, Betty Stevenson Hallam, Katherine Earl Stevenson, and Callie F. Timberlake.

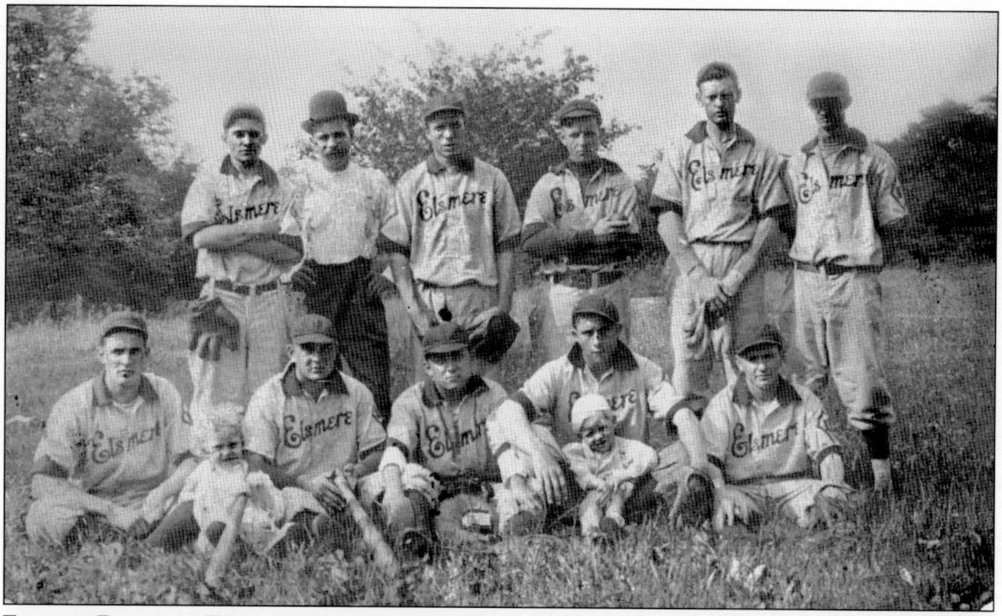

ELSMERE BASEBALL TEAM. In the early 1900s, many organizations supported softball and hardball teams. Any place where two empty lots adjoined served as a playing field. At times, fans would turn on their automobile lights when the games went into extra innings.

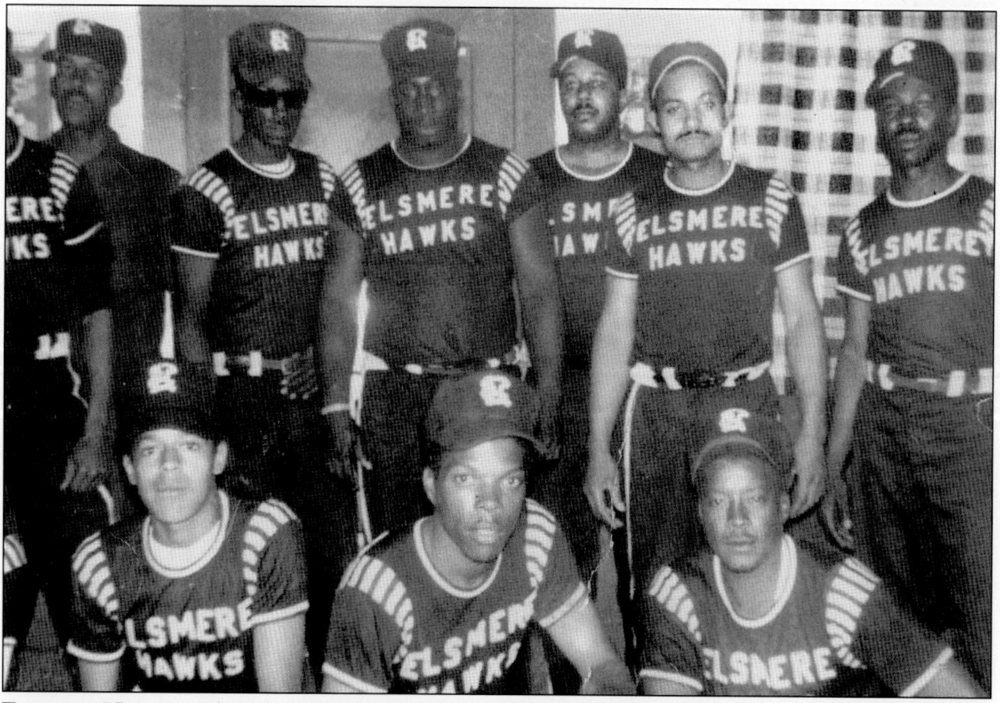

ELSMERE HAWKS. The Elsmere Hawks were a formidable team that represented the Elsmere community with vigor and pride. From left to right are (first row) George Warner III, Moses Walton, and Charles "Smokie" Johnson; (second row) Raymond Lee Johnson, James "Snooky" Luke, Melvin "Bubby" Luke, James "Bobby" Baker, John Richard "Firehead" Chambers, and Willie Willis. (Courtesy of Mary Lewis and Lillie Baker.)

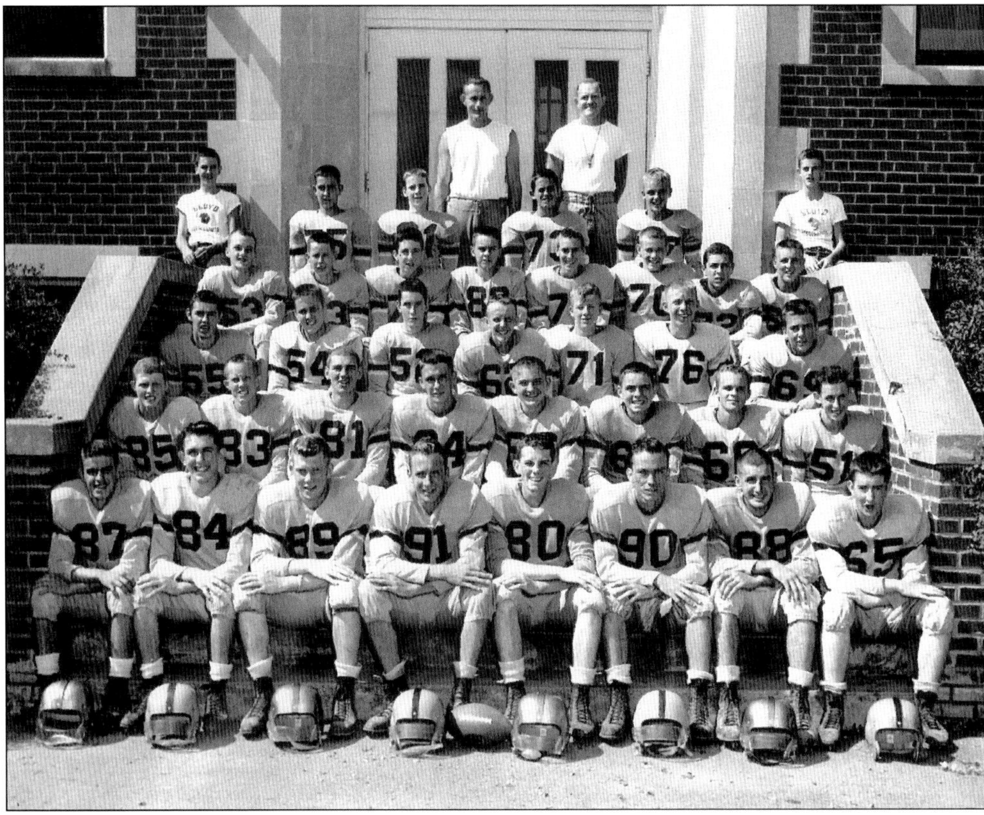

LLOYD HIGH SCHOOL FOOTBALL. The *c.* 1955 seniors shown are, from left to right, Phil Jones (#89); Harry Holmes (#91); Ron Miller (#80); and Ronyl Lindley (#90).

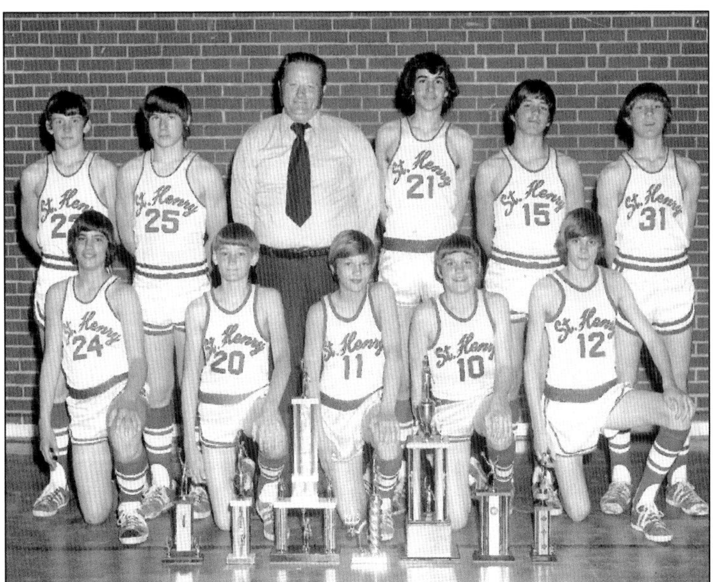

ST. HENRY EIGHTH-GRADE BASKETBALL TEAM. The year of the photograph is 1971–1972. The boys are, from left to right, (first row) No. 24, unidentified; James Staverman; Joseph Zembrodt; Earl Franks; and No. 12, unidentified; (second row) James Hilgeford; Christopher Eisenmenger; coach Gilbert Eisenmenger; Ernie Lussi; Thomas Bredenburg; and John "Jay" Kaiser.

Dempsey Merrell. This photograph is from 1976 when Dempsey was about to turn professional as a boxer. He lived in Erlanger and ran against Gene Snyder for state senator. He was owner of the Village Inn Pizza on Dixie Highway.

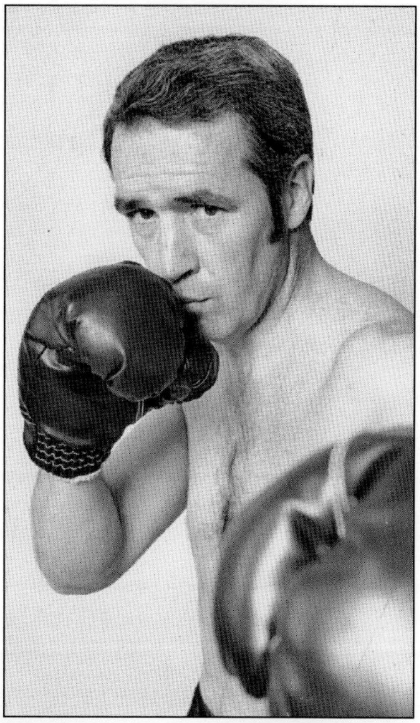

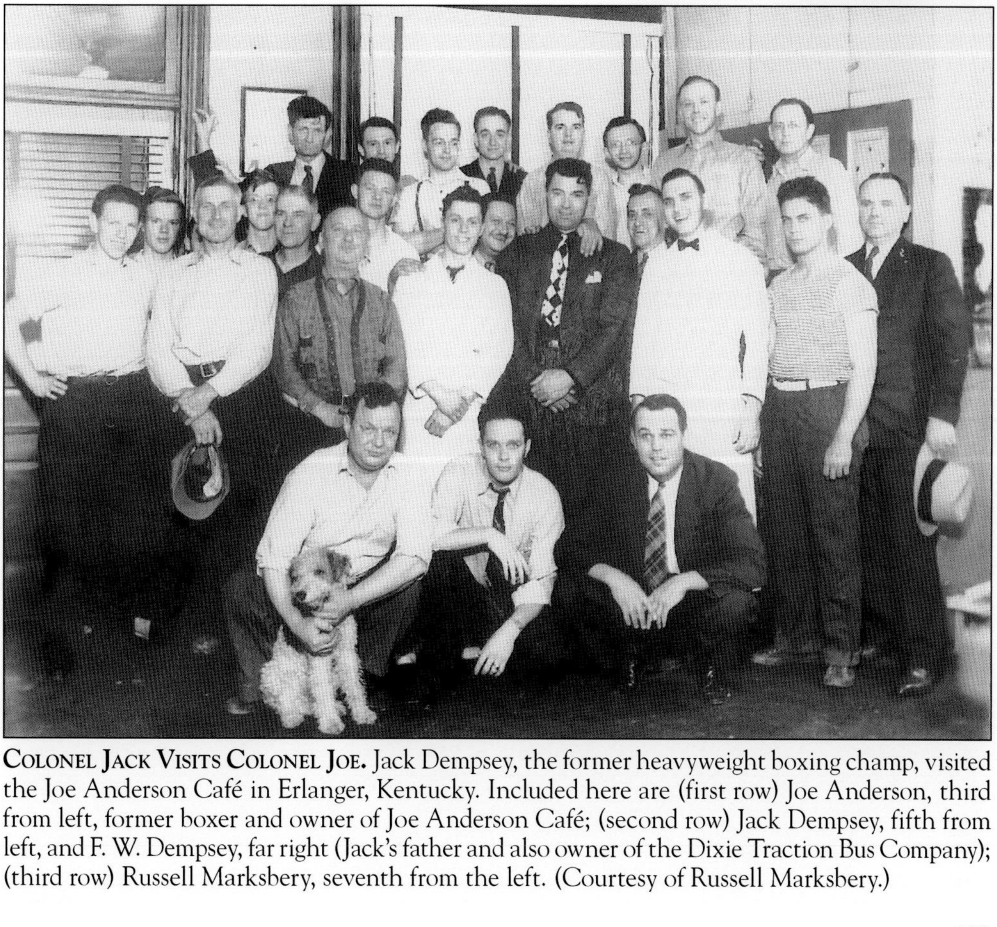

Colonel Jack Visits Colonel Joe. Jack Dempsey, the former heavyweight boxing champ, visited the Joe Anderson Café in Erlanger, Kentucky. Included here are (first row) Joe Anderson, third from left, former boxer and owner of Joe Anderson Café; (second row) Jack Dempsey, fifth from left, and F. W. Dempsey, far right (Jack's father and also owner of the Dixie Traction Bus Company); (third row) Russell Marksbery, seventh from the left. (Courtesy of Russell Marksbery.)

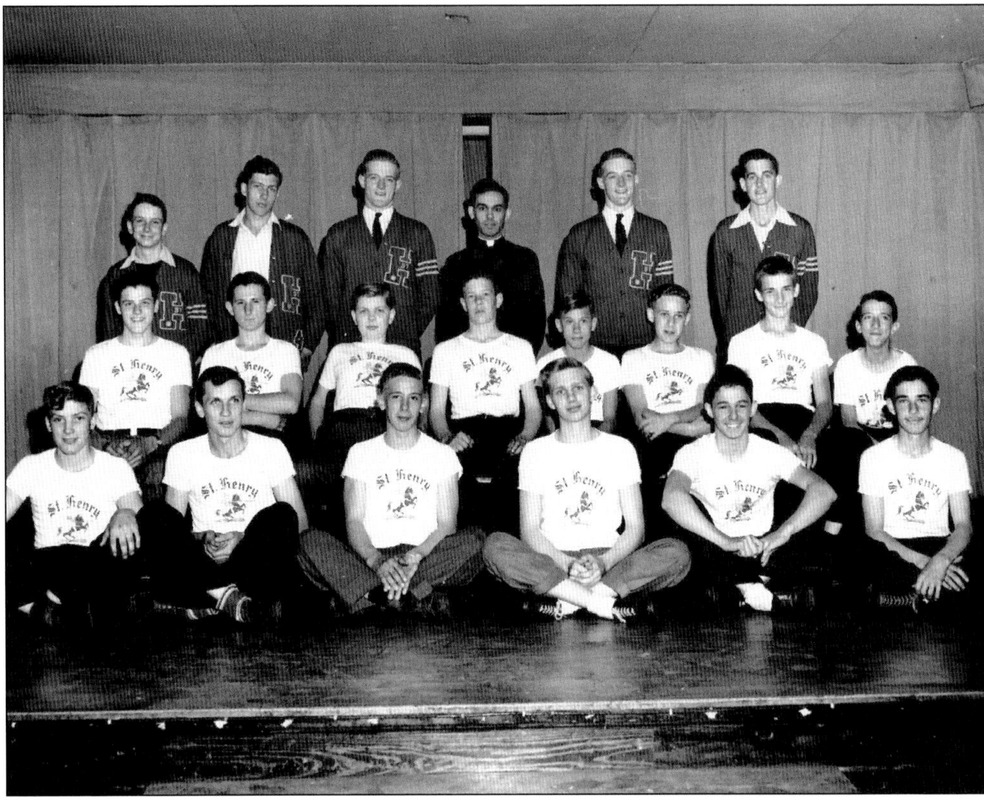

St. Henry Basketball Team. Shown are members of the *c.* 1945 St. Henry basketball team. From left to right are (first row) two unidentified, William Brake, two unidentified, and ? Dorsey; (second row) all unidentified; (third row) Paul Wagner, Walter Perisutti, Richard Flesch, Fr. Paul Ciangetti, Ralph Flesch, and Donald Fussinger.

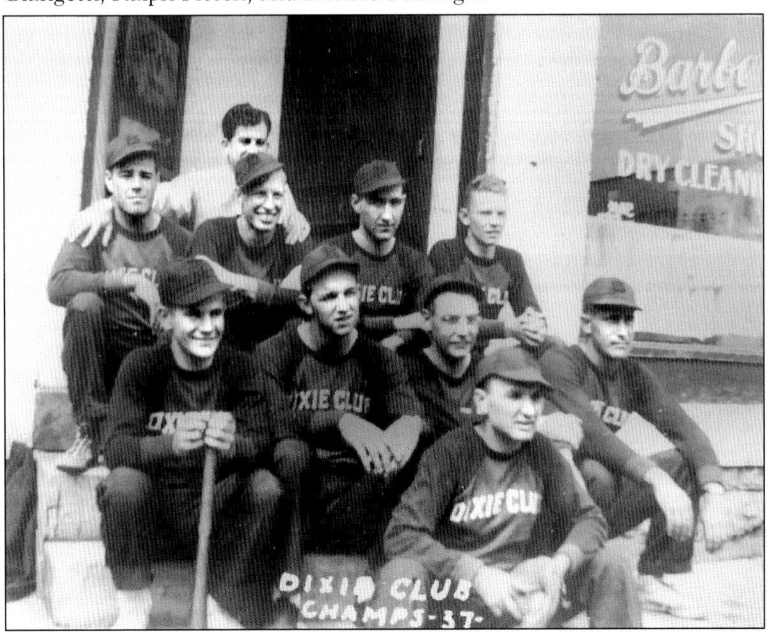

Dixie Club 1937 Team. From left to right are (first row) Chester Bonner; (second row) J. B. Bush, Gerald "Jiggs" Johnson, John Domaschko, and William Scheben; (third row) John Broughton, Walter Dauer, Wilson "Cass" Rose, and Tommy Glacken; (fourth row) Fred Stevens, Dixie Club owner.

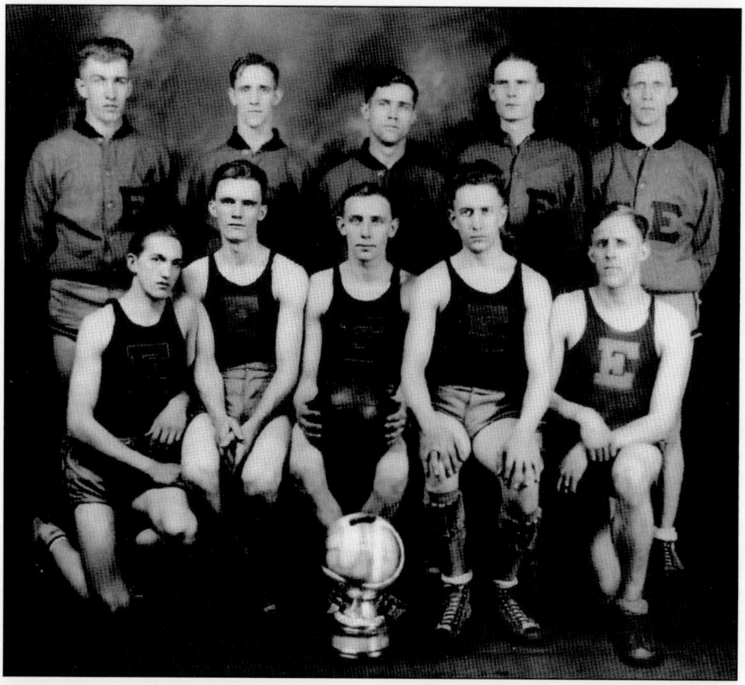

Elsmere Baptist Church Team. This team was the Covington, Kentucky, YMCA Basketball League Champions around 1930. Pictured from left to right are (first row) unidentified, Howard McKinley, unidentified, Ervin Bramlage, and Babe White; (second row) Harry McClurg, William White, Arthur Lindeman, John McKinley, and Russell White.

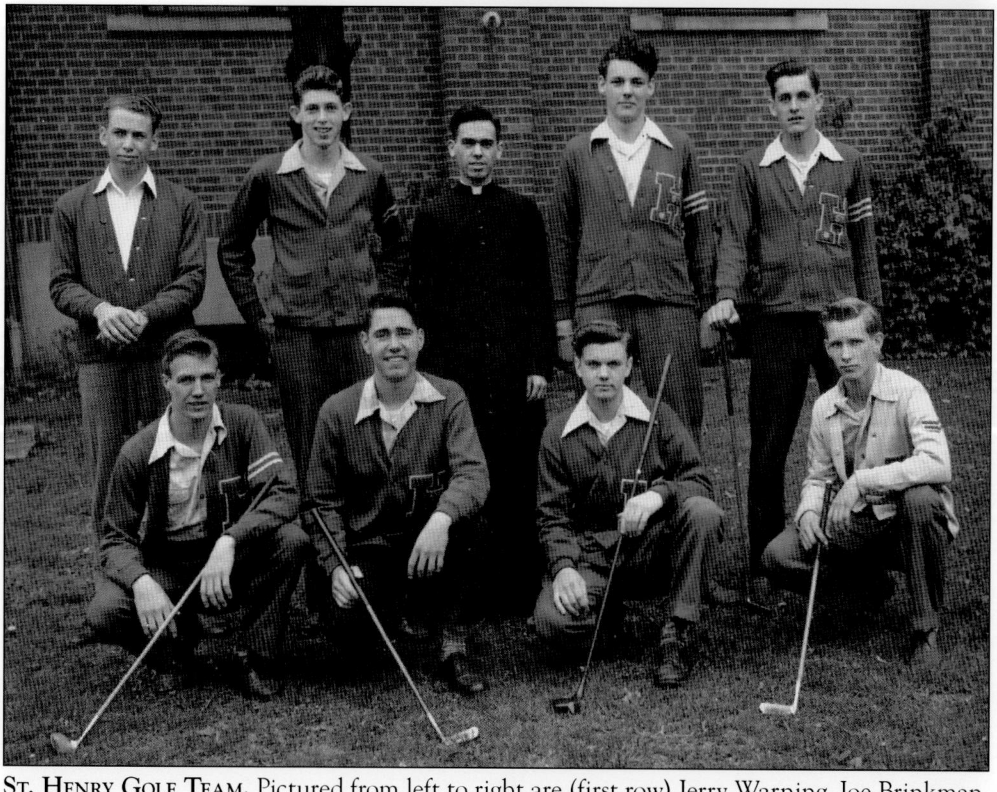

St. Henry Golf Team. Pictured from left to right are (first row) Jerry Warning, Joe Brinkman, unidentified, and Gene Dahlenburg; (second row) Ray Hoffman, Donny Ollier, Fr. Paul Ciangetti, Thomas Schweinefuss, and Donald Fussinger. (Courtesy of Betty Roszmann.)

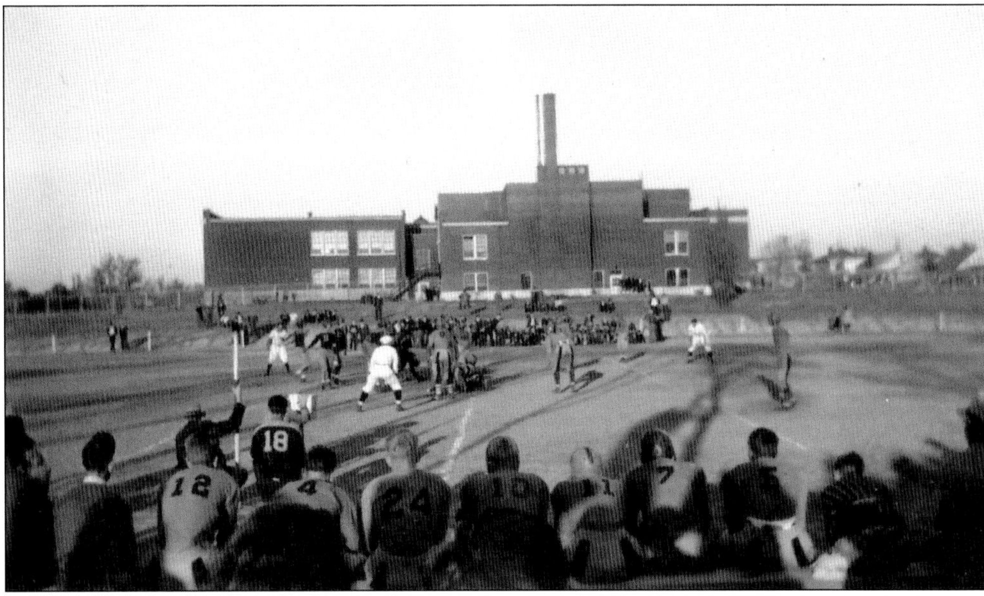

LLOYD FOOTBALL. This *c.* 1937 Lloyd High School football game was played behind what was then the high school. Games were usually played on Friday afternoon because of there were no lights.

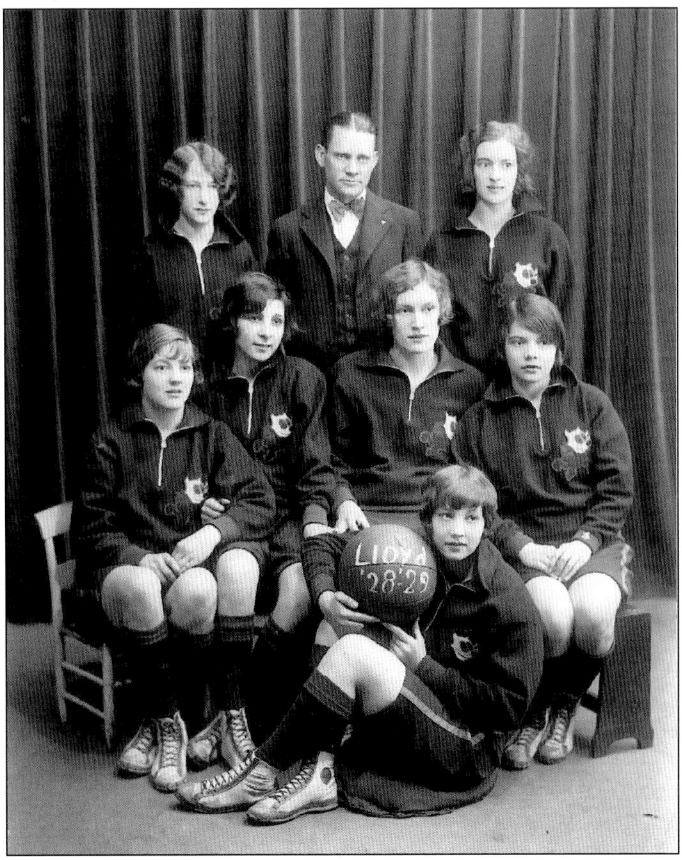

LLOYD HIGH SCHOOL GIRLS BASKETBALL TEAM. Notice the Felix the Cat emblem on the uniform of the 1928–1929 team. From left to right are (first row) Dottie Herrmann; (second row) Ann Penn, Lucille Gutman, Dorothy Dauer, and Ada Mae Antrobus; (third row) Ruth Rafferty, coach Foreman A. Rudd, and Ruth Tanner.

Five

Transportation

Planes, Trains, and Automobiles

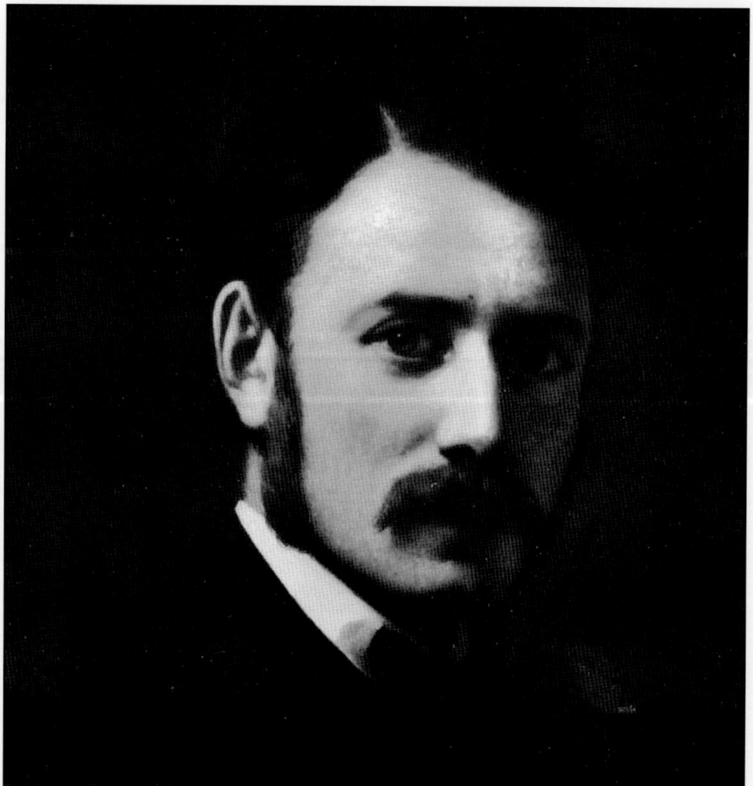

Baron Fredrick Emile d'Erlanger. He was born in 1832 in Frankfurt, Germany. Raised in a family of successful business brokers and bankers who eventually expanded their holding into North America, Emile d'Erlanger gained control of many railroad lines, including the Queen and Crescent Route, which ran through Erlanger. Anna Bedinger suggested the town be named Erlanger when it was incorporated. He died in 1911 in Versailles, France.

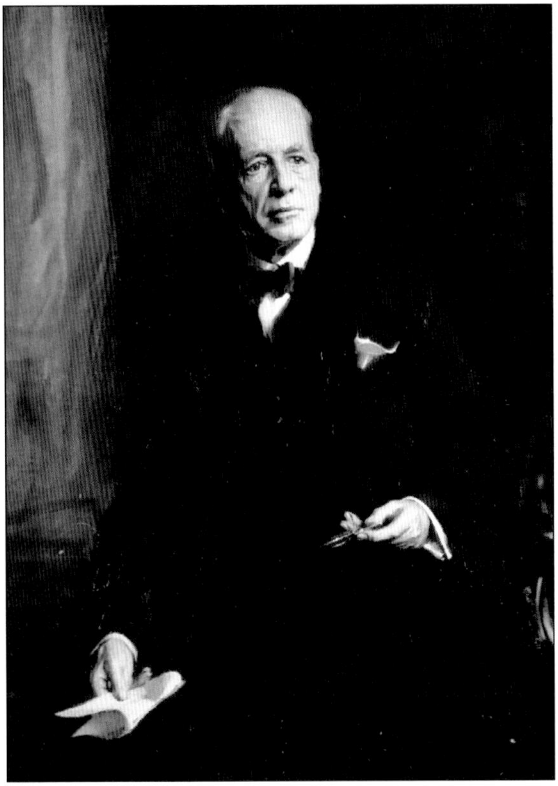

BARON EMILE BEAUMONT D'ERLANGER. Following the death of his father in 1911, he directed much of the family's banking business in North America, including the "Erlanger Firm," as this area was called in London for many years.

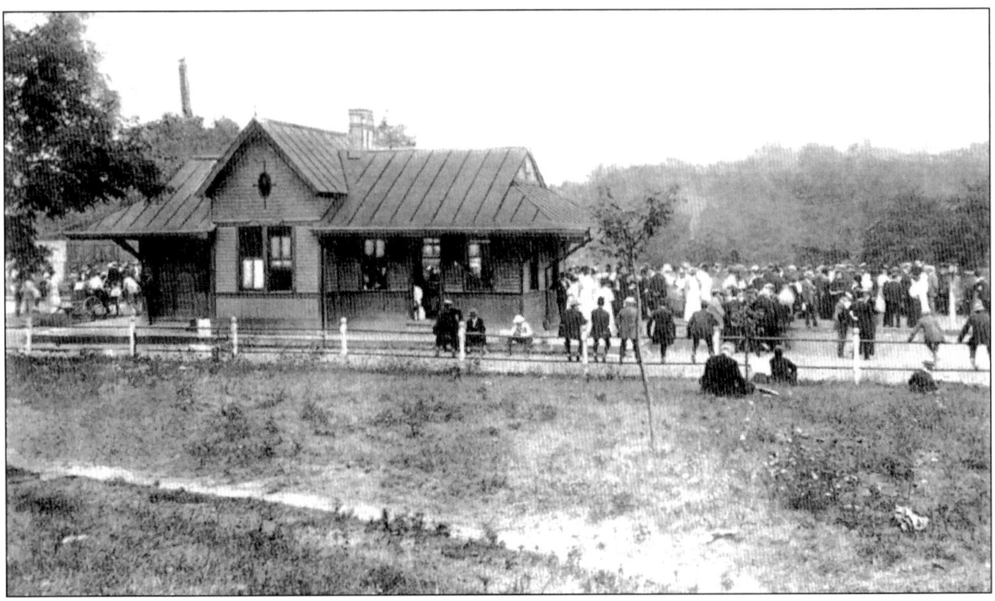

THE QUEEN AND CRESCENT DEPOT. Erlanger, Kentucky, bristles with activity as travelers await their train. The building shown above, though moved from its original location, still stands in a city park and serves as a museum.

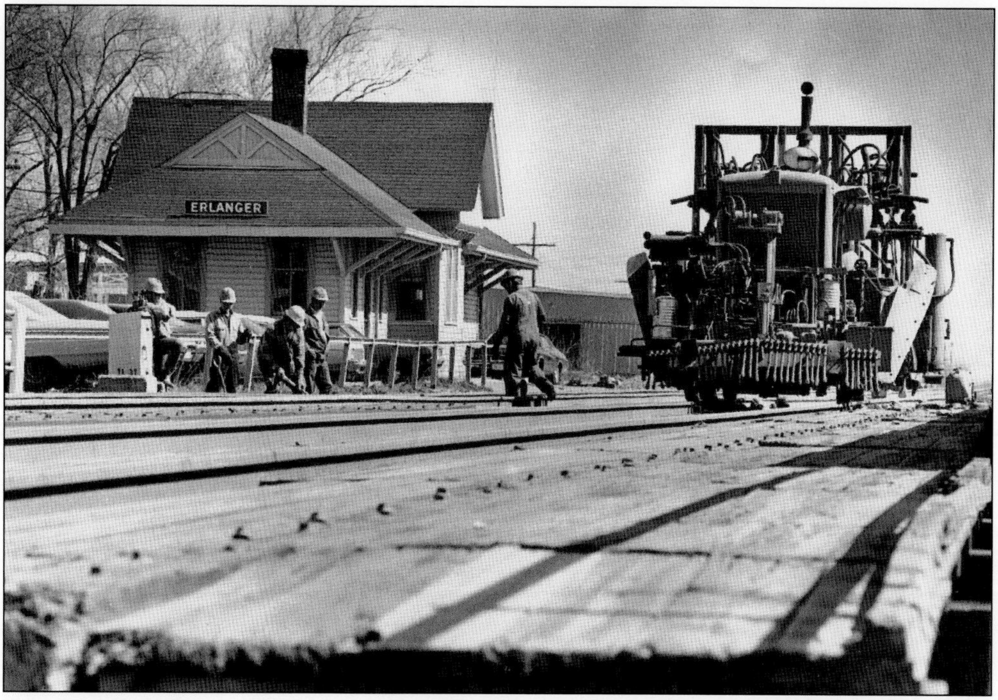

THE ERLANGER DEPOT. In the scene above, workmen and a work engine repair the tracks near the Erlanger Depot.

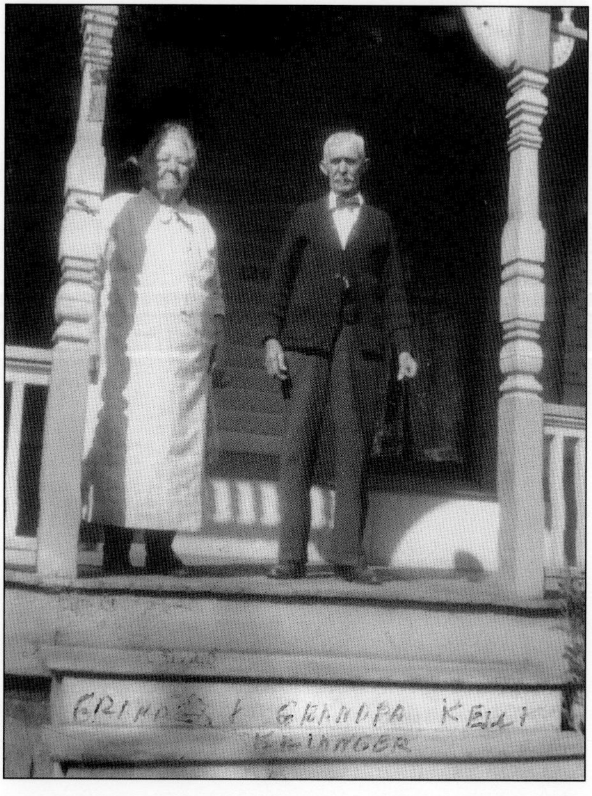

ANNIE MCHUGH KELLY AND REDMOND KELLY. The Kellys were natives of County Galway, Ireland, where Redmond was born in 1854. He worked as station manager of the Erlanger Depot in the early 1900s. They are seen standing on the porch of their home, the station manager's house on Crescent Avenue, around 1925.

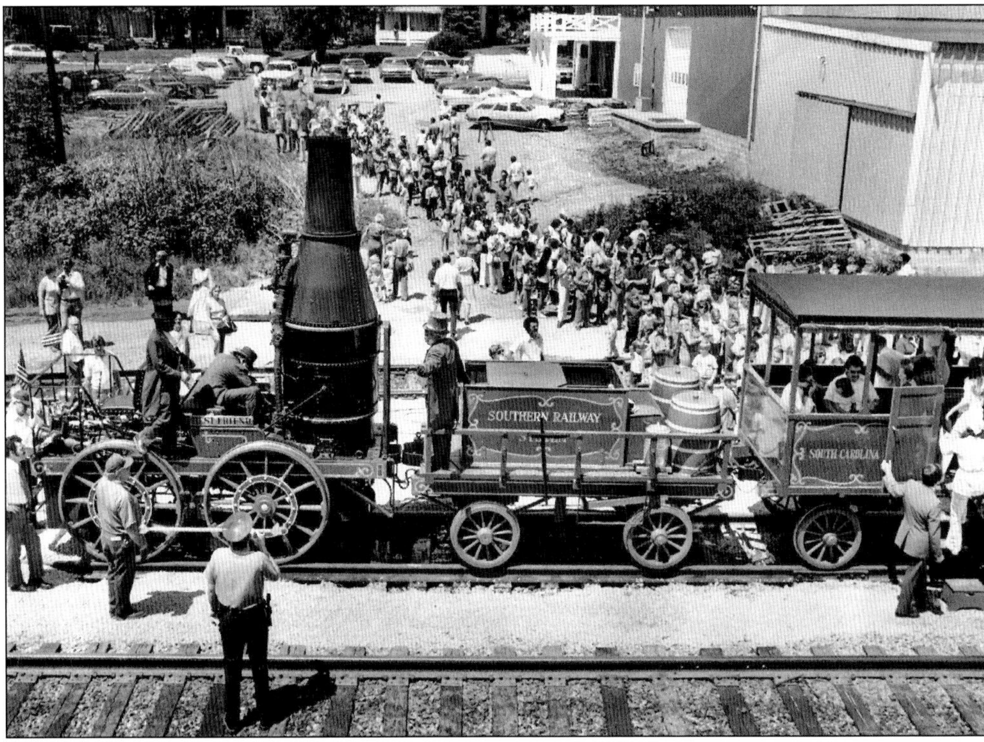

THE BEST FRIEND OF CHARLESTON. This was a replica of the first steam-powered locomotive used for regularly scheduled passenger service in the 1830s. It was said to be the first locomotive built in the United States. This scene is behind the Boone Kenton-Lumber Company on Crescent Avenue. It was on display offering rides in the 1970s.

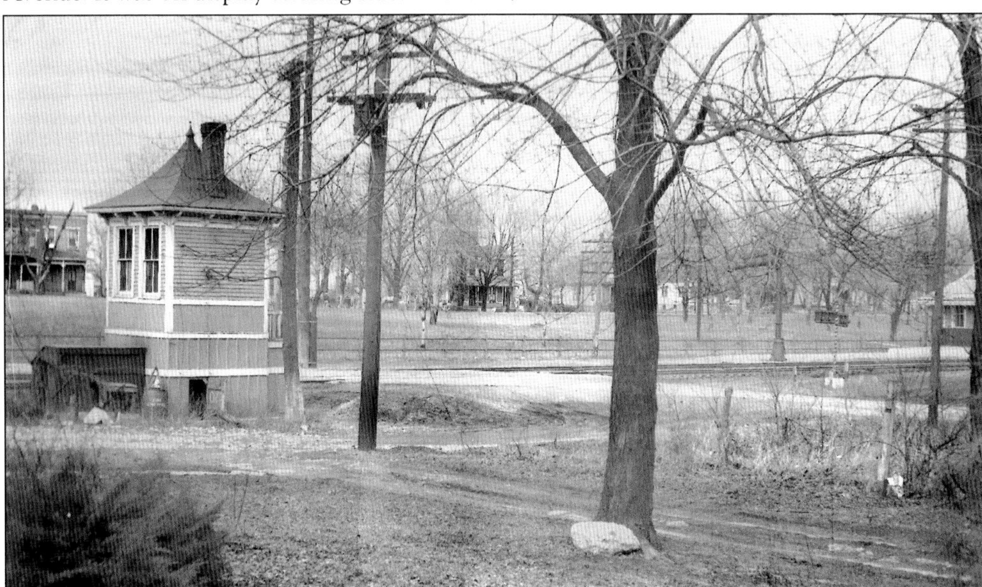

RAILROAD CROSSING. This *c.* 1936 scene shows the Lexington Turnpike (Dixie Highway) where it crossed the tracks in Erlanger before the building of the underpass. The watchman's station is on the left, and the depot would be located farther to the right.

ELSMERE (SOUTH ERLANGER) DEPOT. The depot was located 10.4 miles from Cincinnati, Ohio, at the end of Carlisle Avenue, in Elsmere. In the background appears the wooden Garvey Avenue bridge. The bridge was replaced by the present-day concrete bridge in 1949. Sadly, the depot was destroyed by the Southern Railway along with many others along the rail line.

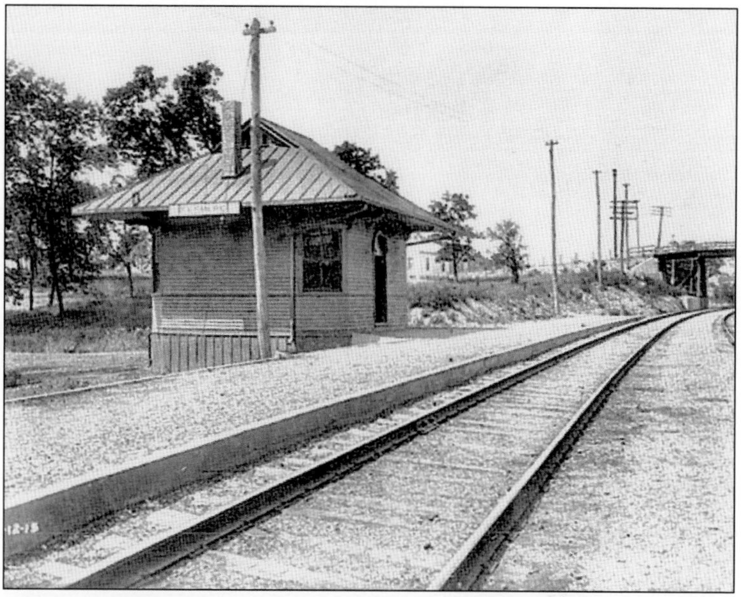

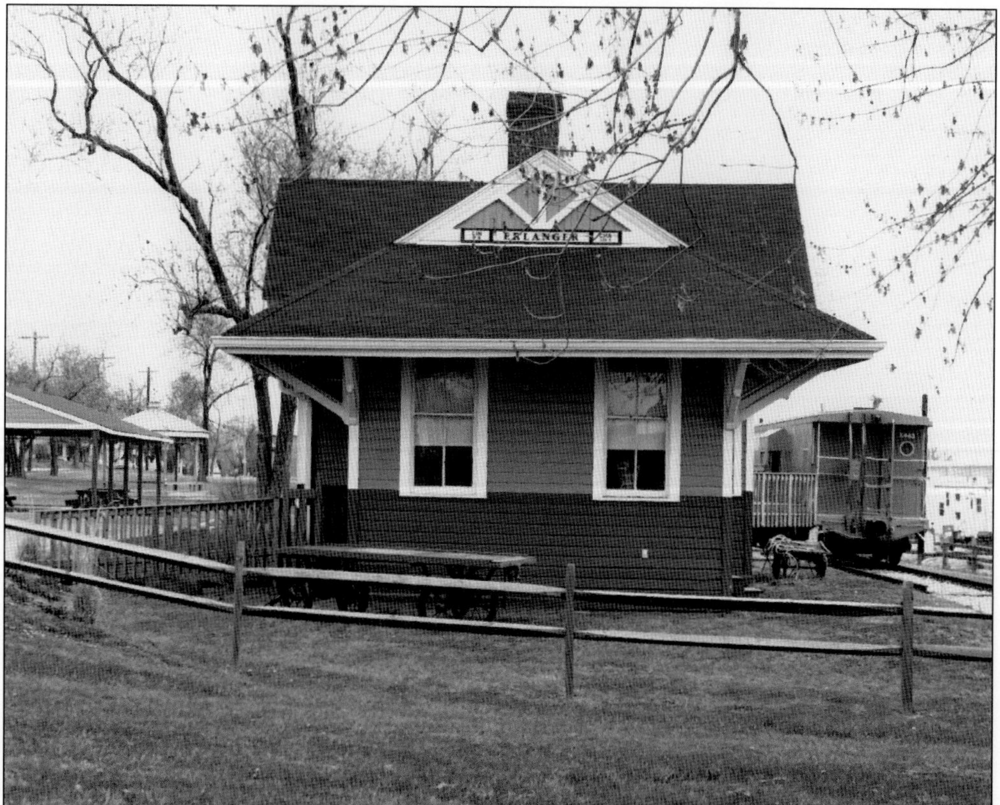

ERLANGER RAILROAD DEPOT. The 1877 depot stands in the railroad park as a memorial to Erlanger's history. Every September, the Erlanger Historical Society celebrates Heritage Days at the restored depot and city park. The next stop south would have been the depot in Elsmere.

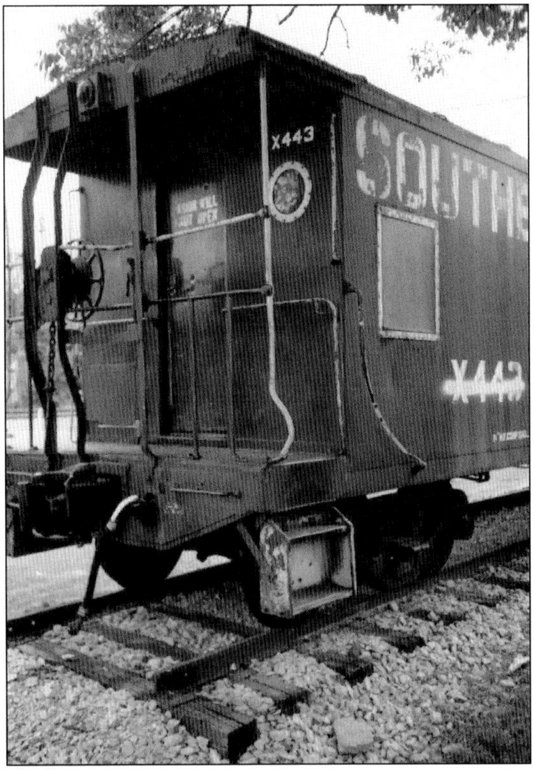

Old Caboose. This old Southern Railroad caboose was one of the last to be built with a bay window. It was given to the Erlanger Historical Society and is on display at the depot museum.

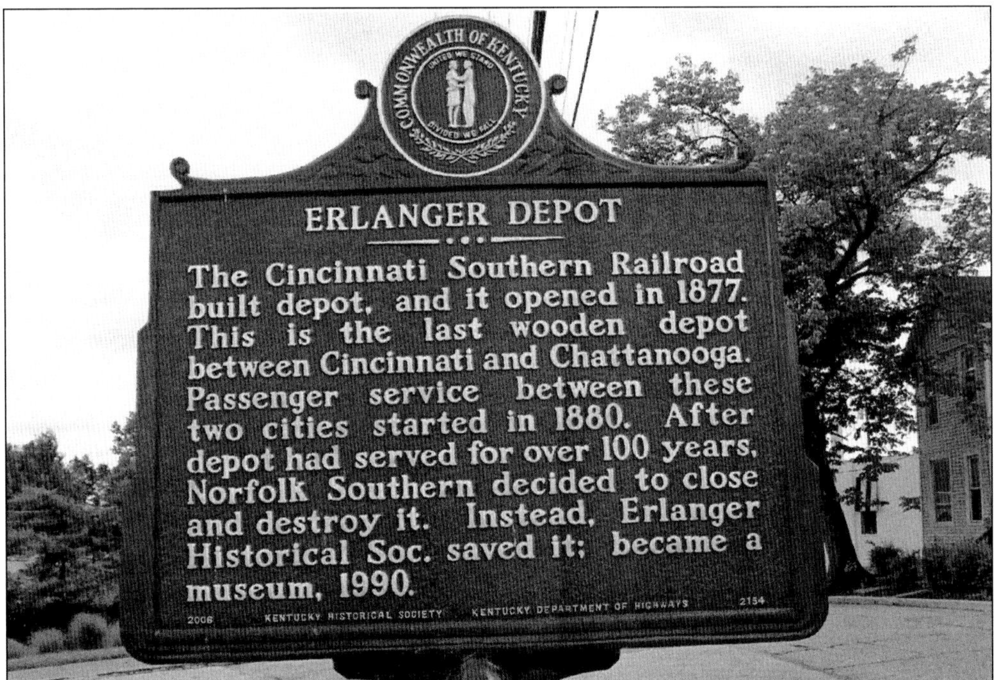

Erlanger Depot Marker. This Kentucky highway marker is located on Crescent Avenue. This historical marker was dedicated in September 2004 at the Erlanger Heritage Celebration.

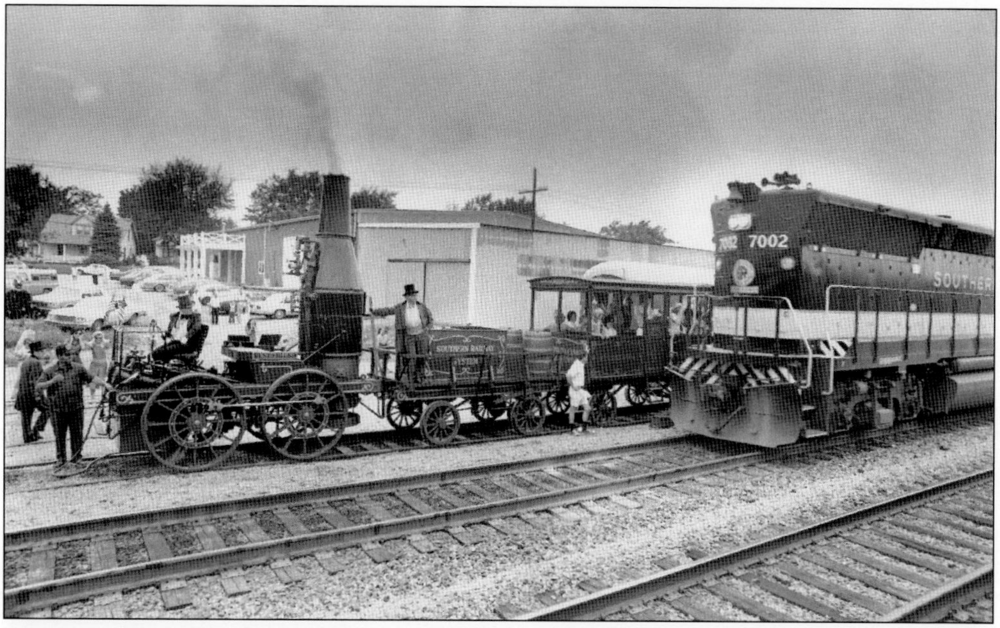

Day in the Park. The Erlanger Women's Club hosted the celebration in the railroad park and was lucky enough to get the Southern Railroad to send *The Best Friend of Charleston* steam engine to Erlanger. A large amount of Northern Kentucky citizens enjoyed a ride on the train on a beautiful sunny Saturday afternoon in the 1970s. *The Best Friend of Charleston* is decommissioned and no longer travels the country.

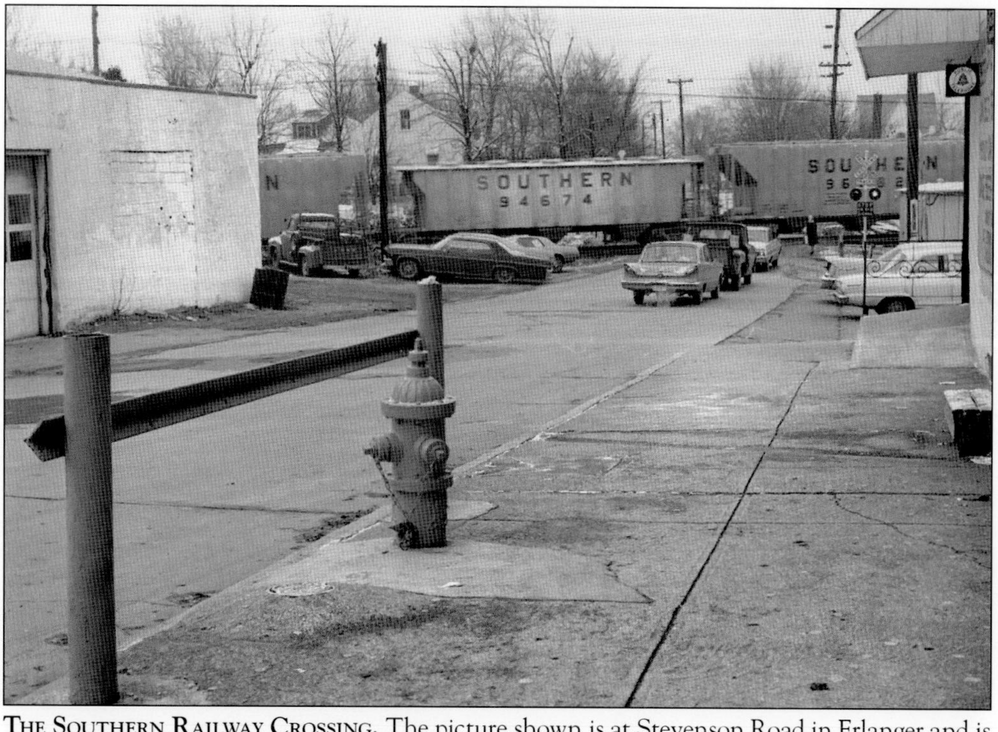

The Southern Railway Crossing. The picture shown is at Stevenson Road in Erlanger and is as familiar today as it was when this picture was taken in 1966.

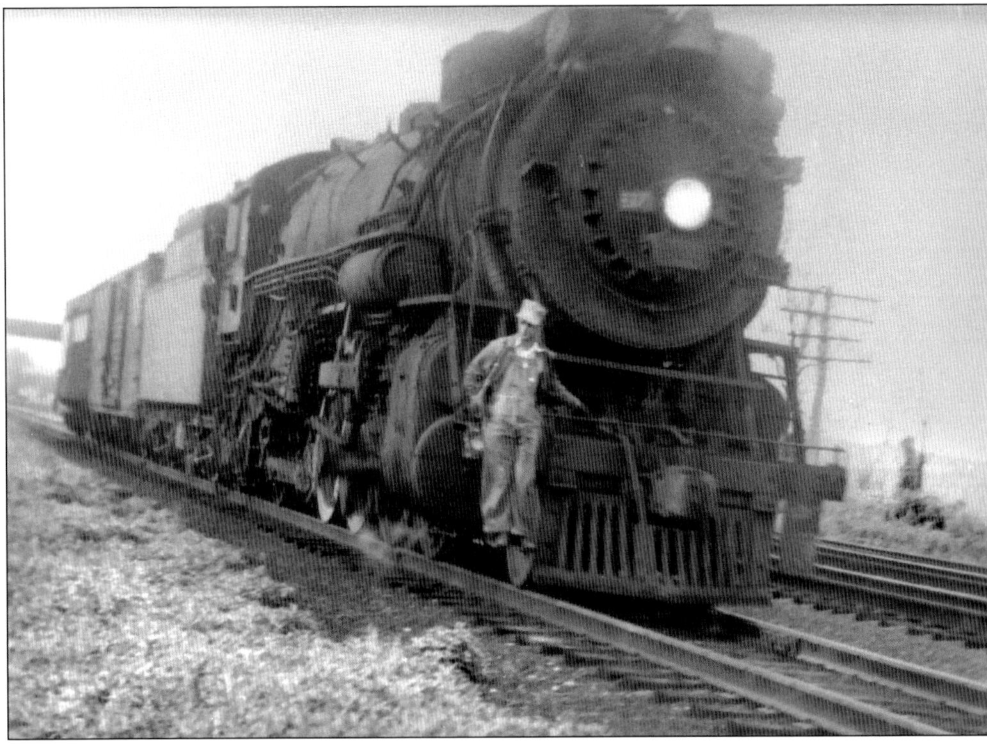

Steam Engine. Traveling the old Queen and Crescent Line, the route went from Cincinnati, Ohio, to Chattanooga, Tennessee. The steam engine always stopped at the Erlanger Station after the 60-feet-per-mile incline over 6 miles in order to replenish the water needed to power the steam engine. The water was supplied from Silverlake in Erlanger.

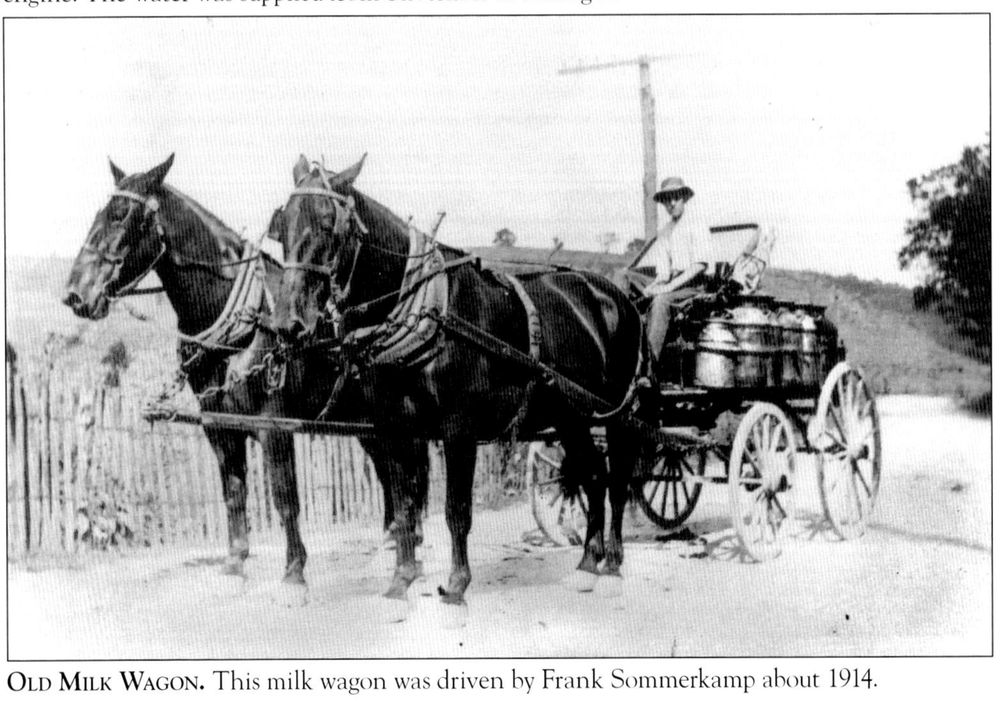

Old Milk Wagon. This milk wagon was driven by Frank Sommerkamp about 1914.

THE DIXIE HIGHWAY. The highway is pictured as it looked in the early 1950s. This view is looking north from where Bartlett Avenue intersects. Note the elm tree in Michels Service Station.

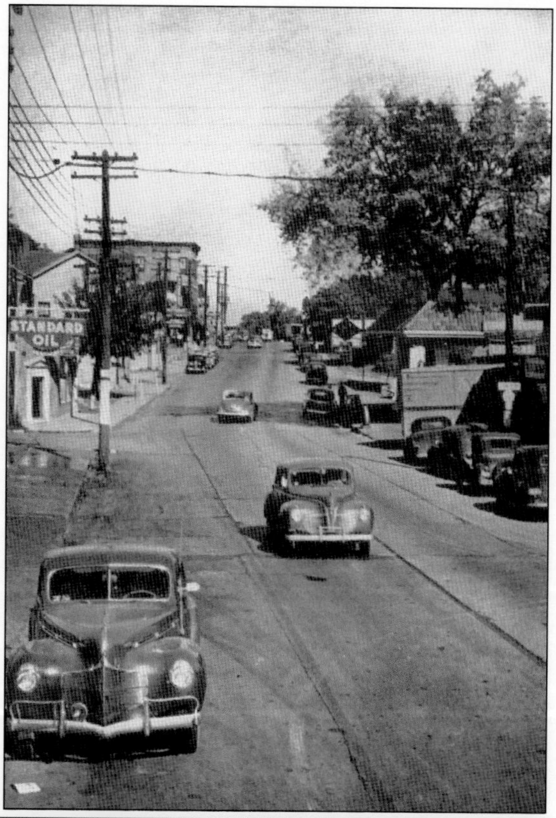

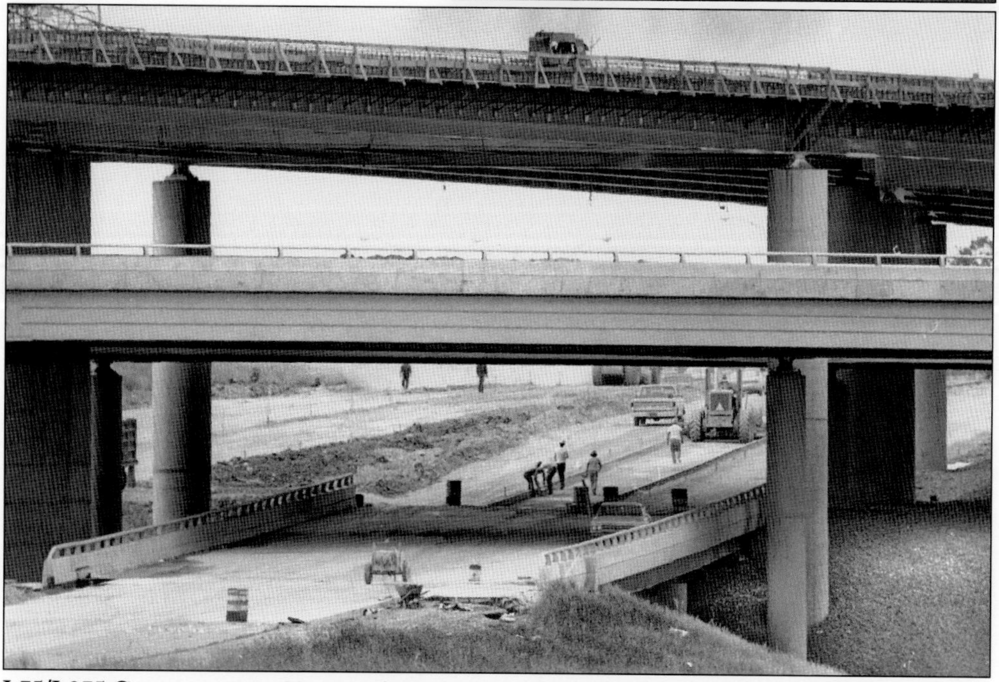

I-75/I-275 CONSTRUCTION. Here is a frontal view of the construction of the I-75/I-275 Interchange near Erlanger, Kentucky, around the 1970s.

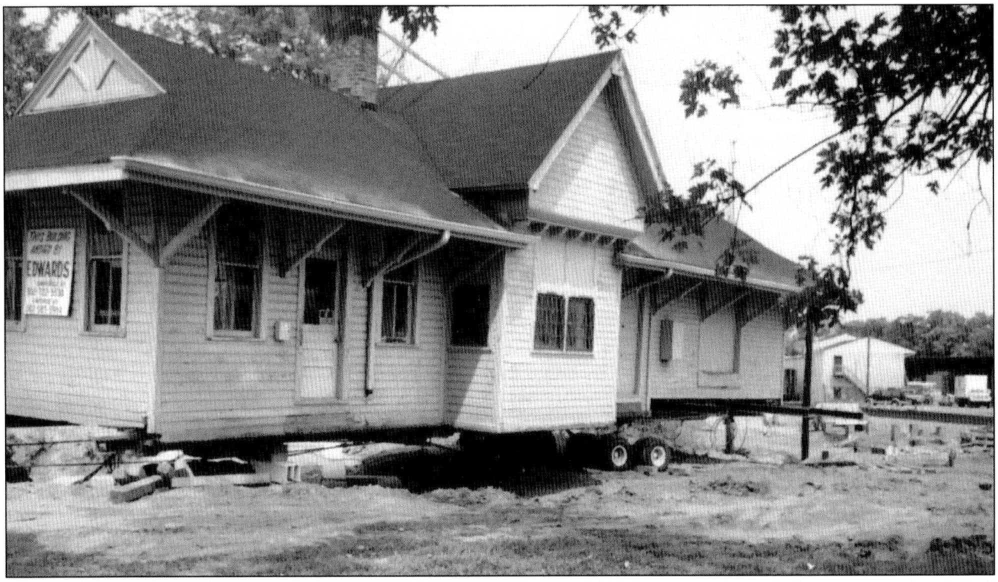

MOVING THE ERLANGER RAILROAD DEPOT. In 1992, the old Erlanger railroad depot was scheduled for demolition, but the Erlanger Historical Society and the City of Erlanger convinced the Norfolk-Southern Railway to donate the depot to the city. They agreed, provided it was moved. The depot was moved 100 feet to its new location in the railroad park on Crescent Avenue.

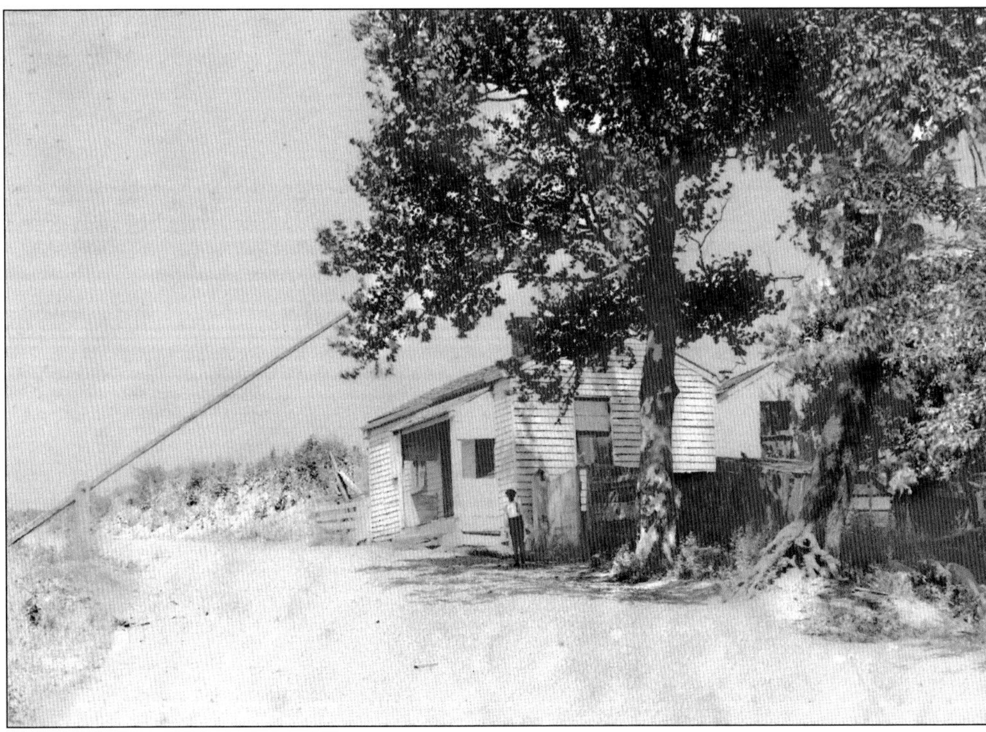

A TOLLGATE. Tollgates such as this one were a common sight for anyone traveling the Lexington Turnpike (Dixie Highway). The turnpike was maintained by private property owners, who in turn were allowed to charge for use of the road. A tollgate similar to this one operated both at the Lexington Turnpike and Bartlett Avenue and at 114 Erlanger Road in Erlanger.

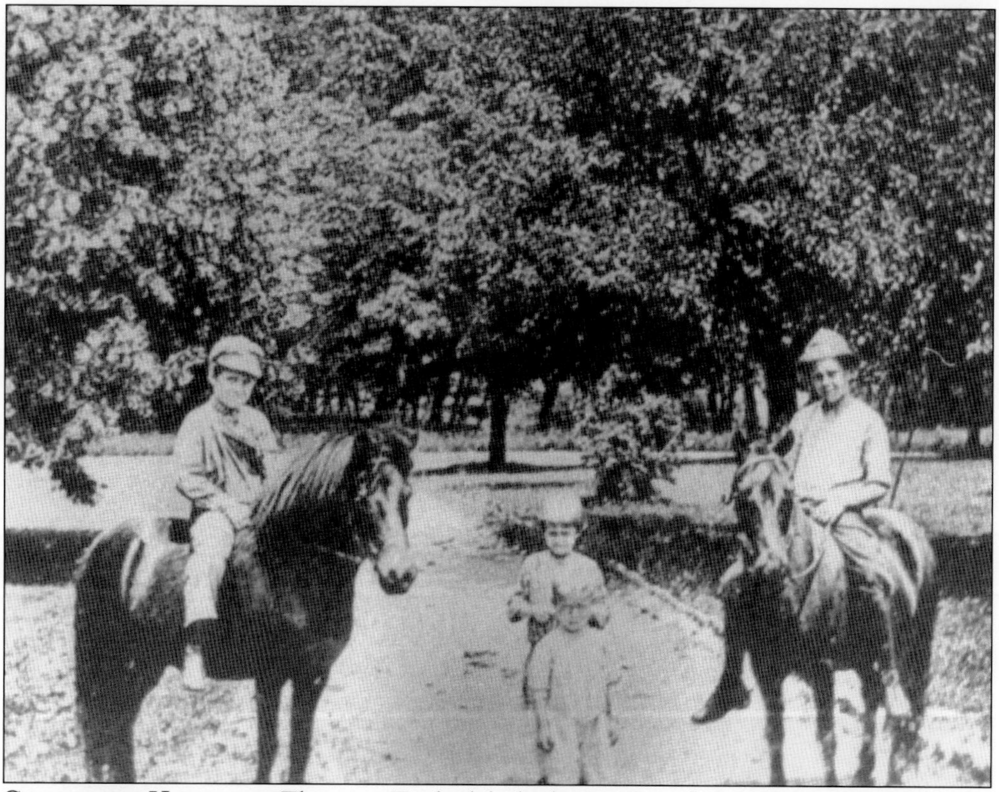

CHILDREN ON HORSEBACK. Thornton Timberlake built a two-story home about 1826 on property that is now Stevenson Road. It faced the turnpike and was known as Sugar Grove. This photograph was taken in 1888.

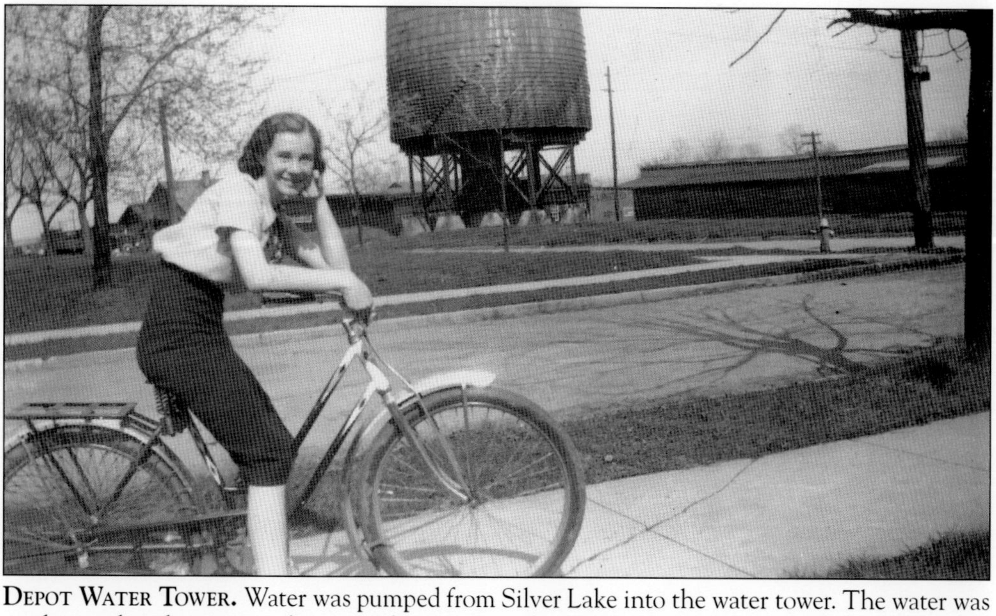

DEPOT WATER TOWER. Water was pumped from Silver Lake into the water tower. The water was used to replenish water in the steam locomotive after the long climb from Ludlow to Erlanger. Rae Collis Mitchell posed in front of the tower about 1937.

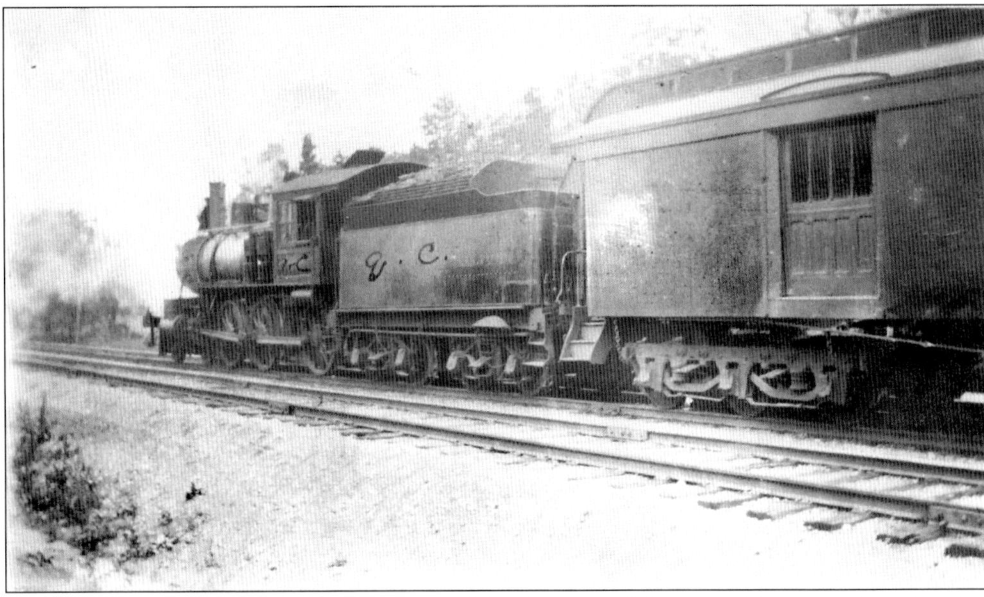

Steam Locomotive. Pictured is an engine of the Queen and Crescent–Texas Pacific railroad. It is parked near the Erlanger Depot.

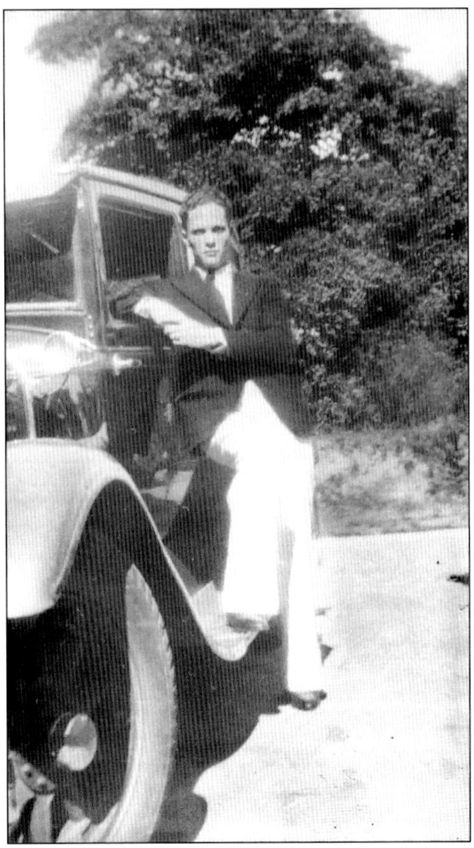

Aubrey Martin. Martin shows off his new car around 1928.

A 1928 VINTAGE CAR. Brady Johnson and Mildred Keeney enjoy a break after a Sunday drive. (Courtesy of Catherine Keeney.)

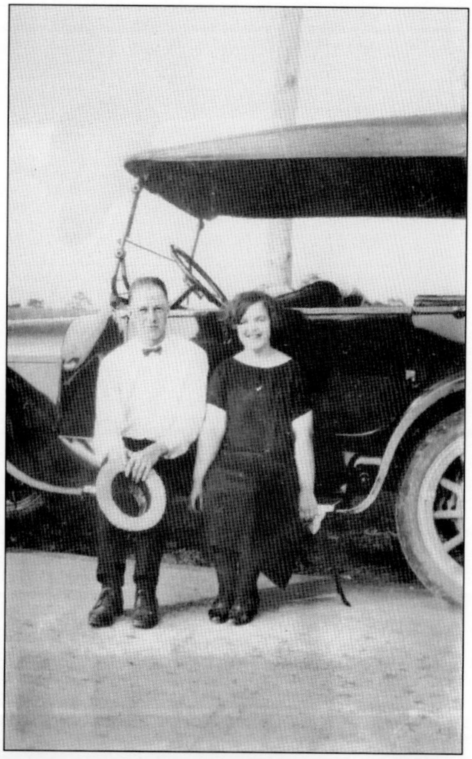

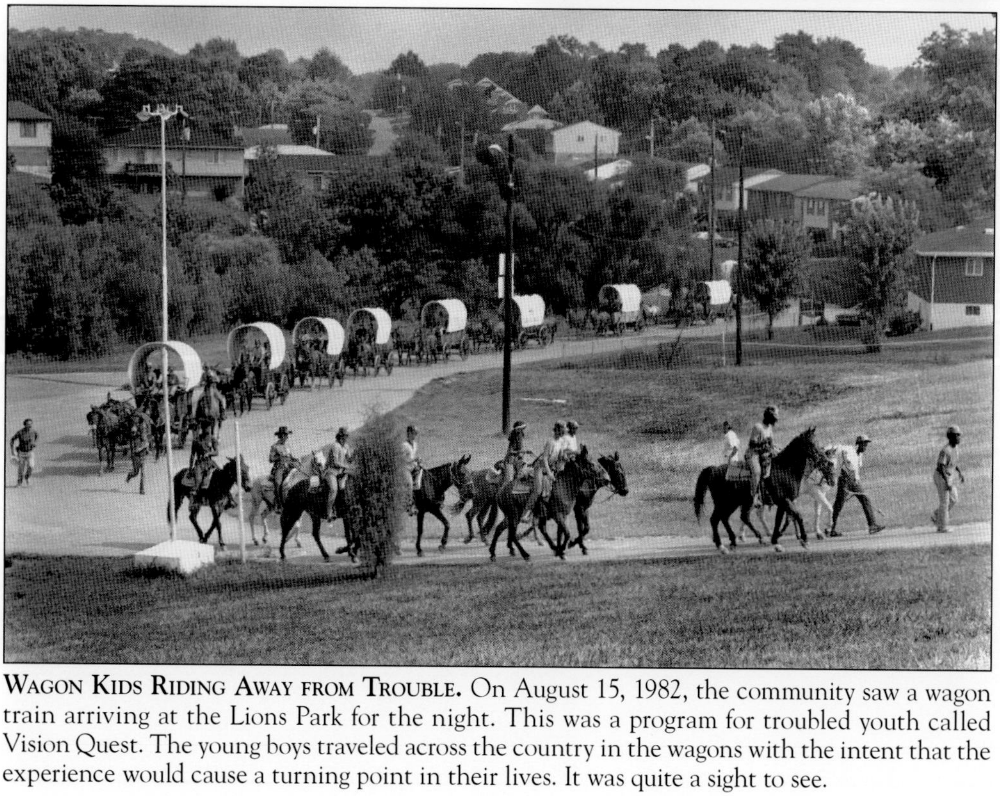

WAGON KIDS RIDING AWAY FROM TROUBLE. On August 15, 1982, the community saw a wagon train arriving at the Lions Park for the night. This was a program for troubled youth called Vision Quest. The young boys traveled across the country in the wagons with the intent that the experience would cause a turning point in their lives. It was quite a sight to see.

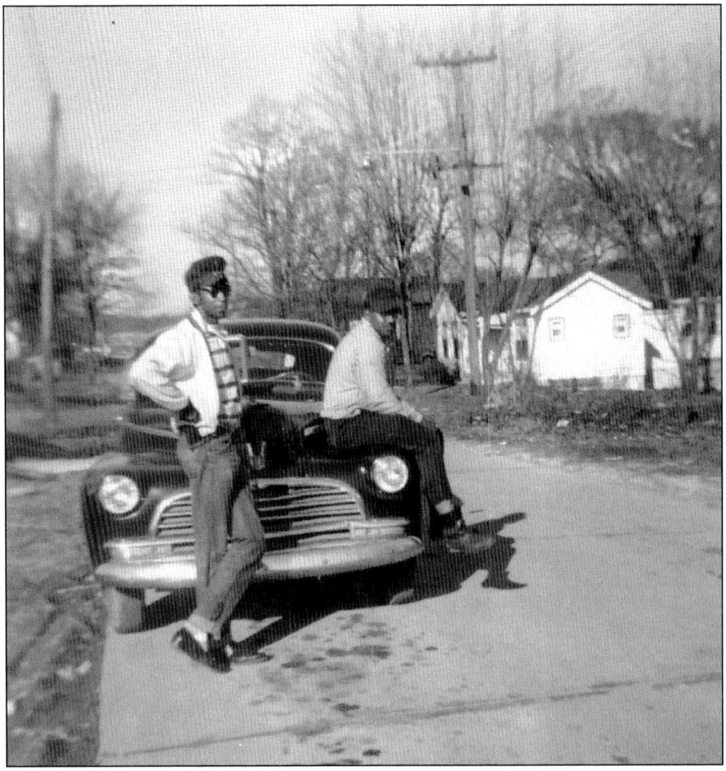

Bruce Bonner and Bobby Baker. Bruce (left) and Bobby are hanging out on Fox Street in the 1950s. (Courtesy of Lillie M. Baker.)

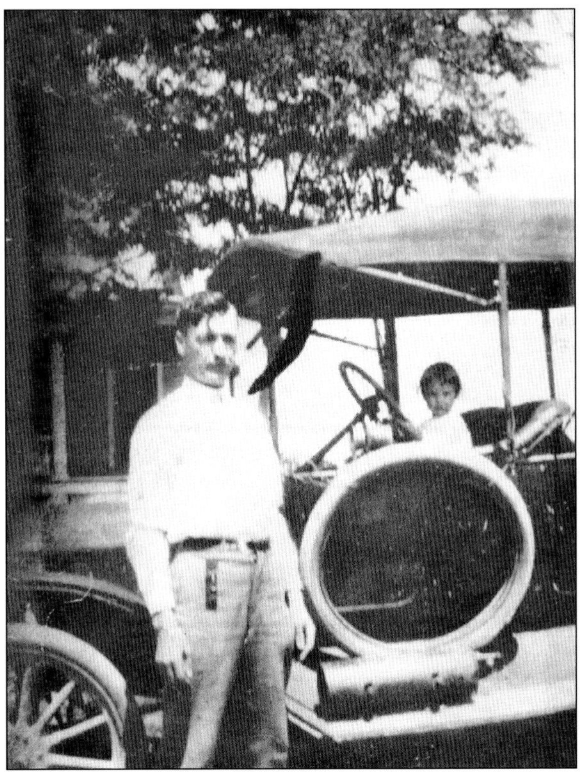

Dr. Harold Keeney. The doctor is pictured with his vintage car.

Sulky Ride. This is a photograph of Dorothea Wolking Kemphaus sitting in a sulky about 1912.

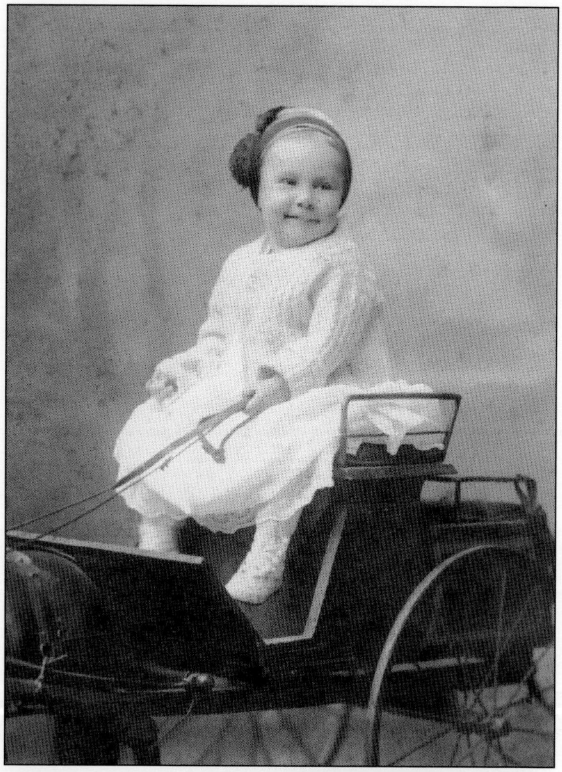

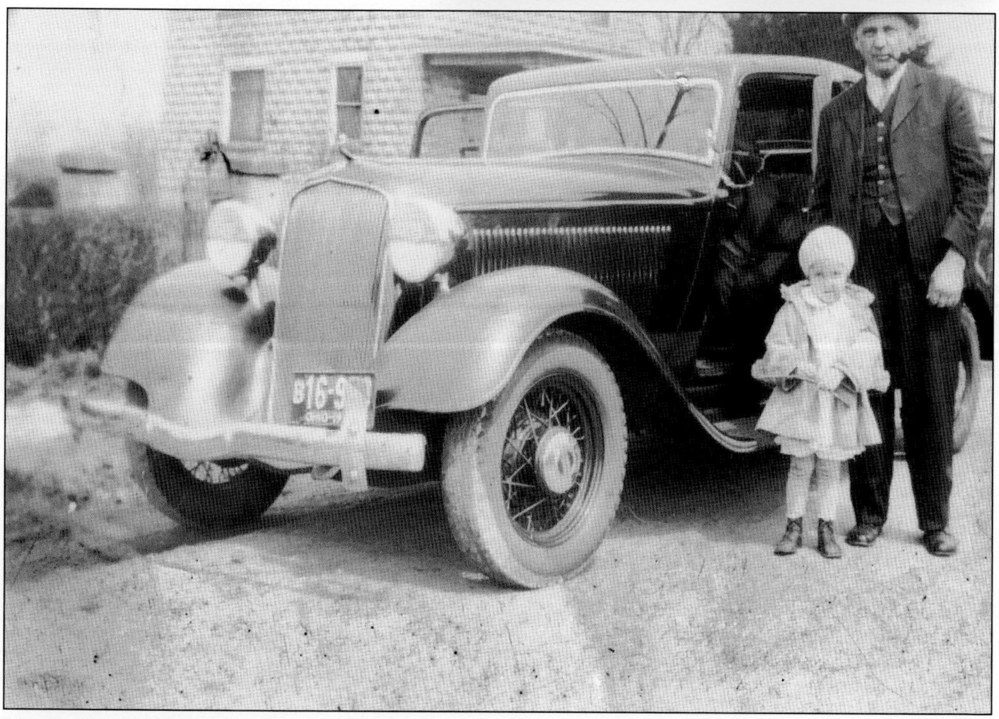

Mary Ann Waginger. This 1933 photograph shows Mary Ann Waginger and Ben Wolf, her maternal grandfather. They are standing in front of the Waginger home at 3226 Riggs Avenue.